Structures of Authenticity in Ruskin Bond's Fiction
Children, Cognition and Truth-Telling

Structures of Authenticity in Ruskin Bond's Fiction

Children, Cognition and Truth-Telling

Bandana Bal Chandnani

ADHYAYAN

ADHYAYAN PUBLISHERS & DISTRIBUTORS
New Delhi-110002

Published by
ADHYAYAN PUBLISHERS & DISTRIBUTORS
4378/4B, 105, J.M.D. House, Murari Lal Street
Ansari Road Darya Ganj, New Delhi - 110002
Ph.: 011-23263018, 011-23277156, Fax: 23280028
Email: adhyayanpublishers@yahoo.com

Structures of Authenticity in Ruskin Bond's Fiction
Children, Cognition and Truth-Telling

Edition 2011
ISBN 978-81-8435-297-9

Printed in India

Published by Harish Chandra Yadav for Adhyayan Publishers & Distributors, Delhi. Laser Typesetting at Jain Computers and Printed at Tarun Offset Printers, Delhi

Preface

> Two roads diverged in a wood, and I—
> I took the one less traveled by,
> And that has made all the difference.
>
> Robert Frost, "The Road Not Taken"

One of the stalwarts of Indian English literature, Ruskin Bond is a versatile writer widely lauded for his children's writing, skilful execution of short story and novella, taxonomic delineation of flora and fauna, truthful and genuine portrayal of the marginalized, lucid and clear style and optimistic humanism. His humane sympathy for the oppressed and 'quiet heroes' invests his fiction with a unique power that places him at a high pedestal. His writings always emphasize the essential nobility of man, despite his weaknesses, to engender compassion in the hearts ofthe readers for them. The objective of this study is to examine the evolving Indian reality in Bond's fiction and shaping of his narrative art.

The present book is structured into seven chapters. The first chapter delves into the life of Bond and evaluates the impact of personal, social, geographical, political and literary influences on his worldview, aesthetic principles and writings. Bond and his writing are the two faces of the same coin. His writing interprets him and vice versa. The second chapter is an extract of the rendezvous with Bond. It precisely and comprehensively explores the art of Bond.

Bond's creativity achieves the heights when he writes for the children and about the children. He has conjured up magical literary landscape where inquisitive, spirited and precocious children have an important role to play. He delineates his child protagonists with the deftness of a psychologist and superb story telling skills. The third chapter traces the development of Indian children's literature in English, Bond's remarkable blending of the canon of Indian and Western Children's Writing and his contribution in the field of children's literature. The fourth chapter evaluates Bond's heart warming relationship with nature. Bond possesses an impeccable understanding of nature. His heart warming relationship with nature and the stimulating magnificence of the dominant images of the hills, trees of the Himalayas and varied big or small animals are perceptible through every leaf that covers his work.

The fifth chapter analyses Bond's sensitive and vivid portraits of the various facets of Indian milieu. It centres on delineating the unobserved and unrecognized strata of society and minute observation of the social landscape, bringing out the marked note of Bond's humanism. A creative wordsmith, Ruskin Bond has put together with dexterity stories where complex concepts are woven into the warp and woof of a simple and lucid narrative. His devotion to the muse of writing gets reflected through his spontaneity of expression, enchanting and expressive narrative, genuine humour, elaborate description, captivating images and floating rhythm. The sixth chapter deals with the narrative art of Bond. The conclusion presents an assessment of Bond's contribution and his enduring place in Indian English Literature.

The present book appraises Bond's choosing of less travelled path: by creating and flourishing Children's Literature, exploiting eloquent and impeccable narration, conjuring up the enchanting world of flora and fauna, skilfully employing the literary form of the short story and presenting creative truth in a realistic way. His writings free the body and mind from the shackles of fast paced commercialism, competition and'complicated present day life.

While writing this book (a revised version of my doctoral dissertation) I have incurred a number of debts and gratitude which I acknowledged with pleasure. I gratefully acknowledge the indefatigable help and support given by my supervisor, Prof. Sushila Singh of Banaras Hindu University. Her precious advice and incessant motivation enabled me to sail smoothly amongst the threatening- storms on the sea of life. I have no words to express my gratefulness to her so I dedicate this book to her.

I have benefitted much from the advice and encouragement of Prof. Shormishtha Panja; Department of English, University of Delhi, Prof. K.P. Singh, Centre of Advanced Study in Botany, BHU, Prof. S.D. Singh, Principal of DA V PG College, Dr. Sangeeta Jain and Dr. Indrajeet Mishra, Department of English, DA V PG College Varanasi.

I put on record my deep sense of appreciation for the courtesy and help I received from the librarians and the staff of the Sayaji Rao Gaekwad Central Library, Banaras Hindu University; National Library, and British Council Library, Kolkata; Library at Jawaharlal Nehru University and Sahitya Akademy, New Delhi.

I am extremely grateful to Ruskin Bond a writer of great gifts and truly generous person who most amicably answered my innumerable questions during the interview session. I am deeply indebted to him for his kind help. I owe Ruskin Bond big time. If there is anyone who has inspired me to look within my own country and find abundant beauty, then it is he. Meeting Ruskin Bond and reading his writings have changed my perception of life.

My deepest gratitude goes to my family for their unflagging love and support throughout my life. This book would have been simply impossible without them. I am indebted to my parents for their unconditional support to pursue my interests. I am also thankful for the encouragement and cooperation of my brother Deepak, sister Usha, sister-in-law Versha and my lovely nephews Dhawal and Kushal. At the end, I bow in deep gratitude to the Lord Almighty and my spiritual Guru Pramila Bhagwan for blessing me through all tests in the past years and having made my life more bountiful.

Bandana Bal Chandnani

Abbreviations

A Face in the Dark and Other Hauntings: Collected Stories	AFD
A Flight of Pigeons	AFP
Collected Fiction	CF
Children's Omnibus	CO
The Best of Ruskin Bond: Delhi Is Not Far	DNF
Friends in Small Places: Ruskin Bond's Unforgettable People	FSP
The Hidden Pool	HP
Landour Days: A Writer's Journal	LD
The Lamp Is Lit: Leaves from a Journal	LIL
The Night Train at Deoli and Other Stories	NTD
Panther's Moon and Other Stories	PM
Rusty the Boy from the Hills	RBH
Rusty Goes to London	RGL
Rain in the Mountains: Notes from the Himalayas	RIM
Rusty and the Leopard	RL
Strangers in the Night: Two Novellas	SN
Scenes from a Writer's Life: A Memoir	SWL
The India I Love	TIIL
Time Stops at Shamli and Other Stories	TSS

Contents

1

From Divided Loyalty to Double Inheritance: Making of the Writer

> Those who professed a religion of non-Indian origin or, coming to India, settled down there, became distinctively Indian in the course of few generations, such as Christians, Jews, Parsees, Muslims.
>
> Jawaharlal Nehru

Owen Ruskin Bond, an admirable raconteur, has chiselled a niche in the treasure-trove of the Indian fiction in English by his outstanding *modus operandi* of child delineation, invigorating style and authentic portrayal of Indian life. The evocation and adoration of nature and record of his relationship with the natural world is a recurrent and predominant feature of his oeuvre. It has earned him the title "Our very own resident Wordsworth in prose." His altruism, love and reverence for mankind and for life make him one of the greatest humanists of our time. He invokes the least known locale in his cameo that reverberates with humble hill folk inhabiting his Arcadian world of the mountains. He raises their experience and their unassuming life to the sublime. His art combines humanity with humour, amusement with sympathy and irony with kindness.

Bond is an Indian author of British descent. During his teens he was perturbed by the dilemma of identity. The question, "where did he belong: England, the land of his forefathers or India the land of his birth as well as of his parents?" always disturbed him. N.P. Gist commenting on the quest for identity that an Anglo-Indian community has often undergone in India writes:

> One of the problems the Anglo-Indian community has always faced is one of *Identity*. Throughout much of the 18th century, Europeans and Indians variously defined them. Under these circumstances it was not easy for Anglo-Indians to develop a clear conception of their own identity. Europeans tended to think of them as Indians with some European blood; Indians thought of them as Europeans with some Indian blood. The prejudices against them, real or imagined, or the prejudices that they themselves had against other Indians, were an obstacle to both group and individual identity. (*Blending of Races* 39-59)

The Anglo-Indian's alienation from both the British and the Indians forced them to think of themselves as a people apart. It has not been easy for them to provide a satisfactory answer to the question, "Who am I?"

In 1951, Bond moved to Jersey and then London, in search of his roots when he was just seventeen. But soon after his short stay at New Jersey, he realised that his experiences, cultural codes and socialisation were all rooted to India. Even London failed to ease his soul. Far from returning 'home' to England, he suffered the trauma of displacement - loss of country, loss of family and friends, change in life style, insecurity and financial problems. He realised his bliss lies in the East. His mind and memory consistently turned to things Indian. Having been born, raised and educated in India, Bond had very little in common with the Anglo-Saxons other than their pigmentation. He felt himself an alienated soul and an outsider in the crowd of his own creed. His maiden novel *The Room on the Roof* which invokes his love for India and his Indian friends was accepted for publication, albeit his yearning for India was too powerful to let him remain abroad for long. Commenting on such dilemma of writers, Salman Rushdie in his *Imaginary Homelands: Essays and Criticism* says, it is a writer who poignantly faces the trauma of existence. They fictionalise the places of their choice, make their literature a medium to express nostalgia and thus compensate the loss:

> It may be that writers in my position, exiles or emigrants or expatriates, are haunted by some sense of loss, some urge to reclaim, to look back, even at the risk of being mutated into pillars of salt ... physical alienation from India almost inevitably means, that we will not be capable of reclaiming precisely the thing that was lost; that we will, in short, create fictions, not actual cities or villages, but invisible ones, imaginary homelands, India's of the mind. (10)

Bond's desire to retain his identity and love for the hills compelled him to return to India in less than four years, never to leave it again "come floods or fury" (SWL xv). It was while being away from the land of his birth - India - he got a chance to reflect upon the predicament of his identity. The quandary of split nationality and the inner conflicts were resolved in favour of India that made him to declare himself an Indian in a truest sense: "I am an Indian—in the broadest, all-embracing, all-Indian sense of the word" (SWL xv-xvi). Bond thus belongs to the tradition of C.F. Andrews, Sister Nivedita and Annie Besant who had merged their national and racial identity with the rich composition of Indian culture. His literature thrives with the passages where he unveils his affection and fondness for his beloved country, India. His commitment to Indian sights and sound is complete. The feeling of homesickness and nostalgia which he experienced while being away from India, the land of his birth, is beautifully encapsulated here:

> The affection, the camaraderie, the easy-going pleasures of my Dehra friendships; the colour and atmosphere of India; the feeling of belonging—these things I missed ... Even though I had grown up with a love for the English language and its literature, even though my forefathers were British, Britain was not really my place. I did not belong to the bright lights of Piccadilly and Leicester Square; or, for that matter, to the apple orchards of Kent or the strawberry fields of Berkshire. I belonged, very firmly, to peepal trees and mango groves; to sleepy little towns all over India; to hot sunshine, muddy canals, the pungent scent of marigolds; the hills of home; spicy odours, wet earth after summer rain, neem pods bursting; laughing brown faces; and the intimacy of human contact. (SWL 154)

Ruskin Bond was born on 19 May 1934, to Aubrey Alexander Bond and Edith Clerke Bond, in a Military Hospital at Kasauli, a hill station near Sanawar, in Himachal Pradesh. He was the third generation of his family in India on his father's side and the fourth generation on his mother's side. He was baptised in the Anglican Church in Kasauli, and christened Owen Ruskin Bond, after John Ruskin, the famous Victorian author. Perhaps, Ruskin's father who was much impressed by the ideologies of John Ruskin hoped that one day the boy would grow up to be aesthetically inclined like the celebrated writers. Bond seldom uses Owen as his other Christian name. An extra Christian name seems to be quite superfluous to him. Besides, Owen (in Welsh) means 'brave,' and he amusingly confesses "I am not a brave person. I have done some foolhardy things, but more out of ignorance than bravery (SWL 19)."

A few months after the birth of Ruskin, Aubrey Bond took a job in the princely state of Jamnagar as tutor-guardian to the royal children. The first five years of Ruskin's life was spent in Jamnagar: among old towering palaces full of mystery and romance. The circumstances in Jamnagar provided him a chance to interact with Indians. He was exposed to Indian culture more than the average British child in India. Unlike the children of most British colonials who were sent to England to study during their formative years - famous among them being Rudyard Kipling, Rumer Godden and M.M. Kaye, Bond received his education in India. He spent his early childhood in the princely state of Jamnagar. Memories of life at the palace are among Bond's earliest (SWL 2-7). He grew up around the little princes and princesses. He remembers his shyness with the young princesses and his favourite flower, the cosmos "waving gently in the softest of breezes" (SWL 5). He was equally comfortable with his Indian cook, ayah, (nanny) and gardener, indifferent to the barriers of caste or social structure. Aubrey Bond never objected Bond's socialising with Indians. Having spent first five years of his life in Jamnagar, Ruskin learnt to read and write at home, developing rather early a taste for comics and the classics of children's literature, read to him by his father from *Alice in Wonderland, Peter Pan* and so on. Aubrey taught him to write in good hand. By the time he started going to school, he was around seven-year-old and could already read and write. Ruskin's sister, Edith Ellen, was born in Dehradun in 1936, where his mother had gone for the baby's delivery. She was just a year and a half younger to Bond. A forceps birth and polio virus had caused irreversible brain and limbs damage. She remained handicapped and in need of care throughout her life. Ruskin's brother William was born in 1942 in Dehradun. There was an eight-year gap between William and Ruskin. Ruskin was in school when William was growing up. So there were not many things that the brothers could do together. Ruskin was quite a sensitive and self-centred child. Bond's biographer Ganesh Saili writes in *Ruskin, Our Enduring Bond*:

> There are people, however, who remember him as a noisy naughty boy, who kicked and screamed and always wanted to have his way. It probably illustrates the two sides of his nature: the reflective nature, which helped him become a writer, and the zest for life that shows up occasionally in his more boisterous moods. (27)

In 1939, when World War II broke out, Aubrey who was in his early forties left Jamnagar to join the Royal Air Force (RAF). He was assigned to the cipher section of Air Headquarters in New Delhi. In the meantime, young Ruskin along with his mother and baby Ellen went to live with Grandmother Clerke in Dehradun. It was because Aubrey could not obtain family accommodation right away. At the age of seven, Ruskin was sent to a boarding school - Convent of Jesus and Mary at Hampton Court, in Mussoorie, where he spent a miserable year. His spirit stifled and he found himself caged in the suffocating atmosphere of the convent. He never really settled down at Convent and hated the place each day of the period that he was there. It was not a cruel place but it lacked character of any kind. It really was a staging post or a waiting room for boys and girls going on to bigger schools in the hill station. The nuns were unsympathetic and strict, the food was awful, the facilities were meagre and punishments harsh. He had been knuckled for not tuning with choir and this made him averse to singing. The only relief in this grim place was the letters from his father which he regularly received, comforting him that books, tours and stamps would be waiting for him when he returned. At school he often planned to run away with a boy who shared his desk. They never got the opportunity to run away. But that did not stop them from planning to escape from a prisoner-of-war camp, as it was. In "Running Away" the unfulfilled dream of running away from the authorities and from adult made world get an outlet. The narrator child Rusty, Bond's alter ego, in the story getting sick of his school, shared his dream with his class-mate Daljit. Daljit too was dissatisfied with school and wanted to sail to magical places like Mombassa, Yokohoma, San Diego, Valparaiso, London etc. Both the boys ran away from the school, getting into a Delhi-bound train from a wayside station, skipping Dehradun for fear of being caught. The truant boy had reasons enough:

> I was sick of school and sick of my guardian. But that was not all. I was in love with the world. I wanted to see the world, every corner of it, the places I had read about in books—the junks and sampans of Hong Kong, the palm-fringed lagoons of the Indies, the streets of London, the beautiful ebony-skinned people of Africa, the bright birds and exotic plants of the Amazon. (Bond, *Rusty Runs Away* 47)

The childhood of Bond had undergone many trials and tribulations. It was the insecure and troubled period of his life. The persistent quarrels of Bond's parents resulted in their divorce. It left a deep scar on his soul. The untimely death of his beloved father disturbed the natural development of shy and sensitive Ruskin. Even today that trauma of childhood haunts him and makes him comment: "...when I see married people quarrel, I am full of fear and trepidation, for them and for their children. An unsettled childhood can give you a terrible sense of insecurity. Perhaps it's the real reason I never married" (Bond, RIM 242). The heterogeneous taste and temperament of Bond's parents Aubrey and Edith, and the age difference of fifteen years between them brought discord in their married life. They were totally an incompatible match. Aubrey was a serious man, too much of a stay-at-home, happy making the morning butter and sorting through his stamps in the evening. Edith was a fun-loving lady who enjoyed going to dances, picnics, and parties. Her vivaciousness and beauty made everyone to look at her twice which was a cause of resentment and jealousy to Aubrey. Ruskin was a mute witness of the family tensions as he was too young to understand such matters.

One day, in the mid-term, much to Ruskin's bewilderment, his mother turned up unexpectedly at the Convent and withdrew him from its constricted environment. He was to find himself not at his grandmother's place in Dehradun but at the railway station to catch the night train to Delhi, without an escort or a chaperone. To Ruskin's utter delight, his father in full uniform met him at Delhi. Soon he came to know the separation of his parents. Although his father had tried to reconcile with his estranged wife but failed to do so. Gradually, Ruskin learnt that the other reason for their separation was his mother's liaison with a Punjabi business man, Mr. Harbans Lal Hari, a dealer in second-hand cars, who owned an auto repair shop. Hari was also married but left his wife for Ruskin's mother. The arrangement of the children after divorce was made in such a way that Ruskin was to be in his father's custody, while Ellen would stay in Calcutta with her seventy-year-old paternal grandmother, Gloriana Bond. William, the younger brother, would stay with his mother. The arrangement made Ruskin happy because he was very close to his father and extremely enjoyed his company.

Bond never recovered from the nightmare of his parents' separation throughout his life. He blamed his mother for deserting them, more at a time when his father was suffering from the frequent bouts of malaria. Some of this hurt and anger can be detected in his stories like "Coming Home to Dehra," "Room of Many Colours." Here he laments for not receiving the attention and nurturing from his mother that he needed so much when he was young. He writes that his mother frequently ran off when he was very young, leaving him with a lasting sense of insecurity. Security and stability were provided to him by his father. He questioned his parents' marriage. He writes,

"People who marry young, even those who are in love, do not really know each other. The body chemistry may be right but the harmony of two minds is what makes relationships endure" (SWL 3-4). It was much later, as an adult that he came to understand the viewpoint of his mother and her needs and the mismatched relationship of his parents. But he always remained traumatized by his parents' clashes and consequent separation. Even today, he remembers many of his parents' quarrels until they got separated. The reason of his remaining a bachelor is quite explicit in the light of such experience. Reminiscing those sad days, he says: "That early feeling of insecurity was never to leave me, and in adult life, when I witnessed quarrels between people who were close to me, I was always deeply disturbed—more for the children, whose lives were bound to be affected by such emotional discord" (SWL 3). The trauma of insecurity has been revealed in his stories especially through adolescent characters like Rusty in *Room on the Roof* and Kishen in *Vagrants in the Valley*.

Ruskin's father profusely compensated for the vacuum caused by the absence of mother. He bestowed his sole love and concern on Ruskin despite his failing health. His rejuvenating and friendly company and his affection never made Ruskin realise the absence of his mother. The comforting company of his beloved father helped him to overcome the loss of his mother. He was deeply attached to his father and lovingly created and recreated him in his fiction. Aubrey gave Ruskin his time, companionship and his complete attention despite his poor health. He taught him literature, maths, geography and political history through fun activities. He also encouraged him to keep a journal, which proved to be Bond's only training as a writer. Bond reminisces:

> I must have been eight or nine when my father gave me a small diary, and I began my first tentative forays as a writer—or wordsmith, as I have sometimes described my calling....this

> indulgence was a discipline of sorts and was to stand me in good stead in later years. It made me neat and meticulous, and helped me form the habit of keeping notes and filing away facts: not, perhaps, essential attributes for a writer, but useful ones. (RIM 211)

Bond began the journal entry just with the listing of singers, records, movies, and Hollywood trivia. But later on this journal record gave him the discipline of writing regularly and recording everything he saw and observed. Aubrey used to take Ruskin on nature trails where they viewed and enjoyed wild flowers, trees, birds. This splendid panorama of nature became a permanent part of Ruskin's psyche at an early stage and has become an inseparable part of his literature. The father and the son enjoyed together various activities - trailing nature, watching movies, exploring old monuments and tombs and collecting stamps. The time spent with father was the happiest time of Bond's childhood. At many places, he recounts his intimate relationship with his father and happy moments shared with him:

> I had a very close relationship with my father and was more than happy with him in Delhi....When he was free he took me for long walks to the old tombs and monuments that dotted the wilderness that then surrounded New Delhi; or to the bookshops and cinemas of Connaught Place....He was, in fact, the only friend I had as a child. (Bond, DNF 147-149)

During the period 1942 to 1943, Ruskin lived with his father in the temporary wartime Air Force hutments. Aubrey Bond could not keep Ruskin with him so he sent him to the boarding school at Simla: Bishop Cotton Prep School (BCS). In 1943, he was admitted to the school. The school was known as the "Eton of East," which was then and still today is - a highly prestigious school with impressive alumni. In those days the school had British teachers and 80 percent of the student body was European or Anglo-Indian. However, after the independence the demography was reversed: the Indian students gradually increased to 80 or 90 percent, while the remaining 10 or 20 percent were children of the Anglo-Indians or the Europeans who had stayed on in India. Before joining the school Ruskin enjoyed an idyllic period with his father in Simla. His father took him to restaurants, book shops, on long walks and places associated with the lore of Rudyard Kipling. It was here his father told him Kipling's story of the phantom rickshaw. He also showed him the shop where Kim got his training as a spy from the mysterious Lurgan Sahib. Thus through his father he became familiar with many of Kipling's characters and settings before actually going through it.

Compared to the old Mussoorie Convent, BCS was a luxury and the young Ruskin could get adjusted easily in the congenial atmosphere. In 1943, nine-year-old Ruskin was placed in Ibbeston House - the other Houses being Curzon, Lefroy and Rivaz. The year went by quickly and at the end of the school term, he was back with his father in Delhi for the three-month-winter break. His father had taken a flat in Scindia House. This suited him perfectly, as it was only a few minutes from cinemas, bookshops and restaurants. He and his father soon became regular cinegoers. Ruskin and his father saw at least three movies a week that must be something of a record for an Air Force Officer and his little son on vacation from school. He greatly enjoyed the company of his father: "Helping my father with his stamp collection, accompanying him to the pictures, dropping in at Wenger's for tea and muffins, bringing home a book or record—what more could a small boy of eight have asked for?" (SWL 22) When Ruskin returned to school in 1944, his father was transferred to Calcutta. Now his father was very far away to visit Simla during the school breaks but he made up for it by writing to Ruskin regularly. These letters gave Ruskin a sort of window to his father's world - news of

Calcutta, Granny and Ellen, the stamp collections and records. In *Scenes from a Writer's Life* Bond reproduces the last letter of his father written to him from Calcutta before his death. This was the only letter and a few post-cards he was able to retain. The letter shows interest in Ruskin's school work, provides guidance on improving his writing style and anticipates the holidays when Ruskin would visit Calcutta at the end of 1944.

Ruskin was enjoying a good time but for his father it was a trying period. Frequent bouts of malaria had undermined his constitution and a severe attack of jaundice killed him. The blissful period of Bond's life received a jolt with the death of his dear father. The untimely death of his indulging father - his emotional anchor, was the shattering and traumatic episode of his childhood. This childhood memory associated with the episodes and images of the period, determined much of his later thoughts (Bandyopadhyay, *Children's Literature* 53-71). Bond came to know about the death of his father when he was in his school. Mr. Murtough, a kind but inept teacher, broke the news of his father's death that made the matter worse to handle. No one had made an arrangement for Ruskin to attend the funeral of his father who was everything for him. This made it difficult for him to reconcile with this irreparable loss. Even after years he failed to accept the death of his father. Secretly he wished his return: "As there was no evidence of my father's death, it was, for me, not a death but a vanishing, and to this day, I subconsciously expect him to turn up (as he indeed often did, when I most needed him) and delivered me from bad situations"(Saili, *Ruskin Our Enduring* 38).

Bond confronts the pangs of the loss of his father by writing "The Funeral." Bond, in this short story, exposes the insensitivity of adults who amongst themselves decide what is good for the orphan child. The child protagonist was shattered when his dear father suddenly died. He resented for not being allowed to attend the funeral. The protagonist of the story, like Bond was unable to understand the words of the Missionary: "God has need of your father ..." (Bond, CF 227).

The child questioned himself: "And had God, in the same way, laid claim to the thousands of men, women and children who had been put to rest here in these neat and serried rows? What could he have wanted them for? Of what use are we to God when we are dead" (CF 227). The despondency of the child in the story poignantly becomes visible with the touching narration: "The boy said nothing. He sat in the darkest corner of the darkened room, his face revealing nothing of what he thought and felt. His father's coffin lay in the next room, the lid fastened forever over the tired, wistful countenance of the man who had meant so much to the boy" (CF 225). The silence of the child pulls at reader's heart. The course of cruel destiny that has befallen him even stirs us: "The house was full of people—friends, relatives, neighbours. Some had tried to fuss over him but had been discouraged by his silence, the absence of tears. The more understanding of them had kept their distance" (CF 225). The moving story, "The Funeral," thus, brings us close to the irretrievable loss that Bond faced at a very young age.

The young Ruskin returned to Dehradun in winter vacation to live with his mother and his stepfather, Mr. Hari. The first home coming after his father's death was an agonising experience for him. No one had come to receive him at the railway station and he had no idea about the new address of his mother. He was hoping to meet his mother but she was not there. So, he took a tonga to the only place he knew - Granny Clerke's house. In "Coming Home to Dehra," he records the experience. This heartbreaking story tells about the narrator's return to Dehradun after the death of his father to find his mother and stepfather's indifference glaring in the face. The memory of the father and the nostalgia weighed down him. The cold reception at the hands of his mother and stepfather made him feel more the vacuum created by the absence of his father. The distressing experience is thus narrated:

> Going home was something that I had always looked forward to. But going home had meant my father, and now he had vanished and I was left quite desolate ... I suppose if one is present when a loved one dies, or sees him dead and laid out and later buried, one is convinced of the finality of the thing and finds it easier to adapt to the changed circumstances. But when you hear of a death, a father's death, and have only the faintest idea of the manner of his dying, it is rather a lot for the imagination to cope with—especially when the imagination is a small boy's. There being no tangible evidence of my father's death, it was, for me, not a death but a vanishing. (CF 440)

Ruskin's stepfather, Hari was a *la dolce vita,* a party-going man who loved drinking, dancing and hunting. He had little or no time for young Ruskin. He was not rude or unkind to him but was inconsiderate for a boy of ten who had just been dumped on him because he had no other place to go. He did not make any attempt to relate to Ruskin and that was just as well. He had not the sensitivity to make a go of being a 'father.' The frenzied partying and hectic life style of Hari and Edith made them indifferent towards the need of a growing teenaged boy, Ruskin. He tried to fend off his ensuing loneliness and changed family life through books and the company of a few friends. The company of the books provided him an escape from the gross reality of his situation. It was during the period that he became totally absorbed in books and writer in embryo:

> My father died when I was ten, and for the next few years books became a scare commodity in my life, for my mother and stepfather were not great readers. In my rather lonely teens I was to discover that books could be good friends, reliable companions, and I seized upon almost any printed matter that came my way, whether it was a girl's

> classic like *Little Women*, or a *Hotspur* or *Champion comic*, or a detective story, or *The Naturalist on the River Amazons* by Henry Walter Bates. (DNF 158)

Bond pays homage to his bibliophile father for introducing him into the wondrous world of books and inculcating in him the habit of reading and writing and thus sowing the seed of his creative zeal. But he feels it was his own sense of loneliness which transported him nearer to the world of books. Bond's reading passion gradually turned into his religion. He read ravenously almost everything that came on his way. About his love for reading he says, "I think it is fair to say that when I was a boy, reading was my true religion. It helped me to discover my soul" (SWL 67).

The books that most influenced him were Charles Dickens' *David Copperfield* and Hugh Walpole's *Fortitude*. He felt in David's story his own tale narrated. He empathized with David Copperfield - in loss of parents, sense of insecurity and struggle for a meaningful life. His ambition for becoming a writer got an impetus: "I think it would be true to say that Copperfield set me off on the road to literature. I identified with young David and wanted to grow up to be a writer like him" (DNF 160). The discovery of two book shelves during this period helped him in accessing books of various kinds and that gave him considerable pleasure then and in the years to come. The first discovery he made in the Forest Rest House where he went with his parents on *shikar* trips. Here he got the chance to read books of M.R. James (*Ghosts Stories of an Antiquary*), P.G. Wodehouse (*Love among the Chickens*) and A.A. Milen (*The Red House Mystery*). He found a rare collection of books, by many Victorian novelists at his granny's house. These books played formative role in his development as a reader. He had almost devoured all the books in that small collection including such diverse works as *Little Women* and *The Invisible Man*. He says that those readings have made him "to this day remain ready to read almost anything provided it has tone, style and substance"

(SWL 40). The Ideal Book Depot had a large lending library from where he could access books easily. For two or three rupees a week he could borrow as many books as he liked, and in this way he read many of the best-sellers of the time – Betty Smith's *A Tree Grows in Brooklyn*, Priestley's *The Good Companions*, A.J. Cronin's *The Green Years*, William Saroyan's *The Human Comedy* and comic novels of P.G. Wodehouse. The love for reading continued in his later life, and that has influenced his art. Bond informs that he has read "over fifteen thousand books" (RIM 247) of many western and Indian authors, prominent among them being Dickens, Wordsworth, H.G. Wells, Walter de la Mare, Rudyard Kipling, Somerset Maugham, J.B. Priestly, Lewis Carroll, Mark Twain, G.K. Chesterton, Thoreau, Rabindra Nath Tagore, Mulk Raj Anand and R.K. Narayan. It is his passion of reading books that has paved the way to his creativity. In *Treasury of Stories for Children*, Bond says:

> Although I never went to college, I think I have read as much, if not more, than most collegiate, and it would be true to say that I received a large part of my education in second-hand bookshops. London had many, and Calcutta once had a large number of them, but I think the prize must go to the small town in Wales called Hay-on-Wye, which has twenty six bookshops and over a million books. It's in the world's quiet corners that book lovers still flourish – a far from dying species! (xiv-xv)

Apart from books there was company of some old people that lessens his loneliness. The patient listener Ruskin got on well specially with old people who had a lot to share. Sixty-year-old Miss Kellener, a physically challenged tenant of his grandmother, was a good company to pass time and a good friend to offer delicacies from her well stocked larder. She told Ruskin stories of her life and about her growing up in different parts of India. Bond writes that older people often found him to be a patient listener. About his friendship with old people he says, "I seemed to get on with old or elderly people, and at this point in my life had no desire to make young friends" (SWL 37). Bond, thus, saw two microcosmic versions of the world: one of his mother and stepfather and the other of a caring maternal grandmother and her tenant Miss Kellener. He disliked the wantonness of the formers but felt an affinity for the latter. An elderly gardener of his grandmother, Dukhi and Mrs. Kennedy, engaged to look after her sister Ellen, were other good companions of Bond during the troubled period. Young Ruskin was fond of Dukhi who had become a symbolic gardener in many of his stories like "A Job Well Done," "The Funeral" and "The Room of Many Colours." Dukhi fostered Bond's love for nature by teaching him about the different flowers, their names and their cultivation.

Back in BCS, Ruskin was given charge of the Anderson Library, which he turned into his private retreat. He frantically read everything he could lay his hands on. He worked his way through most of the libraries during this period. He ardently read real adventures, spy stories, murder mysteries, comics, novels, plays. He was impressed by the short stories of H.E. Bates, William Saroyan and A.E. Coppard. He says, "I was to find that the short story or novella best suited my temperament: snatching at life and recording its impressions and sensations rather than trying to digest it whole" (SWL 75). At BCS when he was thirteen, he attempted to write his first book - a memoir, entitled "Nine Months." It referred to his school term - describing events at the school during the course of an academic year. He caricatured his teachers in it. The manuscript, which filled two school note books, was confiscated by a teacher who tore it to shreds. Thus, his first effort at writing came to an end.

Bond "was the angry young man, in revolt against rules, traditions, conventions, examinations, authority of any kind" (SWL 75). He opposed the school authority, in revolt particularly against Mr. Fisher who was the headmaster. Mr. Fisher and his wife were insensitive to children, discouraging and discriminating towards them. He lost his house captaincy for complaining against bad food and inadequate amount of its serving. He was a hero amongst his peers for his indomitable spirit. He often played pranks and answered back that upset his teachers. Bond acted out his schoolmates' inner desires because they did not have the spirit to rebel against authority. Once he even submitted the examination paper with the observation: "Exams are rubbish!"(Saili, *Ruskin Our Enduring* 35)

After his senior Cambridge with a second division, in December of 1950, Bond bid goodbye to BCS forever and swore that it was the end of his formal education. He reminisces: "I was sixteen that year, and I felt I was wasting my time in school. Dickens hadn't done much schooling, I reasoned; nor had Jack London or Joseph Conrad or the Bronte sisters or other favourite authors. I had only to write a book and I would be in their glorious company!" (SWL 75) He decided to continue his education through self-study by accessing books from libraries and second-hand bookshops. He returned to the house of his mother and stepfather but he did not feel comfortable with them because of the anger which he had against his mother for getting married to Mr. Hari and deserting his father. All he wanted at this juncture of his life was freedom and some measure of privacy, so that he could get on with his life and passion of writing. Domestic discord with parents became an integral part of his life. One day, after a quarrel with his mother, he left home and spent a few days on train platforms and park benches. But soon he realised that he could not live like a vagrant, he returned home, announcing that he would stay with them only until he found a job. He was given a room on the roof of the old building in which his parents lived. The room had its own entrance and window from which he could view the Himalayas and magnificent and beautiful trees. The long cherished desire of his to have a room of his own was fulfilled. The surrounding beauty kindled his passion for writing.

Bond spent most of 1951 wandering and loafing around in Dehradun, absorbing its flavour and observing closely Indian life - washermen, wrestlers, trains and playing football and cricket. He made many Indian friends - Somi, Kishen, Daljeet, Haripal and Ranbir and his sister Raj, to whom he was attracted - visiting their homes, playing badminton and taking bicycle rides in the outlying areas of Dehradun. He wore Indian clothes, ate Indian delicacies, accompanied his friends to the Sikh and Hindu temples and listened to the folktales and religious stories told by his friends' mothers. The aunt figures in his stories are drawn from these story-telling-listening experiences.

During this period, Bond seriously contemplated his life and his career. He yearned for privacy and freedom and was eager to express himself through his writing. He started to write for publication in 1951. His journal entries not only revealed the thoughtful and sensitive part of his personality but they also indicated that he was developing a distinct style of writing - the ability to express deep felt emotions with simplicity, touching descriptions of nature and people, a sense of humour, extreme honesty and self-analysis, and an amazing understanding of life for one so young. He submitted a story to *The Illustrated Weekly of India* and *The Sunday Statesman* but when it was rejected, he sent it to *My Magazine* of India, a small magazine published from Madras. His first published work was a couple of mystery stories that appeared in *My Magazine* for which he received five rupees. He found that most editors lost interest in his writing when they discovered that he was only seventeen. So, he tried to give the impression through his writings that he was old. Ruskin's first story was published in *The Illustrated Weekly of India* in 1951. It was called "My Calling" - a light humorous piece about a schoolmaster at BCS. *The Weekly* published the next one as well. It was called "The Untouchable" - a straight forward piece, no excess, no flourishes and very spare. It fetched him fifty rupees. He was convinced that he was a writer on the strength of a few stories sold to *The* Hindu's *Sport, Pastime* and *The Tribune* of Ambala.

For some time now, Ruskin had been toying with the idea of going off to England to fulfil his dream of becoming a writer. He felt that in England he would be closer to the literary world and his dream of becoming full-fledged writer could be shaped. His grandmother, Ellen Clerke had always been worried about his future, especially because of Mr. Hari's declining business. She had taken out an insurance policy in his name. The policy matured in 1951, and the money was sufficient to pay for his passage to Jersey in the Channel Islands where Aunt Emily lived. At his mother's request, Aunt Emily agreed to let Ruskin move in with her family to Jersey, to stay with her, until he found his bearings. From Aunt Emily's house Bond would be close to the literary world of London, where he had hopes of publishing his books. However, his decision led to inner conflict. One journal entry mentions: "Perhaps I am rotting here, perhaps the West will do me good. I have achieved nothing. I have achieved nothing but happiness (SWL 114). At the age of seventeen, Ruskin took a train out of Dehradun, bidding farewell to the comforts of home, the warmth of friends, to head towards a land unknown, with lots of dreams and aspirations especially with a desire to be published. Ruskin was now ready to take on the world. It was not easy giving up the things familiar. His last entry around this time in the Dehradun Journal says:

> To love and be loved is the greatest happiness . . . Men and women leave the age of childhood behind, and are so busy with their buyings and sellings, their ambitions and their hopes, their loves and their hates, that they forget they once lived in a land where dreams were real. I will not forget my childhood, I shall not surrender it. (SWL 130)

During his trip to the West, Bond realised for the first time how deeply he loved India. He states that "... no sooner had I set foot in the West, than I wanted to return to India and to all that I had known and loved" (SWL 23). In Jersey, Bond was terribly homesick for India. The irony of his situation was that in India he was a foreigner because of his race and British parentage, when he came 'home' to Jersey, he was not only in a place that was foreign to him but where he was regarded as an outsider because of being an Anglo-Indian. On the Jersey Islands he experienced a new alienation - more subtle, elusive and private and was characterised by increasing feeling of loneliness and rootlessness. The place provided neither companionship, nor cheer, "to a lonely and sensitive boy who had left home and friends in search of 'better future'" (Bond, TIIL 55). In *Lamp Is Lit: Leaves from a Journal*, recollecting those days he says that it was "The loneliest period of my life....And I yearned for all that I had left behind in India" (xiii). The nostalgia and homesickness overpowered him. He realised that his inclination and cultural identity lay not with Jersey but with India:

> It was while I was living in Jersey, in the Channel Island, that I really missed India. Jersey was a pretty island, with wide sandy bays and rocky inlets, but it was worlds away from the land in which I had grown up....I knew I did not belong there and I disliked the place intensely. Within the days of my arrival I was longing for the languid, easy-going, mango-scented air of small-town India. (SWL 131)

Bond's sense of dislocation was further intensified because of not getting along well particularly with his aunt, uncle and cousins who were "champions of Empire" (SWL 142). They constantly criticised him for being too Indian. They got irritated by his love for India, his Indian accent and regular correspondence with friends in Dehradun. They wanted him to forget his ties with India and be more British in his "preferences and attitudes" (SWL' 143). Their attitude about India was a matter of surprise for Bond because his uncle was a south Indian Christian and his aunt an Anglo-Indian. He resented their criticism about his Indian friends.

To support himself financially, Bond tried his hand at various jobs but could not succeed. He mentions in his writings how foolish he appeared whenever he ventured into anything else apart from writing. In "All You Need a Paper" he boldly confesses that he could do fairly well only one thing - putting pen to paper. Ruskin worked diligently during the day but spent the evenings in his attic room, shaping the journal entries he had made in 1951 into a first-person account of his friends and experiences in Dehradun. These journal entries took Bond vicariously to the places he missed and helped to resolve his cultural confusion: "I was only seventeen. But out of my loneliness I produced a novel, raw, naïve and imperfect, but brimming with life and joy and truth, my own truth, for to be true to oneself is to be true to others" (LIL xiii).

Mr. Bromley, a senior clerk in the Public Health Department where Bond worked for sometime was impressed by the dedication of this young author. He loaned Ruskin money to buy a typewriter to enable him to prepare a presentable manuscript for the publishers. By the end of 1952, Bond had already submitted the manuscript to three publishers in London and one of them, Andre Deutsch publishing house, liked his work but suggested him to visit London in order to discuss a few changes. The formalities and rules of jobs, the colonial attitude of Aunt's family and the invitation of the publishers from London made him think about moving out of Jersey. He felt his dream of becoming a writer would be jeopardised in Jersey. One day during his solitary wanderings he resolved that he was going to be a writer, "come hell or high water" (SWL 142) and in order to do so he had to move to London. This resolve was further strengthened when a few days later, he happened to quarrel with his uncle over an entry he had made in his diary in which he had expressed his resentment over the colonial attitudes that still prevailed in his uncle's family.

Bond had by then saved £12 from his salary and after giving a week's notice to the Public Health Department packed his literally battered suitcase and took the Cross-Channel ferry to Plymouth. He left Jersey for London with lots of aspirations. Though he was lonely but he was not afraid and discouraged. Now he would have freedom to be on his own completely that he always desired. In London too, he had done various jobs to support himself. He worked as a clerk by day and was writing away in the evening. His hectic job and difficulties of life did not prevent him from pursuing the literary life.

Bond lived in London like a nomad. He flitted from one lodging to another in various residential districts. He preferred north London because it was more cosmopolitan with a growing population of Indian, African and continental students. After the insularity of Jersey, Bond found London liberating and relaxing. Theatres, cinemas, bookshops, museums, libraries helped him in his self-education. Bond came in contact with the British Broadcasting Corporation and gave short talks on its Home Service program on such topics as "My Two Homes" and "Spring Festival." He also made friends with many Indian students and attended their cultural events but far from leading an insular life with Indians only, he made friends with students from Vietnam, Thailand and Europe as well. Among his many friends was a Vietnamese woman, Vu-Phuong, to whom he had proposed. But she left London to visit her parents in Vietnam. He never heard from her again. He had treasured the memory of that unrequited love and wrote about it in "The Girl from the Copenhagen." Bond's love stories never end happily. The beloved remains unattainable because of the difference of age, class or caste. The unhappy ending of his love stories has much to do with Bond's failure in love affairs, one with Vu-Phuong and the other with an Indian girl.

London had given him access to the publishing world. Diana Athill, editor and junior partner at Andre Deutsch had taken a personal interest in his career and in publishing his novel *The Room on the Roof.* On Athill's advice Bond restructured the book from a first person journal to a fictional narrative in the third person. The eager young author was open to suggestions and after two more drafts the novel was accepted for publication. Describing the mindset of publishers and his unyielding spirit, he writes:

> How I worked at that book! I was always being asked to put things in or take things out. At first the publishers suggested that it needed 'filling out'. When I filled it out, I was told that it was now a little too descriptive and would I prune it a bit? And what started out as a journal and then became a first-person narrative finally ended up in the third person. But editors only made suggestions; they did not tamper with your language or style. And the 'feel' of the story—my love for India and my friends in particular—was ever present, running through it like a vein of gold. (SWL 148)

Bond had been away from his roots for three years but the bond was as strong as ever. The longing to return had never left him. His perturbed mind could not find solace in a place away from India. Throwing light on the loss and homesickness, one experiences while being away from one's land, Salman Rushdie writes: "... the writer who is out-of-country and even out-of-language may experience this loss in an intensified form. It is made more concrete for him by the physical fact of discontinuity, of his present being in different place form his past, of his being 'elsewhere'" (*Imaginary Homelands* 12). Bond realised that he did not belong to the country of his forefathers but of his birth. He missed India and longed for the company of his friends at Dehradun. The pressures and pulls to return home were too strong to resist: "And I yearned for all that I had left behind in India. Alone, I walked the waterfront, the rainswept, windswept sea wall, talking to myself, promising myself that I'd be a published writer some day soon, and return to the sensuous welcoming arms of the land I had left" (Bond, LIL xiii).

The longing to return home - India started overpowering his entire being. He was not sure of how he would make a living when he finally returned to India. He did not have any proper qualifications for good jobs and even the possibilities for free-lancing then was not much in vogue. After spending over three years in Jersey and England, in 1955 he returned with his first book accepted for publication. He was brimming with confidence that he would make it as a successful writer in Dehradun. The book advance of £50 helped him in buying a ticket to India. He had also collected a small fee from the BBC and together with his savings from his job at Photax, Ruskin bought a ticket on the S.S. Batory, a Polish passenger liner and set sail for India. Since then he has been living in India and never ever thought of going out of India again even for visiting. Bond says in "Author's Note" in *Rusty Goes to London*:

> After returning from England when I was twenty-one, I have not left the shores of India. I suppose this says something for my attachments to this country, as well as for a secret fear that if I were to go abroad again I would never return. During that lonely year in Jersey, I felt as though I had been banished from India for ever. So I am not taking any chances. Rusty's adventures, as man and writer, will have to continue in India and for his Indian readers. (vii)

Upon returning, Bond set up his base in the hills of North India. He chose the charming landscape of Dehradun to begin his career as a freelancer. It was also a euphoric moment because he could be now near his old friends and the cherished known places in Dehradun. It could also provide him the proximity of the hills and rivers, above all, the freedom of being on his own, a dream desire of his life. Somewhere, he was also aware of the fact that Dehradun is not the place to make a career, especially in writing. It was a risky vocation bordering on eccentricity. But the call of the hills was difficult to resist. His nature-soaked heart has always craved for the proximity of hills. He says he could not fall in love with cities: "my heart was always in the hills and small towns of north India" (LIL 16). Off and on in his work, he discloses his love for hills and its importance in one's life. In the "Introduction" of *When Darkness Falls*, Bond shares his adoration for the hills:

> ... I chose the hills for the purpose of *living* rather than as a congenial place for writing. The mountains make a man realize just how insignificant he is. At the same time, they allow one to remain an individual instead of being swallowed up in the crowd. I enjoy visiting cities; I enjoy travelling over the plains of India; I am fascinated by the desert; but it is always good to come home to the hills. (x)

In Dehradun, Bond started living in a rented first floor flat in Astley Hall. The landlady, Bibiji was his stepfather's first wife. Although Bibiji was against her husband Hari and Bond's mother, she had no grudge against humble Bond. She also felt pity for him because of his lean and thin structure. She took him under her wing and soon he had his own room on the roof. She fed him with rich Indian delicacies. He learned that Mr. Hari had gone bankrupt in business in Dehradun therefore his mother, sister Ellen, brother William and two half- brothers were shifting to New Delhi with Hari. Bond had to do anything to support himself financially. But he did not want to get involved in any tedious and full time office job which could be an impediment to his career of writing. He could not think of compromising with his career on any account. He continued his freelancing with gusto. He bombarded every newspaper and magazine in the land with short stories, essays, articles and even poems. In those days there were hardly any book publishers around to encourage the budding writers (apart from those who brought out text-books), so that one really had to concentrate on journalism. About payments he says: "Payments varied from five to fifty rupees per article, but for several years

I manage to eke out a living as a freelance. That man is strongest who stands alone!" (RIM vii) His ambitious stories went to *The Illustrated Weekly of India*. In 1956 it serialised *The Room on the Roof*, followed a year later by its sequel, *Vagrants in the Valley*. He wrote short articles on a variety of subjects ranging from ghosts to buffaloes for *The Sunday Statesman* and *The Illustrated Weekly* and a couple of other well-known papers - Baburao Patel's *Mother India, The Hindu's Sport* and *Pastime, The Tribune* of Ambala, *Sanik Samachar* and *The Leader* of Allahabad. The most noteworthy was *My Magazine of India* from Madras. Whatever manuscripts came back from the more famous magazines and newspapers with slips of regrets, Ruskin re-mailed those to *My Magazine*. *My Magazine* then paid princely sum of Rs. 5 for a story. Bond was eking out his livelihood somehow as a freelancer. He recalls the publishing condition of those days:

> At that time there were only some half a dozen English language magazines in India and almost no book publishers (except for a handful of educational presses left over from British days). The possibilities were definitely limited; but this did not deter me. I had confidence in myself (too much, perhaps), plenty of guts.... (SWL 155-156)

The three years in Dehradun were difficult ones. He soon realised that he could not continue like this. In his age group, anyone who wanted to do anything worthwhile was moving away from the slump the town was going through. He too had to move on to a big city to look for a regular job. In 1959, he left Dehradun for Delhi to live with his mother and stepfather albeit by paying rent. It was not easy and in the first year he had no job. But soon he started working for CARE (the Cooperative for American Relief Everywhere), an international relief agency. Here, he had to write reports to help channel funds to the right place. Bond felt suffocated in the hectic and humdrum life of Delhi. The prickly heat, the treeless colony, hot dusty winds constantly oppressed the body and soul of Bond. In an attempt to escape the city life, he walked across the main road and into the fields, finding old wells, irrigation channels, camels, buffaloes and sighting birds and small creatures.

From 1959 to 1963, Ruskin wrote travelogues, essays and stories for children. His job left him with very little time to launch into longer works. He continued recording his impressions, in his journals. Bond has found his vocation. In "Bus Stop, Pipalnagar" he says: "Moods and moments are for geniuses," "it's really a matter of working hard" (Bond, NTD 63). By the end of 1963, Ruskin had his fill of big city life. He gave up his job and said good-bye to the rush and tumult of Delhi and moved to the foothills of Mussoorie - "Queen of Hills" near his beloved Dehradun. He reminisces, "I was tired of a desk job. It could well have taken away my freedom and I could well have lost my dream of becoming full time writer" (Saili, *Ruskin Our Enduring* 93).

The phase of difficulties did not end even after returning from Delhi. Those were trying days for him as he had to work hard for a living. Avenues were few except for a few odd magazines that paid small amounts; there were no other opportunities for a free-lancer. Meanwhile he had discovered *The Christian Science Monitor* in Boston, *Blackwood's* in Edinburgh and *The Asia Magazine* in Hong Kong to publish his works. His children's books also began to publish in different parts of the world. It sustained him through the difficult days; Bond, however, survived: "As a writer, I have known hope and despair, success and failure; some recognition but also long periods of neglect and critical dismissal" (TIIL 132). He feels this neglect and criticism is indispensable part of a writing career. For aspiring writers, his advice is simple: "Inspite of discouragement, dedicated writer carry on. Never despair, is their motto, and if you do, then works on in despair" (Bond, LD xii). Commenting on Bond's devotion to writing, Ganesh Saili tells his interviewer: "I have seen him go down to Rs.200 in the bank balance but never did any thought of giving up writing cross his mind. He always wanted to be a writer and there was nothing to equal joy of putting pen to paper for him" (The Hindu, 2005).

At last, Bond's life had taken a new turn dispelling the clouds of slow success and unnoticed career. After a long interim of depression and self-doubt in his middle-years, he returned to his vocation first as a children's writer, a move that rejuvenated his creative power. The turning point really came during the 1980s. The advent of large publishing houses, like Penguin and Rupa in India proved a revival of interest in his writings. In 1996, Penguin India published Bond's complete stories and novels in the omnibus. The publication covers almost thirty books of Bond. He has also published two autobiographies. The first one *Scenes from a Writer's Life* (1997) describes his formative years of growing up in Anglo India. It covers the first twenty-one years of his life. The second book *The Lamp Is Lit* picks up when Bond returned to India after two-year stay in England. It records his early forays into the literary magazines of the 1950s and 60s along with some examples of his work at the time. His *Rain in the Mountains: Notes from the Himalayas* comprises a collection of essays and articles from various journals published long ago. His manuscripts are housed by Dr. Howard Gotlieb in his archives at the Mugar Memorial Library, Boston University.

The Penguin India brought together the episodes from Rusty's life in a sequence. It gave it certain continuity so that the saga of Rusty could continue over five volumes. The events of the life of Rusty a quiet and sensitive British boy who first appeared in *The Room on the Roof* were put in order in which they might happen, not in the order in which they are written. Bond says in the "Author's Note" of *Rusty the Boy from the Hills*:

> Stories featuring Rusty (my alter ego) go back to my beginnings as a writer, when the sixteen-year-old Rusty appeared as the central character in *The*

> *Room on the Roof*, my first novel. Since then he has turned up in stories written at different periods of my life—sometimes as a small boy, sometimes as a schoolboy or teenager or young adult. These stories first appeared in magazines, then in diverse collections. They formed scattered episodes in the life of Rusty. (vii)

The events are arranged in five volumes to give us a complete picture of Rusty - growing up from a seven year old to a young man. The first of these books, *Rusty the Boy from the Hills* traces Rusty's development from early childhood to his early teens. Rusty is a quiet, imaginative and sensitive boy who unlike his counterpart Swami in R.K. Narayan's *Swami and Friends* is not mischievous. He lives in his grandparents' custody in pre-independent Dehradun. His evident love for flowers, trees, animals and the mountain is the underlying theme of the book. Though he is not the adventurous sort himself, the strangest and most extraordinary things keep happening around him. He is, in fact, a child of nature like Wordsworth's Lucy, given to wandering in the woods of Simla, listening to the calls of the cuckoo, looking for the nest of squirrel to restore the baby squirrels to its mother. His world is peopled with birds and animals rather than human beings. The second book *Rusty Runs Away* takes Rusty's story forward to his adolescent years. It captures exciting moments from Rusty's life, his running away from his school in the company of mischievous Daljit and later by escaping from the strict confines of his guardian's home and finding friendship and adventure with Somi, Ranbir, Kishen and others. In discovering this new life, the teenaged Rusty also discovers a different kind of India from that in which he grew up. The book traces five years of his life that sees his father and grandmother pass away in quick succession and Rusty is left in the care of a guardian, Mr. Harrison in Dehradun. Soon, he is sent away to boarding school. One day, overcome with restlessness and an ambition to cross the seas and travel the world,

Rusty decides to run away from school. The third volume *Rusty and the Leopard* marks Rusty's rebelliousness and his eventful progression into manhood. *Rusty Goes to London* traces his life in Jersey and England the country of his forefathers and his coming to the conclusion that India is his home and not England. He returns to Dehradun and settles into his role as full-time author. *Rusty Comes Home* is the fifth and final volume which contains some captivating stories about Rusty's friends and fleeting acquaintances, about human nature and the supernatural element.

Bond finally settled down in, 'the honeymoon capital' of northern India, Mussoorie, the place, he believes of his genetic beginning. Mussoorie was a relatively inexpensive hill station those days. Things are here rather different now; it has become a rich man's playground. It is often described as "Delhi's Chandni Chowk on a Hillside," though *Landour Cantonment* where Bond lives is much calmer. Earlier Bond lived in Mussoorie proper, in Maplewood Cottage just below *Wynberg-Allen School* until 1976. Now he lives in Ivy Cottage Landour 7,000 feet from the foothills of the Himalayan Mountains, with his large adopted family. The windows of his house open out on the forest and the distant snow-peaks of the Himalayas kindle in him the waves of inspiration. Even today, he is as productive as ever and gets many of his ideas by reminiscing while gazing out of the window of his apartment towards the Lower Western *Himalaya,* the *Pauri* Hills and the *Doon Valley.* From his perch atop Mullingar Hill at Landour Cantonment, he can always reach into his rich life experiences, especially his childhood and early adulthood for yet another story line or another evocative character. Like Emily Dickinson, Bond received his life view from the window in his house. Both the writers Dickinson and Bond are introspective in nature and unravel the mystery and misery of the world, serenity and beauty of nature looking through the window of their house. Through the narrator of the story "The Window" Bond emphasises the power of window:

> ...from the window of my room I owned the world....the window was more fun than anything else. It gave us the power of detachment: we were deeply interested in the life around us, but we were not involved in it. 'It is like a cinema'... 'The window is the screen, the world is the picture.' (CF 14-16)

People have this conception that Bond like a recluse is living alone amidst nature and recapturing its vibrant hues. But such is not the case. He is in fact the eldest member of a family of eleven which over the decades has grown around him. In 1970, Prem, a hill boy came to work for him and started living with him. Prem got married and filled the void in the life of the bachelor Ruskin with grace of children and grand children. Bond always feels indebted for the love and pleasure that the family of Prem provides him. It has become an integral part of his personal life. It gives him the warmth and emotional security of a happy home without virtually going through marital experience. Expressing his gratitude for the family, he says: "If it were not for the family that has grown up around me, making me a prisoner of love, I doubt if I would have remained rooted to one place so long – Mussoorie and its surroundings" (SWL xvi). The children Rakesh, Mukesh and Savitri and grandchildren Siddharth and Shrishti of Prem infuse a life force in his single life, an ideal situation for a creative writer:

> I have become a family man by virtue of remaining a bachelor. In many ways, this is the ideal situation for a writer. All the noise, merriment and bedlam of a large family living together has become an integral part of my own life, and for the most part it's joy to my heart and music to my ears. And for me, it makes up for the lonely childhood years when I felt distanced from family and could find happiness only in the homes of friends or between the covers of books. (SWL xvi)

Bond got recognition at a very early stage of his life. In 1957 he was awarded the John Llewellyn Rhys Memorial Prize for his epoch making first novel, *The Room on the Roof* written when he was just seventeen. It is an annual award given to a quality work of fiction written by the British Commonwealth (which then included India) under the age of thirty. The hero of this semi-autobiographical novel is named significantly as Rusty - possibly one who was likely to rust in the dust. But he successfully overcomes the hurdles of life and carves out a distinguished place for himself in the world showing an unwavering faith in life. The novel deals with the growing up of a British child in a changing India. Although he believes himself to be of British blood, Rusty, the tale's orphaned protagonist finds himself strangely attracted to the colourful crafts, the spicy scent of Indian food and the energetic hubbub of the local bazaar. Rusty discovers that he is of mixed English and Indian heritage and leaves to make his own way in the town of Dehradun when beaten by his overly strict English guardian. He starts living with Kapoor family, tutoring their son Kishen and occupying a room on the roof. Tragedy strikes when his naïve romantic relationship with Meena Kapoor, the mother of his young student ends with the sudden death of Meena in an accident. The novel *Room on the Roof* made its author something of a celebrity in India, not only because of his young age but because he was able to capture the spirit of the land and its people so sensitively through his fiction. Throughout his twenties Bond continued to write novels, not turning to writing for children until he had reached his thirties. Since then, he has written numerous stories and poems that capture his nostalgia for his boyhood days - the natural beauty and tranquillity of his grandparents' home and the close, secure and loving relationships that he experienced with friends and his adopted family.

In ,1987, the Indian Council for Child Education recognised his pivotal role in the growth of children's literature in India and selected him as an outstanding writer of children's literature. He received the Sahitya Akademy Award for his book *Our Trees Still Grow in Dehra* in 1992. He became one of the ten authors to be honoured and published by the Penguin Books in 1995. He was awarded the Padma Shri for his life time contribution to Indian English Literature in 1999. In 2003, he is being awarded the N.D. Mehra Memorial Award for his contribution to children's literature at the New Delhi World Book Fair. Today, greater than these awards are the large numbers of children who have become avid readers of his works. His works have become an integral part of school syllabi all over India. He has endeared himself to his readers by his versatile, original and engrossing style of story-telling in a variety of genres. He has been conferred Doctorate *honoris causa* by the Banaras Hindu University. His works have been published for over fifty years by at least thirty different publishers - a unique record of sorts. Many of his books have been translated into French, German, Danish, Dutch and Spanish. His novella *A Flight of Pigeons* was adapted into the acclaimed Merchant Ivory Hindi film *Junoon* by Shayam Bengal. His 'Adventures of Rusty' adapted into the Hindi television serial *Ek Tha Rusty.* The Bollywood director Vishal Bharadwaj made a heart-warming film based on his popular novella for children *The Blue Umbrella.* The movie bagged the 2006 National Film Award for the best children's film.

The literary career of Bond that has spanned over five decades now, by way of innumerable short stories, essays, poems, novellas, memoirs, travelogues, articles, columns in leading newspapers, reminiscences and documentaries, have achieved pinnacle of perfection. Bond's goal as a writer is to be a "simple storyteller" who gives pleasure to both adults and children (LIL x-xi). He has charted out and peopled a unique literary landscape where he advocates the romance of day-to-day lives of commoners. He is a writer of the earth, supremely content to walk, desiring no wings. The artistic force of his enchanting writing gets intensified by the breadth of his experience.

Simplicity and quietude in life and in art is a part of his lasting appeal. He has got tremendous critical acclaim for his nostalgic, heart-warming, tongue-in-cheek and inimitable style. He writes simply without recourse to bombast. He is out to tell a good story and creates believable and identifiable characters with which the readers can identify themselves.

The optimistic fervour and the unyielding spirit of the commoners dominate the creativity of Bond when he portrays 'little' India. He sensitively paints the sensuous images and nuances of his beloved country, India. His India emerges as a happy, rapturous and glorious land where there is laughter and joy, love and hope, where dream comes true, where the people are friendly and accommodate all, where people do not surrender to circumstances and have learned to live and laugh amidst the clouds of trouble. The people about whom he writes - fictional or real, British, Anglo-Indian or Indian are true to life and are marked by a sense of dignity. The personae of his discourse are ordinary folks belonging to villages and small towns who reaffirm the value of peaceful co-existence, grace and honesty by their conduct and character. It is Bond's unpretentious yet accomplished style that captures the imagination of his readers. Arvind Krishna Mehrotra says, "The interest in the emotional lives of small-town folk is reflected in obtrusive style of Bond's writing" (*Illustrated History* 222). Some of Bond's stories present people who, consciously or otherwise need each other: people in love or in need of love, the cumbersome adolescent in edgy relationship with kith and kin and with the milieu, a timid lover trying to come to terms with his bewildered emotions, the vagabond and destitute in need of support and care. Some are gently satirical studies about village and small-town braggarts and petty officials. Several others mourn the tragedies of human error; the gradual erosion of the rich beauty of the hills and the gentle people living in the rural heartland. But the enduring charm of his stories lies in their assertion of the dignity and 'quiet heroism' of the characters he describes. All the stories are rewarding for the authentic portrayal of love, loss, achievement, pain and struggle.

The literature of Bond is a harmonious amalgamation of the songs of experience and the ceremonies of innocence. He skilfully blends these two aspects, innocence and experience: by describing the serenity and beauty of nature; by portraying the ingenuousness and precociousness of children; by recounting the lament of old people for the bygone days; by narrating the unyielding spirit and shattered dreams of neglected and ignored class of society - beggars, cobblers, drivers, retards, vendors, sweepers, prostitutes, watchmen; by illuminating the encounter with mischievous ghosts and other horror-stricken supernatural elements. His fictional world is enriched with dreams and aspirations of undemanding simple people whose dreams flutter in the dust like their unnoticed life. He accepts the world as it is and loves human beings as he finds them without moralising on their vices. His characters, despite being commoners - a failure, a destitute, a criminal, an old kite maker, a wayside station *khalasi* (watchman), survive and illumine the pages of his fiction because of their originality and universality. Sharing the reasons of interest in these commoners, Bond says in *Friends in Small Places*: "Meet some of the people I can never forget. Not because they were of great importance or stature but because their individuality made them stand out from the commonplace. It was not money or success but pride in themselves that set them apart" (vii).

Bond's novella *Delhi Is Not Far* celebrates the unsung sagas of the common masses, their unfulfilled dreams, their complacency, their fear and their unnoticed life. His interest in impoverished people of small-town-India comes to the fore in Pipalnagar - a world burgeoned by the simple folk and their ordinary life, where each day is like another. There is not exactly despair but resignation, indifference to intercourse of life and to both living and dying. Nothing momentous happenings occur here. The narrator of the story Arun lives in a tiny room. He shares it with lizards, mosquitoes, thieving rat and an itinerant beggar who occasionally shares his sagging *charpai* (bed). One day he stumbles across a homeless boy, Suraj. Being enchanted by the beauty of Suraj's long limbs, hesitant smile and eyes full of secrets, Arun offers to share his room with Suraj. Arun befriends Kamla, a delicate twenty-three-year old prostitute. The trio Arun, Suraj and Kamla adopt one another. With a miniaturist's skill, the author paints the town folk of Pipalnagar around the unlikely family. The dreams of common masses of Pipalnagar are common. *Pan*-chewing barber Deep Chand dreams to open a more up-to-date saloon in Delhi where he might give the Prime Minister a hair cut. Pitamber, the rickshaw-*wala* wants to trade his cycle rickshaw for the less demanding scooter-rickshaw. Aziz, junk shop owner, who at eighteen, already collected dust, age and disease (Tuberculosis) would be happy with a junk shop in Chandni Chowk. Arun, a struggling young writer of detective novels in Urdu waits for inspiration to write a blockbuster. One day he will pack his meagre belongings and take the express train out of Pipalnagar, a sleepy town. The epileptic and homeless orphan Suraj, a hawker of knick-knack is surprisingly optimistic about his future. Kamla, the young prostitute knows that she cannot escape from her plight. She has learnt to live with her drunkard husband. The novella ends without anyone realizing his or her dream. But these common folk of Pipalnagar would go on living. Even with unfulfilled dreams they are not angst-ridden individuals; they would delight in life and share the suffering of one another and celebrate ordinary joys together. Few authors can write with such sensitivity and skill about 'little' India as does Bond. Meera Khorana appreciates Bond's stories that are drenched with deeper aspects of life, which spring from the life of humble and modest people and their positive aura: "At the heart of [Bond's] writings the value placed on simplicity and a selfless attitude toward life. Although the stories deal with the pleasures of humble people, their loves are enriched by meaningful experiences and a profound insight into life" (Khorana, *Twentieth Century* 123-26).

Bond loves to observe the hues of life and is keen to paint it through colourful vibrant strokes. He is at ease with the dew of the morning, the sensuous delight of the day, the silent blessings of the night, the joys and sorrows of children, the striving of ordinary folk and the ridiculous situations in which one, at times, finds oneself. It is his enthralling style and humanistic bend that suffused interest in his otherwise commonplace theme. Bond's gentle and noble heart creeps around every expression and description. The sincerity in description provides charm and relevance to his common and crude realism. With the same zeal and insight he describes, the *gulmohar* trees in their fiery summer splendour, a raindrop on a blade of grass, a hoopoe on the grass, a blue jay performing aerial acrobatics, a lizard on the rock, the scent of wet earth after the first rain, a hidden pool behind the rocky mountain and grassland, barefoot boys riding buffaloes and chewing sugarcane, a tea shop to a way side station, a *dhaba* on the road connecting the cities. The fervour of his genuine compassion never wavers in portraying the commoners like waifs, orphans, restless adolescents, frustrated old men, beggars, tonga and truck drivers, mentally challenged people, watchmen, sweepers, thieves, blinds and others. His literature, in a true sense, is a paean of the marginalised. He, with compassionate outlook depicts the pleasant and unpleasant and hideous and elegant aspects of life. His belief "man being a very imperfect creation" (Bond, *A Town Called Dehra* 172) motivates him toward total acceptance of life. The absence of evil in his works is due to his unflinching faith in the inherent goodness of humanity. Commenting on this aspect, Nirmal Sadhu says: "Simple people day-to-day situations and important persons and places of the Doon valley are described with sensitivity. Only a writer of deep understanding and observation can draw so much from the otherwise eventless, dreary life in the hills"(Nirmal Sadhu, *The Tribune,* 2004).

India is a vast and complex country, "a melting-pot of races and religions" (Bond, *Tales and Legends from India* 11). Vividness and variety exist in every aspect of Indian life - topography, climate, culture, language and life style. There is multiplicity of the life lived in the vast spaces of India. Avtar Singh Bhullar writes in *India Myth and Reality*: "...in India a host of languages, people, religions, castes, classes etc. make the nation so complex and entangled that even after years of effort to understand this "queer nation" one is liable to remain perplexed about the nature of Indian 'reality' and of Indians in general"(1). Indian reality denotes many India existing and flourishing simultaneously in Indian sub-continent. The reality of a board meeting in a five star hotel in a metropolis, or the reality of a flood-ravaged village in Bihar, or the reality of an expatriate who returns to his motherland rejecting the lucrative offers, or the reality of a growing child in the Himalayas, or the exploitation of women in family matrix, all are but different angles of the one circle India. Every writer sees and interprets India through his own perspective. He sets his telescope to the area of his liking and explores almost contradictory facets of the Indian reality. Some like R.P. Jhabvala focuses on dirt, squalor and the poverty of India, some turn their attention towards religion and philosophy of India and glorify them like Raja Rao and Manohar Malgonkar, some discuss the myriad of social problems and advocate for its reform, like Mulk Raj Anand, Bhabani Bhattacharya and Kamala Markandaya. Some like Shobha De shoots out their subject matter from urban life and glamorous world and others scan the Indian villages for their subjects. Bond stands apart from these writers. His India lives and breathes in the hills and he kindles his cameo with its landscape, its simple folk and their challenging life. The life and setting presented by him retain a sylvan character - unspoiled, unsoiled and tranquil. His literature like painting reveals the soul of the piece through harmonious and varied subtle colours and effects.

Bond, despite his British descent does not write about India from a Eurocentric perspective. His mirroring image of India is marked by his love and attachment for India and its milieu. The hallmark feature of his literature is deeper understanding of Indian culture and its convincing portrayal. The Indian sensibility that he invokes is more authentic than the writers who exploit the Indian realities to attract foreign readers. Bond's Indian and English identity merges into one when he draws a character. His characters are never ridiculous and laughable caricatures but are genuine and true to life. He never seems to dangle between the divided loyalties. His double inheritance proves an asset for him. Endowed with remarkable openness, he is always ready to receive impressions coming from all sides. He himself feels proud of being a man of double heritage. The special attributes of both the cultures have enriched his vision and make him liberal and more adjustable. He states: "Being a child of changing times, I had grown up with divided loyalties; but at the end of the journey I had come to realize that I was blessed with a double inheritance. And I was determined to make the most of it" (SWL xvi). Bond seems comfortable with both the cultures: Indian and English and there is no sense of tension between the two. He truly bridges the two cultures and does not seem to have characteristics bias of either an Indian or a British author. Commenting on Bond's successful assimilation of the two cultures, Bill Aitken writes: "Ruskin's childhood that straddled two cultures ... could have produced a bitter adult ... Instead he glides unperturbed through both worlds of westernised and unsophisticated India..." (Singh, *Creative Contours* 179).

According to historian Patrick Colm Hogan, as a result of post-colonialism and globalisation, a person's contact with different cultures increases and constitutes a challenge to their identity. In general, he argues that people react in one of two ways, assimilation or syncretism. Assimilation is the full acceptance of the other culture while syncretism is a combination of the two cultures where the person chooses what seems best from each culture. Hogan argues that syncretism is the attitude most common among post-colonial writers. Bond seems to have assimilated the Indian culture and made it his own.

Bond's immersion to Indian culture and traditions and his penchant to the soil of mother India provide authenticity to the ambience presented in his work. In the words of Mulk Raj Anand: "... he has gone far beyond other British writers into the heartland without any assumption of superiority and without imposing his own idea of India like other orientalists. He has approached our land as a native in the manner of Verrier Elwin" (Singh, *Creative Contours* 8). Having lived his whole life in India, barring those four years when he was discovering his main roots, he knows the country as an insider, writing with an accuracy and emotional engagement about the land and the people of small town - Pipalnagar, Deoli, Shamli, Shahganj, Shahjahanpur. Nripendra Singh calls him an "Indophile Britisher who by choice and predilection becomes a naturalized Indian whose knowledge of the Indian airs and homes is more authentic and sensitively accurate than those of the Indian critics whose knowledge of the Indian countryside is ridiculously bookish and unfaithful" (Singh, *Contemporary Indian English Short Story* 45). His book *The India I Love* is written to express his love and long association with India and its various aspects. The following quote conspicuously encapsulates his perception about India: "The India that I love comprises the goodwill and good humour of ordinary people; a tolerance for all customs; non-interference in others' private lives; a friendly reciprocation at all times; a philosophical acceptance of hardships; love and affection, especially in children" (TIIL ix). The warmth of his attachment with India is also observed by Nirmal Sadhu: "His love for his country - India is not adopted country but his motherland as much as it is for any one of us - becomes apparent in every word he writes and every phrase he composes."

In fact, there is a lot of commonality between Bond and Narayan, in the sense that both the writers have brought their own little world of Dehradun and Malgudi endearingly alive and close to the heart of their readers. Narayan's writings lovingly talk about the ordinary folk of Malgudi, their struggle to accommodate themselves in the changing world and the old value systems. Like Naryan's Malgudi, Bond too brings alive a part of India: Garhwal hills, the subtropical Siwaliks and Dehradun. He amazingly invokes the settings, the customs, the occupation and the struggle of gentle folk and catches the uniqueness in the ordinary. His fiction could be termed as local colour literature. His delineation of character nuggets on hill life bears the mark of realism which at time is more poignant than Narayan. Some of Narayan's Malgudi books provide a fictional map of the place in the inside jacket. Bond's stories too supply us with a similar and familiar set of locations that might easily be drawn on an imaginary map, the Mall, with its bakeries and shops, the familiar trees and flowers, the run-down once magnificent hotel or house that belonged to so-and-so and the all important cemeteries. His fiction like travelogue writing helps the readers to locate the place. Bond and Narayan both focus the thwarted aspirations of their *homo fictus* and record them with humanitarian approach and comic gift. The comical scene is created through humour in Bond and through wit in Narayan, through self- deprecation in Bond and through social satire in Narayan. Both were touched by the innocence and simplicity of children and conjured it up in their literature. Bond writes about children mature enough of their age, Narayan about adults young for their age. Both have created believable characters with which the readers can identify their lives and day-to-day problems. Their choice of medium novel and short story and their place of living north and south of India bring variety in their work. Both have tried to present the realities of life around them with utmost sincerity.

The art of Bond is often set in contrast with Rudyard Kipling. Like Kipling, Bond too had lived in India and evoked Indian life especially of Simla, Dehradun and other hill towns. Kipling's vision of childhood and his jungle lores have much in common with Bond. Kipling's voice is interpreted as the voice of an imperialist. His fiction is characterised by his strong plea for the justification and usefulness of the British rule. He assumed the superiority of the British race and propounded a framework of imperial mythology through his fiction. Bond's opinion differs from him. A genuine spirit and an empathetic outlook overpower every picture that Bond sketches. Despite his inwardness with Indian life, Kipling responds in a surprisingly conventional fashion. He fails to comprehend the basic aspects of Hindu mythology and is unable to distinguish between legend and reality. Bond's creative orientation differs from Kipling. His understanding of Indian realities has enabled him to delineate the authentic images of India that are both convincing and artistically satisfying. He gives his readers the true feel of the Indian life that he has seen and experienced. His European blood seems to flow through Indian sensibility. His humane interest in mankind produces sensitive vignettes of Indian life and characters. The vivid and colourful presentation is done in Kipling's work more to cater English reader than to reveal love for the foster country. Bond keeps himself away from sensationalism, from false exotica, away from maharajas, beggars, spies and *shikaris*, away from romantic English women and their far pavilions. He writes about India for Indian readers without an eye on international audience. He does not at any point look to interpret India to the West. Hence there is no glorification of poverty, no slickness and no smugness. There is no artifice to his works, it is written from the core of the heart of a lover who loves to write about his beloved country India. He dabbles in art for soul's sake:

> He observed with great avidity

The Indian way of life
Particularly in the mountainous regions
And wrote about with an élan.
(Swapan K. Banerjee, *The Asian Age,* 2001).

Unlike the diasporic writers Farrukh Dhondy, Salman Rushdie and V.S. Naipaul (who too invoked Indian milieu and landscape), Bond has lived in India permanently in his adored Garhwal Hills. His faithful record of humble people of Garhwall hills, their humble joys and sorrows create an image which is faithfully true to the classical image as a country of simple people having the faith in the essential goodness of human nature. He has nothing to show which runs alien to the self-respecting Indian. Discussing the work of Indo-Anglican writers, Srinivas Iynger criticises their undue interest in the foreign audience than in the Indian audience. Instead of presenting a true image of India they give the kind of the image that the west is supposed to want or expect: "... cobras and sadhus and decadent Hindus and phoney intellectuals and corruption in high places and fantasy and superstitions" (Iyenger, *Indian Writing in English* 697) to please the foreign audience. Bond has affectionately created the variegated nuances of Indian life with absolute genuineness. He does not have a sense of superiority over Indians. He never observes contemptuously the negative aspects of Indian life dust, squalor, heat, mosquito, vagabond, beggar, thief, blind, prostitute and street dancer. For him the bright day and dark night are integral parts of life. He accepts heartily every happenings and sees silver lining in darkest cloud. He celebrates the unyielding spirit of Indians amidst harrowing circumstances. His descriptions are marked by verisimilitude. He loves the landscape, tradition and culture of the country and evokes them in his work. In an interview with Ruby Gupta on being asked "Do you consider yourself as an Indian, writing in English ...?" (Sharma, R.S. *Studies in Contemporary Literature* 163) His response is:

> I do consider myself an Indian writer, writing in English, I don't know that anything really sets me apart from others, apart from the fact may be that I grew up in ... you might say, an English or Anglo-Indian household. So at that age when I was very young, I probably saw India through a rather mixed perspective, if you understand. And as I have grown older and the longer I've lived here, perhaps I've become more and more Indian. But perhaps my childhood and boyhood years, which were formative years - I was still a bit of an outsider looking in, rather than an insider looking out. . . (Ibid., 164)

He selects a genuine Indian subject and creates an adequate Indian idiom to express it. His Indianness is poignant like any other writer, writing in English, as he points out:

> My inspiration or subject matter if you like, has always come from my Indian background and experience—my relationship to people, the landscape, the atmosphere. The West never affected me in the same way. I spent almost four years in the UK, but very little of that time or experience made any impression on me, either as a person or as a writer. (Bond, *When Darkness Falls* ix)

Bond shuns away from the burning social issues like casteism, class-conflict, religious bigotry, the economical condition of the masses or political upheavals. Bond believes that these issues have been "dealt with far more effectively by writers who are more gifted in that direction" (LIL xi). Bond is intellectually not incapable of dealing with them but they simply do not stir him as nature and everyday life does. He puts: "I had always thought that man's relationship with the natural world was a social issue" (LIL xi). He writes about the unsung life of the people living across the road. He weaves a lively and interesting story taking an incident from his life or life of the people around him. He confesses: "...I have no pretensions at writing a great writing, a great sociological novel. I am basically an Indian Charles Lamb" (Sehgal, *Times of India*). His writing is full of passion, one actually feels all the emotions portrayed in his stories. His religious mind sees presence of god in a raindrop than in a place of worship. He is more interested in the unyielding spirit of a destitute than a famous political leader. His contentment with his subject-matter makes him comment:

> ... I'm happy with my theme. Ask me to write a piece on petunias, and I'll turn out an enthusiastic essay on this underrated flower. I might even write a story about someone who grows petunias, because such a person must obviously have sterling qualities....But ask me to write the life story of a great leader or media tycoon or matchbox-maker, and I'm stumped and stymied....I cannot breathe life into these subjects....(LIL 195-96)

Bond's soul lives far from the madding arena of socio-political thoughts. The popular sensational themes possibly do not touch him from within. His credo is to be an undemanding story writer. He is "happy to give a little innocent pleasure to a handful of readers" (TIIL 134). For him the day-to-day life and the gentle hill folks that have become an integral part of his psyche are more captivating than the glamorous world of politics or media. He candidly admits in *The Night Train at Deoli and Other Stories*:

> I have never been any good at the more lurid sort of writing. Psychopathic killers, impotent war-heroes, self-tortured film stars, and seedy espionage agents must exist in this world, but strangely enough, I do not come across them, and I prefer to write about the people and places I have known and the lives of those whose paths I have crossed. (9)

Bond's writing is immensely popular and has merit

in history despite small range. He like Jane Austen is content with his 'little-bit of ivory.' He does not write for the sake of writing or earning immediate fame. Writing for him is 'Sadhana,' a mode of prayer. It gives him immense pleasure that he wants to share with his readers. Salman Rushdie has once said: "Literature is self-validating. That is to say, a book is not justified by its author's worthiness to write it, but by the quality of what has been written" (*Imaginary Homelands* 14). Bond's genius can not be questioned for what he avoids to write. He should be rather extolled for writing humanitarianly and lovingly about Indian villages and small towns, its peaceful rural life, its generous and loving people, its flora and fauna. This is particularly important because as modernisation, urbanisation and westernisation continue to affect India many lives are bound to change. Bond's time capsule of villages and small towns of India will remain with us.

Bond a dedicated writer focuses his attention on something deeper and higher and his genuine subjects sprout out from the core of his heart. His ordinary people and the ordinary setting in which they feature show Bond's love for commoner. His characters struggle for survival. They are not disillusioned by the weariness, fever and fret. He writes affectionately about a poor old vendor in "The Box Man" who hawks his wares, an ayah whose loving care to a child makes her child's "My First Love," an outcaste in "Untouchable" whose presence consoles a child of upper class in the moment of loneliness and fear, a dumb nit-wit Goonga who is often pestered by hooligans in *Vagrants in the Valley*. He sees the squalor, poverty, mystery and muddle of India with an eye of a compassionate observer but he neither affirms them nor negates them. He draws attention towards the unnoticed daily activities which have their own role to play in our preoccupied life. His creativity lies in the fact that he has discovered adventure in small day-to-day happenings. An ordinary happening or scene in his stories leads us to the perception of the inner truth of a character:

> A man is beating out a strip of red-hot tin on his anvil. A boy is filling a bent bicycle-pump with sand (to keep it firm) before straightening it out with his hammer. The entire family, including bearded old men wizened old women ready to take off on broomsticks, and naked grand children, is at work. Handsome people these; and although they live in dirt and squalor, they seem *quiet* and dignified. (LIL 24)

Bond emerges like a trustworthy friend interested to share his varied experiences with his readers. He is a skilled story teller who plays with his material the way he likes. It is by his splendid effort he turns ordinary events into extraordinary and fascinating. The plot generally starts from a punch line and gradually catches the intensity of the moments, and gets the essence. In the story "The Boy Who Broke the Bank" a small remark by Nathu, a sweeper boy —"I haven't even received my regular pay" (CF 35) builds up a rumour. The rumour spreads through the town until everyone begins to withdraw his or her money and the bank is really on the verge of bankruptcy. Nathu does not know that it is his casual comment about late payment system of the bank has become the reason of its sudden collapse: "'Who would have thought the bank would collapse!' he said to himself, and looked thoughtfully into distance. 'I wonder how it could have happened ....'" (CF 39)

Reading a Bond story is like watching a glorious sunset. The story like sunset fades out. But what has been experienced is preserved in the store of memory forever. Thus, he embraced whatever often remained neglected. Within his deliberately chosen limited range, he has produced fiction of everlasting impact. It has soothing effect on his readers and lulls them not to sleep but a unique awareness of the realities of life without registering any complain against it. His work is like an oasis, a green patch in the dreary desert of modern feverish writing that soothes the reader by its therapeutic and rejuvenating effect: "His words are capable of brightening all life and transforming this awful world of ours, with its startling facts and gruesome daily phenomena, into a castle of dreams not fantasized but realised" (Singh, *Creative Contours* 2).

Literature is manifestation of the fulfilled and unfulfilled dreams and aspirations of a writer. A writer's personality and perception, trial and tribulations, faith and frustration get an outlet through his writings. Bond's work is fine example of this. His art is projection of his life. His own mood and spirit is embodied throughout his work. The sensitive portrayal of poor and orphan children, lonely and old Anglo-Indians, neglected and rejected common masses of society, niggles of adolescent and inclination to the world of nature have much to do with his insecure and troubled childhood, lonely youth and single life. It is his devotion to writing and dedication to the heavenly landscape around his abode that helped him to overcome the misfortunes of his life. He has learnt to live amidst suffering, pain and trauma of existence with the thought: "Never lose hope" (RIM 55). Bond's literature promotes the better understanding of life and helps the reader to explore their true potential. The positive attitude of Bond and his emphasis on simplicity infuse zest for life. He prays: "May you have the wisdom to be simple and the humour to be happy" (LIL 2000). His optimistic approach to life, his inoffensive neglect of vices, respect for values and gentler virtues, faith in the essential goodness of man, celebration of 'seemingly invisible' people who survive through 'the struggle of living,' love for serene beauty of nature, for animals, for environment have become the source of inspiration for baffled modern man caught in the labyrinth of 'hurry, worry and fury' and fast-paced commercialism. The reader loves to trail with him in a carefree world of exuberance and freshness and exploring the beauty 'within' and 'in the world around us':

Out of the city and over the hill,
Into the spaces where Time stands still,
....
...cast away care and come roaming with me,
Where the grass is still green and the air is still free. (TIIL 1)

2

Personal Impressions: An Interview with Ruskin Bond

> Talent develops in quiet places, character in the full current of human life.
>
> Johann Wolfgang Von Goethe

Reading Ruskin Bond's fiction has been a transforming experience for me. It became difficult to resist the desire to meet him personally. I started correspondence with him. He readily invited me to his hometown Mussoorie and agreed for an interview. I got an opportunity to meet him at his home, Ivy Cottage Landour, Mussoorie on June 15, 2006, between 5 to 7 p.m.

Bond's cosy cottage is perched on the crest of a hill. The beautiful corridor-cum-garden and its fragrance dispelled my nervousness. Bond made me seated in the drawing room which was more a mini library and confirmed him being a bibliophile. Extensive study of his literature and specific topic of my research filled my mind with lots of queries and doubts. The writer himself was before me to quench my thirst. What else a research scholar could expect? I got the long awaited opportunity and asked him diverse questions. He patiently answered me despite having soar throat. He apologised for not giving me much time and asked me to visit again in winter when he and his Mussoorie are comparatively free.

After initial conversation making me feel at home, Bond accompanied me to his study-cum-bedroom and opened the window that overlooks a breathtaking view of the heaving mountain ranges and magnificent hills covered with opulent oak, the fantastic fir, splendid deodar. The serenity of view and the whiff of chilly wind blowing were soothing and spellbinding. He pointed to the 'Pari Tibba' hill which he has described in his "On Fairy Hill." The window provides him subject matter for his stories: people passing below it, squirrels, insects, monkeys, birds entering his room from it or taking shelter on the window sill and trees beckoning him.

It has given me an immense pleasure and satisfaction to meet and know Bond as a person and as a writer. As I would walk down the memory lane in future this interview would be one of the most treasured moments for me and for those who want to know Bond. I am very thankful to this amiable and charismatic personality for his undivided attention. The time spent with him will always remain unforgettable for me.

My questions pertained to the themes of Bond's stories and his art of writing, particularly his grappling with truth and its narration:

Bandana Bal Chandnani: Do you like to be categorised as a children's author?

Ruskin Bond: I don't mind being called as a children's author, although most of my work during the last fifty years has been for the general reader and not specifically for the children.

BC: Why have you chosen children as the main characters of your fiction?

RB: They are the main characters only in the children stories or in autobiographical stories.

BC: What are the special techniques that you use to

make your fiction interesting for your young readers?

RB: No, there are no such special techniques. I just try to tell a good story, about interesting people.

BC: Once you stated your desire to be like the writer heroes of Dickens' *David Copperfield* and Hugh Walpole's *Fortitude*. What influence have Dickens and Hugh had on you?

RB: Yes, Dickens had a great influence on me and so did many several other writers, including the one you mention Hugh Walpole.

BC: What are the special ideas or issues you love to write for children?

RB: I tell them good stories.

BC: What appeals to you in children?

RB: I like their freshness, directness and innocence.

BC: As the ink has cast its spell on the different characters in the form of children which one is your favourite one?

RB: Memorable ones you could say Binya in *Blue Umbrella* and the boys in *The Hidden Pool.*

BC: How in your opinion do the children differ from the grown-ups?

RB: Not in any particular way.

BC: Tell me about any other children's author who had great influence on your creativity?

RB: The authors of *Alice in Wonderland, Peter Pan, Treasure* Island, all these are important to me.

BC: Do you miss your childhood?

RB: Not particularly.

BC Are you recreating your childhood through your stories?

RB I do recreate my childhood through many of my stories, especially those dealing with my own childhood which you come across.

BC: The children of your fictions are inquisitive by nature. Were you too?

RB: I guess most of the children are inquisitive by nature and I was not different.

BC: What is special about Indian children?

RB: May be they are more affectionate, frank and informal compared to others.

BC: Why do you not write about the children belonging to the upper class or to the educated or sophisticated families?

RB: I just write about the children that I have known; regardless of what class or background they come from.

BC: You never depicted the children enjoying the family ties? They are individuals and they search their own identify. Is there any reason behind it?

RB: Many of my children are individuals and the families are often in the background, because I want to concentrate on the adventures of the children themselves. Children do not want interference of adults. This is the reason some of my stories are very popular among children. They do not like to have too many adults in their story.

BC: What should one keep in mind if one wants to become a children's author?

RB: You must keep in mind the necessity to tell a good story and hold the attention of the reader. The attention span of young reader is shorter than an adult's.

BC: Are you planning any new work for children?

RB: Yes, I am always thinking of something new for them.

BC: Any message which you would like to give to children?

RB: No, particular message.

BC: Your convincing and detailed description, use of Indian vocabulary, use of word image and sound effect made you popular among children. Do you agree?

RB: That's correct.

BC: Whose style and language had an impact on you?

RB: No, not of any particular person. I have developed my own style, whenever I found the need.

BC: It has been said that you communicate through descriptive and simple language. What would you like to say about this?

RB: Yes, I do use simple and descriptive language.

BC: Do you agree realism is key note of your work?

RB: Well, most of the stories are realistic.

BC: I found women portrayed in your works are of two kinds either beautiful and innocent or amorous and seductive like the Rani of Magador. Why not a character in between?

RB: I will think about it. Well, may be in future I would try to write in between.

BC: Your detailed description of flora and fauna is very catchy and interesting. What are the sources of inspiration behind these descriptions?

RB: Yes, I spend a lot of time to get on describing flora and fauna accurately because it is important that we know about the natural backgrounds.

BC: Indian heat, dust, affliction, bazaar, platform, habit, customs are glorified by you while others have looked them down. The essence of Indianness has been beautifully portrayed by you. Your comments.

RB: I didn't glorify it. Yes, I celebrated it. It is a part of life. So, I bring it. There is significance in every aspect of life and whatever people do on their daily basis that has got some significance.

BC: How would you describe yourself as a narrator?

RB: I try to tell a good story in simple and direct way.

BC: You have attributed human qualities to animal characters: a python loves its reflection in the mirror; the crow has its own way of living life; etc. Any reason of this attribution or it is spontaneous.

RB: Lots of children writers attributed the human

qualities to animal characters like *The Jungle Book* by Kipling, *The Panchatantra*.

BC: You have accepted human beings with their faults. You respect their individuality and their peculiarities. How would you take it if I call you a humanist?

RB: Every human being has his own faults and weaknesses. We must accept them as they are.

BC: Some of your myth or anecdotes are often repeated, "like ghosts staying in the peepal tree," "take twenty one steps, your twenty second step will make you fall," "a spinster has a Siamese cat." Do you like these expressions so they are oft repeated? Are these derived from your own experience?

RB: Many stories were written at different periods of my life. So, occasionally repetition does occur. But it is not deliberate, purely accidental.

BC: Can your writing be called autobiographical? Why do you choose to be a subjective writer?

RB: A lot of my writing can be called autobiographical. I'm a subjective writer because that's my strength.

BC: What aspect of Anglo family is still on you?

RB: Not sure.

BC: Which do you prefer short stories or novel?

RB: I prefer the medium of the short story or the novella to the long novel. It is just a personal choice.

BC: "Ruskin Bond's novel is racy and exacting and you read so fast you feel sorry the book is not longer? But you cherish the warm and happy feeling for a long time," your comments.

RB: Particular comment of a critic. That's fine.

BC: Do you like the world of animals more? You never fail to mention about them.

RB: I like animals. But I prefer humans.

BC: Man is a social animal and nature has bountiful affect on him. As we are drifting away from nature we are becoming artificial, your comments.

RB: Well, that's true. What I believe it may not be relevant for everybody you know after all. Somebody who has grown up and spent his entire life in urban atmosphere will not have the opportunity to be close to the nature. But if she or he can discover the natural world it is always very helpful. I am sure in personal life as well as in the attitude towards other.

BC: In the story "Death of a Familiar" I found you are raising the question of existence especially in a populated country 'India,' where man feels himself lost in this vast population. Here are the concluding lines: "The case has already been forgotten, for in the great human mass that is India, hundreds of people disappear every day and are never heard of again."

RB: Well, somebody may hear about them again. But to say for us living here it's always a case in such a country. People do sometimes drift away or get lost.

BC: Your acceptance of the people in India as they are is really praiseworthy and it shows your optimistic approach and humanitarian outlook. What is your comment?

RB: Yes, I've shown. That's correct.

BC: You've shown in *A Flight of Pigeons* how the common humanity of ordinary folk - "Hindu, Muslim or Christian - could sometimes overcome the forces of hate, revenge and retribution." Do you want to teach the lesson of humanity?

RB: Not want to teach anyone. But showing and depicting the better side of human nature. Well, there is also an ugly side. It's there too. But, it can often be redeemed by a glimpse of generosity and kindness.

BC: You have often emphasised the need of a friend through your writings. How will you define friendship?

RB: Two people finding something in common, getting on well. It varies from childhood friends to adult friends and from age to age.

BC: At this juncture, what do you feel about this relationship?

RB: I just think friends are very few and far between, actually, genuine friends. One can become friendly with everybody. But close friends are someone you can go in time of trouble.

BC: Tell me any friend of yours?

RB: Not, particular.

BC: The life of Rusty in *The Room on the Roof* is portrayed like a sea-saw. He gets one thing and then loses it. He meets good ones then gets away from them. Why does it happen? We feel bad when he loses the dear ones.

RB: Yes, it did happen. It may be reflection of my youth of those times.

BC: Do you believe in Indian theory of the Vedas? In the story "Would Astley Return?" you are talking about the Indian theory that soul is more important than body. Astley, says Prem Bahadur pointing out to his dead body. "It was you. Only the husk now, the empty shell. This is the real you, standing here beside me."

RB: Of course, soul is very important. Body is ephemeral and temporary. I am sure in many ways the Indian philosophy has affected me. Although, I cannot say I have studied religion or philosophy deeply. The fact is that living here, and being surrounded by the life; it is both spiritual and physical one gets influenced by it.

BC: Any particular spiritual or mythological book of India that had an impact on you?

RB: Possibly, *Gita Govind* which is by Jaidev. Not to be confused with *The Bhagwat Gita*.

BC: What would you like to comment about your excess use of hyphenated words?

RB: It's a style. Words in English are hyphenated.

BC: What aspects of your work would you like to be explored?

RB: Well, the humanitarian aspect.

The present interview gives a comprehensive idea of Bond's creativity. He writes with the sole aim to amuse his readers with an interesting and gripping story. For this he has developed his own unique style suited to his simple hill folk, ordinary men and women, and young protagonists. Story telling for Bond is like Scheherazade of the *Arabian Nights,* a need, a means of survival, a way to earn his livelihood and to live near the Himalaya, a place of his choice. For Scheherazade it was the fear of death that forces him to write. But for Bond it is love and devotion to the muse of writing that made him a master raconteur. Bond's love and reading of great masters Dickens, Hugh Walpole, Stevenson, Lewis Carroll, shaped his creative art and help him to master a standard and sophisticated English that many Indian writers crave for. The living in close proximity of splendid, snow-peaks of Himalayas, and the inspirational book *Gita Govind,* a beautiful love lyric celebrating life by Jaidev form the content of his writing.

3

Writing Children Writing Human

> And the children (Raki, Muki, Dolly) bring me joy.
>
> Growing up was always a difficult process for me, and I gave up trying many years ago. I decided that there was little point in becoming adult, if I could remain a child and still make a living.
>
> Ruskin Bond, *The India I Love, Rain in the Mountain*

Like rainbow in the sky, flowers in the garden, moon among stars, the spring among the seasons, childhood in the life is adored and glorified unanimously. It is indeed a period in one's life which is not only charming and glorious but also considered to be divine. The vivaciousness and exuberance of children spontaneously grip the attention of beholders and their loveliness and liveliness radiate them with ecstasy. Children have the healing power to embalm fatigued and tensed life of the adult. The sensitive writers with great vision in mind always try to colour the canvas of their creativity with this primary and cherished stage of human life. The world of literature has produced a number of literary figures that have taken great interest depicting childhood and its pleasure. Ruskin

Bond secures an outstanding place among the array of children's writers. He is credited with being, "the pioneer of modern children's literature in India" (Marquand, *Christian Science* 19).

Bond has conjured up magical literary landscape where inquisitive, energetic and precocious children have an important role to play. He delineates his child protagonists with the deftness of a psychologist and superb story telling skills. He weaves the fabric of his children's world thread by thread, using his engrossing and evocative narrative technique, with the sole purpose to enthral his young readers. It is mostly the atmosphere of *joie de vivre* that pervades in his fiction where children enjoy, fight, play, roam and live a protected life. His exceptional knowledge of children helps him in authenticating his writing about children. He has a deep understanding of children and the mind and motivations of adolescents and youths. Ignoring the popular didactic mode of writing, he pays attention to the psychological and emotional needs of young readers. He creates a different world when he depicts innocent children on the threshold of experience. Bond's child persona gradually discovers the truths about themselves. They are not treated as the 'other' but as inexperienced adults who are an integral part of society. They are being created with an awareness of 'self.' Bond enters their mind to understand their peculiar sensibility, imagination and impressionable nature. One feels strongly committed to liking Bond's 'small man,' mischievous and jolly in temperament but kind in heart, commoner and marginalised but universal in approach. Bond's portrayal of life-like children and his unique communication with directness and graceful appeal with children carved out for him a special place in children's literature. Subhadra Sen Gupta writes:

> Through the years Ruskin Bond has taken the craft of writing for children and created an art form uniquely his own. Few Indian writers can communicate with children with the directness and

> simple appeal as Ruskin can. Without, condescension, no preaching and none of the sugary sweet lachrymose silliness that authors think children like...He is too busy giving them the pleasure of good reading. (Singh, *Creative Contours* 231)

A child's perception and approach to life follow a track that differs from that of adult's. The child loves to live in his dreamy and sensuous world. He is rarely affected by the gross and crude realities of mundane life which a grown-up often faces in his day-to-day hectic schedule. His understanding of the world is steered not by any logic or philosophy but by imagination. He views it blindly and passionately and observes it with insatiable curiosity and suspense. He feels connected to literature that attempts to perceive things from his point of view. He "prefer[s] literature that focuses more on child or child-like characters, and their typical feelings and preoccupation" (Tucker, *The Child* 18). He becomes passionate about it if it recounts his journey into his dreamy world and stimulates his aspirations. Aidan Chambers points out in "The Reader in the Book": "If literature for children is to have any meaning at all, it must primarily be concerned with the nature of childhood, not just the nature commonly shared by most children but the diversity of childhood nature too" (Peter, *Children's Literature* 98). The writers who write for young audience keep this in mind while fabricating stories for them. This is the reason behind the block buster success of *Adventures of Tom Sawyer* and *Huckleberry Finn* by Mark Twain, Noddy and other stories of children's adventures by Enid Blyton, series of Harry Potter by J.K. Rowling. Novels by Charles Dickens and essays by Charles Lamb are other important writings which for a long time created an impact on the psyche of child readers because of its empathetic treatment of children.

Bond excels in describing true-to-life children who one can encounter in any village and town of India. The world of his children literature is a world of gay abandon and ceaseless wonderment, a world which is not filled with 'goblins and magicians' but nevertheless a world of 'magic in realism' filled with ingredients of faith, love, courage and joy. The Indian kids can identify themselves with his characters. It is not an alien and unrelated magical world of fantasy like the world of Harry Potter. For Ruskin Bond, writing for children was a result of the way he writes and the genre of short story he likes. He confesses: "I can't write anything too voluminous. I like writing short stories" (Tanu, *Times of India*). The attention span of children in general is short. They avoid lengthy and bulky work. They get attracted more towards short stories than novels. Bond's deliberate choice of short story and novella, his lucid language and digression free plot glue the young readers to his work.

The childhood always enchants Bond and holds him in its magic-spell. He believes that it is a blissful period of one's life. Like Tagore in his work, he salutes the innocence, sanguinity and friendly attitude of children. In *Delhi Is Not Far* Bond quotes Tagore to emphasise his point of view: "Every child comes with the message that God is not yet discouraged of man" (362). Bond's single life brightens when he creates up a world sparkled with the aura of children and their merriment. His ability to communicate the richness of childhood renders his children fiction with deep insight and universality. He always cherishes the memory of his childhood. He delves deep into his own life for the creation of his characters, particularly the children. Once Mark Twain wrote: "If Byron - if any man - draws 50 characters, they are all himself - 50 shades, 50 moods, of his own character. And when the man draws them well, why do they stir my imagination? Because they are me - I recognize myself" (Simpson, *Twentieth Century* 17). The autobiographical element is so dominant in his portrayal of the child characters that his own childhood can easily be reconstructed. He writes and re-writes his rapturous and discontented experiences in his stories. It could be said, 'not a single impression is left out, not a single memory is forgotten of his childhood,' as he says: "Men and women leave the age of childhood behind, and are so busy with their buyings and selllings, their ambitions and their hopes, their loves and their hates, that they forget they once lived in a land where dreams were natural. I will not forget my childhood, I shall not surrender it" (Saili, *Ruskin Our Enduring* 62).

Bond's sensitive treatment of children and projection of their dreamy world, full of fun and frolic make him one of the favourite children's writers. His buoyant and high spirited child characters set in an idyllic backdrop leave an enduring and everlasting impact on the child readers. Bond's child protagonists attract us by their lovely moods and passionate nature, lively and pleasing activities, playfulness and their never ending pranks. They are burgeoning with mischief, sulk on being scolded, fabricate smartly the stories on being caught, quickly get involved in squabbles, easy to win as a friend, startle us by their precociousness and maverick demeanour, squander their time, bewitch us by their shining and innocent faces, get mollified easily on being offered things for their appetite, ride bicycles down precipitous hills, climb mango and *lichi* trees, explore river and mountain paths, take nap under shady trees, without any fear of crime and violence and enjoy wandering around.

The child protagonists of Bond spring up from the Himalayan soil, especially from the neighbouring villages and towns of Dehradun and hill stations of Mussoorie. Bond recreates the everyday experiences of the life and the problems that the children face for survival. Adventure, discovery, love for animals and variegated phenomena of nature, portrayal of mischievous ghosts and running away are some recurring themes, around which Bond weaves the yarn of his children stories. He gets attracted by the unassuming and happy-go-lucky life of children and display of their indomitable spirit in difficult circumstances. He often mentions the unyielding spirit of children of India while supporting their family and bearing the burden of life happily:

> Most children are more than equal to any obstacles that may arise. Like those youngsters in the Ganjam district of Orissa. In the absence of a bridge, they swim or wade across the Dhanei river everyday in order to reach their school....Wherever you go in India, you will find children helping out with the family's source of livelihood, whether it be drying fish on the Malabar Coast, or gathering saffron buds in Kashmir, or grazing camels or cattle in a village in Rajasthan or Gujarat. (TIIL 7)

The best part of Bond's portrayal of children is his involvement, his coming down to their level and his association with their erratic life. His oneness with children has infused 'life force' to his common theme. He does not merely describe a child but becomes a child for the time being. His literature explores childhood hidden behind the layers of adulthood: "A latent childhood remains tucked away in our subconscious. This I've tried to explore" (TIIL 30). The love for children seems to emerge from his own discontented and lonely childhood, his longing for happiness and security when he was a child. The loss of dear father, odds of forced relationship with mother and stepfather, lonely youth left a deep scar on his soul. Even after growing up he was unable to surmount the haunting impressions of those early days. He discloses the personal reasons for his deep attachments with the children:

> I don't suppose I would have written so much about childhood or even about other children if my own childhood had been all happiness and light. I find that those who have had contented, normal childhoods, seldom remember much about them; nor do they have much insight into the world of children. (SWL 4)

Bond found himself being weighed down by both

personal and professional problems during 1970's. He turned to writing for children. He says: "In writing for children one has tò adopt a less subjective approach; things must happen, for boys and girls have no time for mood pieces" (NTD 11). He feels writing for children helped him to get away from himself and to triumph over his personal distress. It also became a means by which he vicariously fulfilled his own needs and yearnings of childhood days, refashioning and restructuring his discontented and grieved childhood into a secure and cheerful time. Bond is aware of the fact that in this world of adult, children are often neglected. They and their opinions are not taken seriously. This awareness makes him gradually more concerned towards them. Because of his insight and empathy for children, he says that he could enter into their minds when he is writing about them. Bond has noticed that the children are mostly guided by their own decree. They have their own individual way of perceiving and interpreting things. They have a world unto themselves, where they weave their thoughts, emotions and feelings and find joy and sorrow in their own way. In his opinion "As children we are all individualists, it is only as we grow older that we acquire a certain grey similarity to each other" (NTD 11). Bond enjoys and celebrates the uniqueness and individuality of children's personality.

India has a rich ancient tradition in story-telling. However, the concept of children's literature in India as a genre and with sole emphasis to child as a protagonist is comparatively a recent phenomenon. There is no doubt the literary history of India abounds with literature that thrives with impressive and fascinating child characters, but the writings that emanate and culminate with child's perspective and interest got a platform and impetus after independence. The reading needs of children till date were served through simplified versions of books meant for grown-ups. They were regaled by loads of stories since time immemorial but those stories were not meant only for children. The children portrayed in these stories have no convincing identical background. They were often romanticized and idealized. Childhood was rarely depicted for its own sake and from its own point of view. Despite having enough ingredients to hold the attention of the young audience, these tales could not be termed under children's literature. Focusing this point, Nita Berry writes in her essay "Value Based Writing":

> It must be remembered that there was no separate literature for children for a very long time. Our early stories were, in actual fact meant for everyone, young and old, from the learned intellectual to the simple, unlettered villager. No doubt, these often contained several levels of meaning. Each age group or class of listeners applied its individual level of comprehension to the stories and these became a vital part of the texture of life. (Menon, *Children's Literature* 168)

The development of children's literature in India has passed through three distinct phases. Initially, the stories from the oral tradition, mythology, religion, folktales, legends, and classics were adapted and rewritten. Then there were translations and adaptations of material already published in England and other European countries and also in different native languages. Original creative writing has developed largely in the last five decades (Jafa, *International Companion* 1076). The really distinctive children's books grew more slowly and in less expected forms. The need of text books, growing interest in the education of children, exposure to western books and spread of publishing houses: Children's Book Trust, National Book Trust, Nehru Bal Pustakalaya, Amar Chitra Katha, Southern Languages Book Trust help to promote the cult of children's writing.

The full history of children's literature in India is closely entwined with the fate of the oral tradition, the folk lore, constituting a major segment of fiction which is rich with wisdom and whose values have been stored by communities. In traditional Indian literature for children 'the pride of place' is given to the *Panchatantra*. It is also known as 'Nitisastra' or the wise conduct of life, where the art of living is espoused through simple and enchanting stories. It teaches worldly wisdom within the framework of a lesson in a most palatable way. Woven around charming animal tales of intrigue, wit, greed, friendship and so on the stories composed by Vishnu Sharma invariably conveyed a moral or a message. It was written to teach the *rajniti* 'practical sense' to three dullard sons of Amarashakti. Vishnu Sharma succeeded in edifying where direct instruction or serious preaching had failed.

The next oldest collection of tales is the *Kathasaritasagara* written in Sanskrit in the eleventh century by Somadeva. These stories are known for the charm of language, elegant style, masterly arrangement and metrical skill. The *Jataka Tales* told by Buddha are another collection of stories in the traditional genre. They are tales of rare wisdom on the Buddha's former births. *Hitopadesa* by Narayana Bhatt, *Brhathkatha* Manjari by Kshemendra, *Singhasan Battisi*, stories of Tenali Raman, anecdotes of Akbar and Birbal and Sheikh Chilli, Lord Rama and Lord Krishna's childhood portrayal in the *Ramayana* and *The Bhagavad-Gita* are all very delightful and have an all time charm about them for children. In spite of the tremendous popularity and appeal of these stories, they cannot really be classified under children's literature or literature solely for children. Though not meant particularly for children, there were enough ingredients in above mentioned ancient tales to capture the attention of young readers.

The concept of children's literature in its true applied sense or as a separate discipline of art with the modern sensibility got momentum from the West. Contact with the European countries and particularly with England and the English language have led to the growth of modern children's literature. The history of children's literature is not very old even in the West. The separate cult of writing for children was not established till the mid 18th century. The children were catered through the books meant for adults. The earlier books from the west were about voyages, shipwrecks and sailors marooned on islands. *Robinson Crusoe* (1719) by Daniel Defoe was the earliest. It enticed with the infinite ingenuity of the hero in his adventure. It was followed by Jonathan Swift's *Gulliver's Travels* (1726). It interested and humoured children in its first and second parts, (in *Lilliput* where its inhabitants are six inches high and in *Brobdingnag* with its inhabitants as tall as steeples). Adventure stories, most of which have been intended for boys, first, became popular in the 19th century: *The Coral Island* (1858) by R.M. Ballantyne, *Treasure Island* (1883) and *Kidnapped* (1886) by R.L. Stevenson. *Alice's Adventures in Wonderland* (1865) and *Through Looking Glass* (1871) by Lewis Carroll also acquired popularity. It attempted to amuse children by creating a fairy world of adventure, fantasy and fun. Anna Sewell's *Black Beauty* (1877), Kipling's *The Jungle Books* (1894-95) use animals to invoke sympathy and to throw light on the complex social structure of human world respectively. The simplicity of the concept and the lack of didactic moral overtones and personified animals have made *The Jungle Books* a lasting influence on the young mind. Mark Twain's *The Adventures of Tom Sawyer* (1876) and *Adventures of Huckleberry Finn* (1884) are finest pieces of literature about adventure of young kids, their struggle in adult made world. Twain here aims to comment upon the problems of racism, child abuse, corruption and exploitation. He paints a vivid picture of Mississippi frontier life and combined picturesque adventure with powerful satire. These above mentioned works had all been for a general audience. Children adopted them as their own because of the exciting and adventurous themes that move around the child heroes.

The most prolific children's writer of the 20th century, Enid Blyton emerged on the children's books scene with her mystery stories *Secret Seven, The Famous Five* and *The*

Magic Faraway Tree. Her books often mirrored the fantasies of younger children where children are free to play and explore without adult interference, more clearly than in most authors before or since. Adult characters are usually either authority figures (such as policemen, teachers, or parents) or adversaries to be conquered by the children. Children are self-sufficient, spending days away from home.

The Indian writing for children in English, in its earlier phase, got inspired by the western children stories. It gradually started embodying Indian spirit and ethos and promoted national pride and culture. It assumed its accomplished form during the second-half of the twentieth century when English reading Indians could feel the influence of the English school of children's writings. In its subject matter, technique and treatment Indian children's literature differs from its western counterpart. The celebration of innocence, edification of manners and cultivation of values through literature and harmonious relationship of children with adults are some important issues of Indian children's literature. Fantasy, adventure, horror, satire, sex instruction, child abuse, confrontation with the miseries faced by the children, revolt with adult world are some focal points of discussion in European children's literature.

In India the trend of separate children's literature with sole emphasis on child centred perception came into vogue only a couple of decades ago. The children were not considered as an individual entity in Indian social and familial systems and so was the case with their literature. Literature to entertain was designed for the entire family. Indian literature and society since ancient times had perceived children as passive receptors with no identity apart from their family or community. Commenting on Indian system that gives less importance to Children's individuality, Manorma Jafa writes: "In these countries (India, Bangladesh, Bhutan, Maldives, Nepal Pakistan and Sri Lanka) the child has remained an integral part of the family. The nucleus of community life and art and literature has developed for the enjoyment of the entire family" (*International Companion* 1076). Sudhir Kakar observes that in Sanskrit literature, children rarely figure as individuals in their own right, with activities, reactions and feelings separate from those of their all-powerful parents (Kakar, *Indian Childhood* 3). The assumption and attitude towards children have received a drastic change. The new wave of thought sweeping the intellectual world is getting momentum. Children have their own space - a room of their own - in the changing structure of family and society. They started taking the leading role both in literature and society and their ideas and thoughts are given importance in public and private matters. The nuclear family system, wave of questioning spirit and western thoughts have much role to play in this changed perception. The media world has tried to exploit this new status of children. Various channels have started keeping in mind the interest and needs of children. Even a range of products is launched to allure them and to capture their attention. The advertisement world is now created in such a way where children have leading role in decision making. The awakening towards the significance of childhood and the renewed status of the child fostered creative writing for young readers. The development of an independent genre of children's literature in India has also been linked with the formation of a pan-Indian identity and the subsequent evolution of the identity of the child as an entity separate from his/her family. Nita Berry is also of the same opinion. She rightly asserts:

> The child was beginning to be recognized as an individual entity with special rights and needs. Also the idea gained ground that children were malleable and could be influenced by good books. Children's Literature ideally offered information as well as entertainment and fostered an awareness of tradition and duties. (Menon 177)

The status of children's literature has changed over the years and it has now received serious critical consideration both scholarly and popular. With child readers identified as a significant target audience, writing for children has become a major branch of literature. There are many writers who had contributed in Indian writing for children in English. The trend to write about children started quite earlier but it lacks the span and variety in its earlier phase. The real spirit of children and childhood was missing in it. Either the children appear for a short period only colouring the background or as a leading character, they were away from convincing portrayal. It was still overshadowed by didactic mode. The first important writer is the Nobel laureate Rabindranath Tagore whose Bengali stories translated into English has great impact in forming the canon of children's writing in English. He celebrates the innocence and exuberance of children in his works. His stories like "Kabuliwalla," "Atithi," "Home Coming" and "Birpurus" and plays like *Dakghar* (*The Post Office*) are remarkable piece of work capturing the impressions from the lives of children. Tagore here sensitively explores the mind of children, their ingenuousness and their imagination. The highly philosophical ideas of Tagore, his contemplation about life and death, belief in the value of truth, humanism take the limelight in his literary explorations. His literature has less affinity with real children, their psychology, their day-to-day life, their dreams, aspirations and problems. So, otherwise appealing, his stories have weak grip on the child readers. In his play *The Post Office*, the child hero Kamal is sick. He desires to meet the king. Tagore intends to portray the urge of the soul (the *Atman*), to meet God (the *Parmatman*) through Kamal's desire of meeting the king. The conceptual ideas of Tagore fail to attract the child readers because "children prefer books that deal with concrete events rather than with abstract discussion, and which have an emphasis upon action in preference to introspection" (Tucker, *The Child* 9).

R. K. Narayan's *Swami* and *Friends* (1935), an evocative and delightful novel, made a good starting in children's writing. Narayan here accounts the adventures of a boy, Swami and his friends Rajam and Mani in the bucolic innocence of the legendary Malgudi. Swami's adventures, his running away from his home, his fighting with his friends, his tall talk, his love for his grandmother and his playfulness fascinate the child readers at their best. The book has made a forte in the children's literature. But sometimes it looses the grip because of Narayan's haggling with "borrowed medium" (Iynger, *Indian Writing* 706). English was not established on the firm track during Narayan's time. *Haroun and the Sea of Stories* (1990) by Salman Rushdie and *The Village by the* Sea: An *Indian Family Story* (1982) by Anita Desai are noticeable children's classics after Narayan's *Swami and Friends*. These writers have occasionally indulged in the delightful occupation of writing for the young. They belong mainly to the mainstream of adult fiction and turn to writing for children to lessen the burdens of life. There are group of writers like Sigurn Srivastava, Dilip Salwi, Swapna Dutta, Manorma Jafa, Pratibha Nath, Polie Sengupta, Ira Saxsena, Nilima Singh, Krishna Naraya and others who have produced work in recent years that is exciting, entertaining, intelligent and not didactic or patronizing at all. These writers have made an attempt to recreate the Indian cultural milieu in English and are evolving a language in which they can go beyond the surface and express themselves in a real and credible manner.

Today Children's writing in India has formulated a distinct voice and identity, reflecting its unique ideology and aims, and drawing on its artistic, literary and cultural tradition.

The Indian English writing for children was not as resourceful and novel as Indian English writing for the adult was when Bond begins to write. Bond's emergence in children's writing started a new canon of children's literature. Deepa Agarwal says, "...perhaps the only writer who can be identified as having a notable presence and a definite philosophy in the field of Children's books is Ruskin Bond" (*The Book Review* 26). There were hardly any successful and devoted children's writers when Bond emerged on the horizon of writing for children. The credit of flourishing a separate corpus of literature for children goes in Bond's favour. He freed children's literature from the shackles of retold Indian mythology, legends and folklores, adaptation of western stories and also from the mode of didacticism. He nourishes it by setting on a new foot of realism. His writing is marked by an individual signature. His canvas radiates with vivacious children who by their individuality captivate us. He is one of the few authors who straddle the gulf between prescribed and popular texts. Praising Bond's art, Prema Srinivasan writes: "This sensitive story-teller from the hills has been able to set a standard for quality book for children in English which can be read with pleasure by the adult as well" (*Children's Fiction* 52).

Bond's love for children and his dual British and Indian heritage lend depth to his writing. He selects his style and subjects with the child reader in mind. His first person narrative helps the young audience to identify easily with the narrator child. He displays a fresh outlook while projecting the world of children, their dreams and high spiritedness. He has consolidated the notion of the child as a cherished and valued member of the society who has his own aspirations to follow and dreams to pursue. Bond has the uncanny capacity of going straight into the heart of reader and unveiling the layers of childhood - universal in its romanticism. His stories have marked the trail for the future writers. Emphasizing his contribution, Meena Khorana writes in her *The Life and Works of Ruskin Bond*: "His stories for children brought freshness, imagination, and, because of his Anglo-Indian background a multicultural identity to Indian Children's Literature" (94).

The cultural code and family matrix of Indian and western society differ entirely. Hence literature, a replica cf the milieu in which it is created, is bound to differ. Commenting on the difference between the attitudes of an Indian writer in relation to a western one, Vrinda Nabar points out:

> The importance of individualism in distinguishing between the two world outlooks, the Western and the Indian, cannot be undermined. In spite of a marginal literary move in the Indian languages toward the western mood canon in this respect, both Indian literature and culture have remained largely impervious to its message. (30)

The remarkable blending of the literary traditions of Indian and English literature is noticeable feature of Bond's creativity. He focuses the individuality of children, their dreams and their adventures like English children's writing. He captures the innocence of children in his fiction like Indian authors. The stories like "The Angry River" and "The Blue Umbrella" brilliantly amalgamate the traditions of Indian and English Children's literature. Sita the young heroine of "The Angry River" bravely fights the destructive forces of nature. Binya the vivacious girl of "The Blue Umbrella" successfully overcomes the self-seeking attitude towards life. The readers are motivated in witnessing the indomitable spirit of both the heroines, Sita and Binya, as they fight the external and internal forces of life.

The story "The Blue Umbrella" is a great example of Bond's ability to present the intricacies of life with much simplicity. With just an old man and a little girl and a few minor characters, he reveals to us all the facets of emotions that make us human - joy, pain, anger, disappointment and hurt and all the tragedies and celebrations that make life what it is. Binya Devi, the child heroine of a moving story "The Blue Umbrella" from Gharwal hills, is hardly ten-year-old. She willingly lends her pleasing smile to anyone who is unhappy. She possesses the heart of a young lady. On a childish impulse, she quickly gets ready to exchange her charmed pendant made up of a leopard's claw for a dainty, blue silk umbrella. The umbrella is owned by a wealthy woman who came for picnic in the hills. Binya's pendant created a stir in the heart of this lady. With a desire to possess the pendant she reluctantly gets ready to exchange her umbrella for it. Binya is very happy, on the seventh heaven, after receiving the blue umbrella. She gets enamoured by its beauty. Her passion sees no limit for her prize possession. She carries it wherever she goes and seldom closes it. It accompanies her everywhere protecting her from storms and snakes, as goes the description: "Whenever Binya went out—whether it was to graze the cows, or fetch water from the spring, or carry milk to the little tea shop on the Tehri road—she took the umbrella with her. That patch of sky blue silk could always be seen on the hillside" (CO 29).

Binya's fawn like movements in dale and forest like Wordsworth's Lucy, her innocence like Tagore's Mini from "Kabuliwala" draw our attention and her love for the umbrella enthrals us. Binya enjoys her raised status in the village. The disparity between Binya's poverty and the richness of the umbrella created a stir of jealousy among the villagers. The school master's wife, a second class B.A. feels extremely degraded in not having the rich possession. She thinks it was quite wrong for a poor cultivator's daughter to have such a fine umbrella while she, a second class B.A. has to make do with an ordinary one. Everyone heaves a sigh of longing for Binya's elegant umbrella. Their jealousy breeds ill will against it:

> Most of the people in the village were a little envious of Binya's blue umbrella. No one else had ever possessed one like it. The school master's wife thought it was quite wrong for a poor cultivator's daughter to have such a fine umbrella, while she, a second class B.A., had to make do with an ordinary black one. (CO 41)

The large heartedness and innocence of children are set in direct contrast with the shrewdness and envious nature of grown-ups. Bond here juxtaposes the two worlds - the innocent world of children and the cunning and manipulative world of adults. The children openly admire Binya's blue umbrella and get thrilled by its sensational touch. It is their sincere appreciation for umbrella that gives them a chance to hold it and experience its thrilling touch. The malicious attitude of grown-ups stopped them to admire it openly. But secretly everyone craves to possess it:

> Most people consoled themselves by saying that Binya's pretty umbrella wouldn't keep out the rain, if it rained heavily; that it would shrivel in the sun, if the sun was fierce; that it should collapse in a wind, if the wind was strong; that it would attract lighting, if lightning fell near it; and that it would prove unlucky, if there was any ill-luck going about. Secretly, everyone admired it. (CO 40)

Bond brilliantly here celebrates the innocence of children by setting them against the world of adults. The children sincerely appreciate Binya's umbrella and give a vent to their true feelings. By criticising umbrella the grown-ups reveal their prejudice and egotism. Away from pretensions, the children openly praise it: "Unlike the adults, the children didn't have to pretend. They were full of praise for the umbrella....They knew that if they said nice things about the umbrella, Binya would smile and give it to them to hold for a little while--just a very little while!" (CO 40)

This little girl Binya by her heroic adventures wins our heart. She frees her umbrella from the clutches of a thief Rajaram, an employee of a tea shop proprietor, Ram Bharosa. From the day Ram Bharosa had seen Binya's umbrella he became so passionate about it that he wanted to own it at any cost. When his all mean attempts to seize it from Binya and her brother Bijju utterly failed, he sent

Rajaram to steal it. The villagers got angry on knowing Ram Bharosa's use of wrong means to get it from Binya. They boycotted him and stopped buying things from his shop. His reputation, business and life all collapsed:

> Ever since it had become known that Ram Bharosa had tried to have the umbrella stolen, the village people had turned against him. They stopped trusting the old man, instead of buying their soap and tea and matches from his shop, they preferred to walk an extra mile to the shops near the Tehri bus stand. Who would have dealings with a man who had sold his soul for an umbrella? The children taunted him, twisted his name around. From "Ram the Trustworthy" he became "Trusty Umbrella Thief". (CO 53)

The story reaches at its climax. Our heart is overtaken not by the malice of the villagers against Ram Bharosa but by the sympathy and love of Binya for this forsaken man. She secretly feels herself responsible for the miserable plight of Ram Bharosa whom the villagers and the children have made the target of their taunts and jeers. She questions her own self - a mere object an umbrella is more important to her, or an old man and his feelings:

> Had it mattered more to her than people mattered? She couldn't help feeling that in a small way she was the cause of sad look on Ram Bharosa's face ... and the ruinous condition of his shop. It was all due to his own greed, no doubt; but she didn't want him to feel too bad about what he'd done, because it made her feel bad about herself; and so she closed the umbrella whenever she came near the shop, opening it again only when she was out of sight. (CO 53-54)

It is through Binya, Bond raises the pertinent question on the concept of material happiness and futility of the whole process. He highlights the Indian ethics which ignore material wealth before the feeling and concern for others. The battle of wills between the old man and the girl takes many unexpected turns. The compassionate heart of Binya wins. She discovers there is more to life than material possession. This little lady, Binya willingly donates her prize possession, the blue umbrella to Ram Bharosa. By her kind gesture, she teaches the great lesson of humanity. Love breeds love. Crooked Ram Bharosa melts. He repays her generosity by presenting her a pendant made up of a bear's claw (more auspicious than leopard's claw) tied in a silver chain. Who says the world cannot be changed? The present story proves that a child can. The projection of an undercurrent of the inherent moral education is very appealing. The novel pays a tribute to the basic goodness of man and underlines better than any philosophical treatise could, that human vice and goodness are not inborn but a result of circumstances. Who we call villain is not devoid of nobility. A touch of compassion, an ability to share and a sense of justice can turn a heart of stone into a heart of gold. Ram Bharosa's case is an example of it. He rises like a phoenix from Binya's kindness, lovely smile and selfless donation.

Bond effectively blends the tradition and canon of Indian and English children's literature in this story. By portraying Binya's free spiritedness, her heroic adventure to save her umbrella from a thief and her passion for it, Bond focuses the individuality of a child as does the English children's literature. The story highlights the innocence of children and communicates the lessons of kindness, sympathy and brotherhood like the traditional children's literature in India does.

Bond's acumen could well be observed in his projection of life-like children. His child protagonists appeal enormously for their love, adventures and inquisitiveness to know the things around them. They pester the adults, at time their friends, with unending and mind boggling questions. They frequently tell lies which are invented truths of their imagination, tease each other, befriend again forgetting the scuffle of one minute before and show concern for peer interests.

The child characters of Bond act and behave as the children do in any part of the world. In their appearance and attire, Bond's children could differ from the children of the world but not in their attitude and temperament. If Tom Sawyer of Mark Twain steals jam from a pot in the *Adventures of Tom Sawyer*, Ranji, Koki and Teju of Bond steal guavas in the story "When Guavas are Ripe." Tom befools Aunt Polly and so do these three children play tricks on Gopal, the watchman of the guava orchard. Aunt Polly punishes Tom by asking him to whitewash the fence. Tom shows excessive interest and indulgence in whitewashing with the intention to allure his friends to complete his work. His trick works. The gullible friends of Tom not only whitewashed the fence but also enriched Tom by gifts for allowing them whitewashing. Teju, Koki and Ranji flatter Gopal, an ex-wrestler and the keeper of an orchard. They praise his prowess and physique and listen to dull stories of his bravery with the sole interest of procuring guavas in return. The old and lonely Gopal was immensely impressed by children's flattery. He treated them with the grand feast of guavas from his orchard. Tom and Huck love adventures. They enjoy hunting and fishing and go for expedition to Jackson's Island. Laurie, Anil and Kamal of *The Hidden Pool* too enjoy themselves the secret pool on the mountain site. At the pool they fish, build dams, take midnight dips, wrestle and ride buffaloes. They go for trekking up to Pindari Glacier at 12,000 feet above sea level, where no one from their town has gone before. Rusty in *The Room on the Roof* runs away from his apathetic and strict guardian, Kishen in *Vagrants in the Valley* from his drunken father, Daljit and Rusty from school. Thus Bond's children follow the trend of running away from home or work like Oliver Twist, David Copperfield, Kim and Huckleberry Finn.

The act of stealing jam or guava, place of expedition on Jackson's Island or Pindari Glacier, reasons for running away from school or home could differ but not the spirit of Bond's children from the children in other cultures. Telling lies, stealing things, playing pranks on others and benefiting in their small enterprises are the common activities of Bond's children. Thus, Bond achieves universality while delineating with accuracy the familiar characteristics of his child protagonists. His close observation of children's behaviour endows his child persona with convincing authenticity: "And here I stand at my window, watching some of them pass by - boys and girls, big and small, some scruffy, some smart, some mischievous, some serious, but all going somewhere - hopefully towards a better future" (TIIL 9).

Children have always rated those people high in the list of their favourites who respect their feelings, trust them and stand by them in times of trouble. That's why indulging and doting grandparents and grown-ups with caring and understanding attitude are always preferred by children to the dominating and disciplinarian ones. Bond colours the canvas of his stories with friendly and considerate adults who love children and are loved by them in return. Michael Heyman says that Bond "depicts relationships between adults and children where children are not wiser, and where they rarely challenge the adults" (253-254). Bond is aware of the fact that the tender body and immature mind of children need protection and guidance, to acclimatise themselves in the world of adults. He invokes loving and nurturing relationship between children and adults - not necessarily parents. Loving portrayal of friendly adults and doting grandparents have autobiographical reasons as Bond says: "In some of my children's stories I have written about fun-loving grandfathers and doting grandmothers, but this was just wishful thinking on my part" (SWL 34).

In Indian family system the children have always enjoyed the friendly and secure company of grandparents. Children reciprocate the love and care of grandparents with the same zeal. The writers with young readers in mind have always exploited this theme. "Idgah" by Premchand is one such touching tale. Hamid, the young hero overcomes the glamour of fancy toys and mouth watering sweets at the fair to return home with a pair of tongs for his grandmother. Khushwant Singh lovingly talks about his grandmother and the spirited relationship between him and her in the story "Portrait of a Lady."

The strange woman in the story "The Woman on Platform No. 8," Aunt Mariam in "A Guardian Angel," grandfather in "All creatures Great and Small," Mr. Kumar in "Ranji's Wonderful Bat," Bansi in "The Last Tonga Ride," Mr. Khushal in "Masterji," Keemat Lal in "A case for Inspector Lal," grandfather in "Grandfather's Private Zoo" and in "The Cherry Tree" are a few loving adults who become the source of children's growth and education and self-knowledge. They take care of the child protagonists by their caring attitude. These kind-hearted adults command respect. They pass on their wisdom to children and enable them to gain confidence and assume responsibilities. The invigorating relationship between children and adults nurture the young readers with positive vibes. This harmonious relationship Bond himself has experienced and poignantly deals with when the children and grand children of his adopted son Prem become dear to his heart: "Prem came to live and work with me in 1970. A year later, he was married. Then his children came along and stole my heart; and when they grew up, their children came along and stole my wits" (TIIL 13).

Bond's fiction reverberates with touching relationship between a child and a grown-up. This set him in direct contrast to Nicholas Tucker's observation. Tucker is of the opinion that adults in children fiction are better off absent or, on the occasions when they are present exist mainly to be the butt of ridicule and humour (*The Child* 108). The western concept gives less importance to the role of adult in children's life or literature. It believes a child needs his own space and total independence for blooming. Adult's interference and dominance eclipse the individuality and potentiality of children. The more a child has access to freedom the more efficient he/she becomes in problem solving. The child protagonists are often shown in clash with adults in western literature. The seminal book for children *The Adventures of Huckleberry Finn* by Mark Twain traces the adventures of Huck and his drifting apart from adult world. Huck does not like to live with Miss Watson who tries to civilise him. He also seeks to free himself of his father's neglect. He enjoys life of a vagabond. He struggles to reach freedom by running away, living freely and refusing to be civilised by those who attempt to fix his crude manners.

Bond seems to go with the Indian thought which stresses the positive role of adults in children's stories. He portrays at least one adult on the side of the children in the interest of verisimilitude. This relationship is marked by harmony. Arup Dutta has also emphasised on the need to have at least one adult on the side of the children, implying therefore that even in the fictitious world of the novel, reality has to intrude - the reality of adult control. Dutta believes the presence of a father figure in a story with children as central character helps to invest the story with credibility:

> Because the father figure always steps into a situation which is beyond the children, he not only saves them from the imaginary peril in the story, but also from becoming super brats. Children, even older ones, have somewhat exaggerated options of what we adults can perform, so the actions of the father-figure do not in any way infringe on verisimilitude. (Writer and Illustrator 45)

The Indian belief has always emphasised the significant role of adult in cultivation of young brains. Children have never left totally on their own to settle their problems. In joint family there are many adults to support or accompany them: grandparents, aunts, uncles and other relatives. The same tendency and approach is revealed in

Indian literature. Ruskin Bond inclines towards the Indian tradition while portraying adult character in his children's literature. He has understood the importance of adults in the life of children. But he uses limited adult characters who form the backdrop of stories. The story wheels in and around children. The child protagonists are free to choose their way without much adult interference. The adults are like northern star who guide the lost ship of children from distance whenever they get struck in storm. The derailed train of children is often brought on the track by the guidance and motivation of the caring adult.

Bond presents two kinds of adult characters: one who acts as possible catalyst and the other who creates hindrance. In general, the adults in Bond's stories are considerate and contact with them exposes children to new vista and a better perspective. They love and rescue innocent and naïve kids from troubles like the fairy Godmother of Cinderella. The good-natured strange woman who gives treat to a lonely child in "The Woman on Platform No. 8," caring Aunt Mariam who takes care of an orphan nephew in "A Guardian Angel," loving grandfather who introduces the child to the world of nature and accompanies him in his pranks while teasing the relatives of grandmother in "All Creatures Great and Small" and in "The Cherry Tree," inspirational force Mr. Kumar in "Ranji's Wonderful Bat," friendly Bansi who gives free rides to his young friend in "The Last Tonga Ride," generous and kind Keemat Lal who lost his promotion in his attempt to save the life of an innocent girl in "A Case for Inspector Lal," the ingenuous Arun who changes Deepak from an experienced thief into an honest man in "The Thief" are thoughtful adults who by their positive attitude and loving approach take care of the children and guide them during trouble. They receive deep reverence of children. They pass on their wisdom to children and enable them to gain confidence and assume responsibilities. The invigorating relationship of children with adults paves the way toward happy selfhood.

The story "The Woman on Platform No. 8" deals with a boy, Arun and his encounter with a benevolent lady. Arun was sitting on platform No. 8 at Ambala station waiting for northern bound train. He heard a soft voice asking him "Are you all alone, my son?"(CF 3) It was a lady with pale face and dark kind eyes. She was dressed very simply in a white *saree*. Her dignity and simplicity commanded respect. The lady offered a treat of *samosa, jalebi* and tea to Arun. The treat strengthened the bond between the strangers. Under the influence of the tea and sweets, Arun began to talk quite freely about his school, friends, likes and dislikes. The lady won Arun by showing her confidence in Arun's capacity of travelling alone. Arun told her that he could travel alone, she quickly agreed: "'I am sure you can' [travel] ... and I liked her for saying that, and I also liked her for the simplicity of her dress, and for her deep, soft voice and the serenity of her face" (CF 4).

Arun extremely got impressed by the simplicity and caring attitude of this lady. But he disliked his class-fellow, Satish's mother, an authoritative and overbearing lady. He got infuriated even by her sound advice. He found himself hating her "with a firm, unreasoning hate" (CF 7). She looked sternly at Arun through her spectacles. She asked him not to talk to strangers. Arun retorted he would because he liked strangers. Satish enjoyed this verbal fighting between his friend and his mother. He was on his friend's side which revealed his dissent against his mother's domination: "Satish was standing behind his mother, grinning at me, and delighting in my clash with his mother. Apparently he was on my side" (CF 6). Arun's dissent pleases the child readers as well. Children in general enjoy those stories where the domineering adults are outwitted by children, "where powerful or mischievous characters defy authority and break most of the conventional rules" (Tucker, *The Child* 20). The glimpse of selfless love between the pale faced kind woman in white *saree* and the lonely boy at the station suggests the victory of human bond.

The children need love, care, protection and encouragement for their all-round upbringing. Manoj Das says in this context:

> Just as a child's body hankers for the kind of nourishment that is indispensable for its growth, the child's psyche also demands elements that are necessary for its growth ... they are simply faith and love, to begin with. No infant can survive even the trauma of birth, not to speak of survival into childhood, without these two elements playing their role at the very dawn of its life. In fact, the very first cry the child gives out is an instinctive assertion of faith - the faith that there is help for its utterly helpless state. Next what the child needs - to stand up, to toddle on despite falls - is courage. (4-6)

Bond's fiction abounds with caring friends and sensitive adults who fulfil the needs of children. Mr. Kumar, owner of the sports store in "Ranji's Wonderful Bat" is on friendly terms with Ranji. One day Mr. Kumar calls Ranji in who is passing from there. Ranji feels relaxed as soon as he enters the shop of Mr. Kumar. He is upset because of not making good score in his last three matches. He will be now dropped from the team if he does not improve in the next game. Mr. Kumar, cheers him up by saying "never mind, where would we be without losers?" and "All players have a bad day now and then" (CO 229). Kumar gives Ranji the luckiest of all his old bats with which he had scored a hundred runs. The bat proves lucky for Ranji as well. He scores many runs. One day he loses his lucky bat. All his happiness and dreams were shattered. Mr. Kumar consoles Ranji saying that he could make all the runs he wanted: "Any bat will do" (CO 234). In order to boost his confidence, Mr. Kumar has given him an ordinary bat, saying it was the luckiest bat. Now when Ranji loses it, he loses all hope of winning any further match. Mr. Kumar discloses the truth. Ranji understands Mr. Kumar's advice, "... it's the batsman and not the bat that matters" and "a bat has magic only when the batsman has magic!" (CO 234). It is confidence not the bat which Ranji needs. Kumar intends to make Ranji realise that he as a player has always been good, is good and will be no matter whether he loses or wins. Mr. Kumar judges him right. A confident Ranji performs well and wins the next match.

The case of Jai in the story "The Eye of an Eagle" is also like Ranji. He takes his lambs for grazing to the hills. He feels disappointed when his one lamb was taken away by a golden eagle. His grandfather consoles him. He gives Jai a long stout stick made of wild cherrywood which he often carries around. He advises Jai to swing the stick around his head if the eagle comes near him or attacks his lamb that will frighten the eagle off. Jai hits the eagles when they attack. He loses his stick while fighting the eagles. He was discouraged on losing the lucky stick. The grandfather comforts him and asks him not to worry because "It isn't the stick that matters. It's the person who holds it" (PM 83). Jai like Ranji comes to realise his own potentiality. Thus Bond's adults not only provide companionship but also guide and instruct children but not in a preachy manner. The loving and nurturing relationship between children and adults is dealt with exquisitely through a child and his doting Ayah in the story "My First Love." It centres on the affection of a child for his Ayah. The child does not like when anyone calls her ugly. He promptly responses: "No she is beautiful!" (CF 513) The child has a strange fascination for his Ayah's size, her "wrestler's arms," "broad quivering hips," "thick, crinkly hair" and "teeth stained red with the juice of innumerable *paan*-leaves," which were at first disconcerting to any other child. When she smiles with pleasure the boy feels, "it was as though the sun had just emerged, lighting up her features with a great dazzle" (CF 513). The course of this pure love affair between a child of six and an Ayah of thirty gets broken when she plans to get married. The thought of separation from his beloved saddens the child:

"While my parents considered this a perfectly natural desire on Ayah's part, I looked upon it as an act of base treachery. For several days I went about the house in a rebellious and sulky mood, refusing to speak to Ayah no matter how much she coaxed and petted me" (CF 517). The child hides himself when the time of Ayah's moving with her husband comes. The nervous and dismayed Ayah keeps on looking left and right and calling the child with the hope to see him. Unable to bear the misery of Ayah any longer, the child comes out of the hiding place. The Ayah gathers the child up in her great arms. Recording the happy moment while parting from his beloved, the child says "... when the tonga finally took her away, there was a dazzling smile on her sweet and gentle face - the face of the lover whom I was never to see again...." (CF 517) Bond's story echoes Bapsi Sidhwa's *The-Ice-Candy-Man* which also reveals the love between the child narrator and her Ayah. The novel features an eight-year-old girl named Lenny cared by her Ayah, an eighteen year old dusky beauty, Shantha. Lenny recalls her first conscious memory of her Ayah thus: "She passes pushing my pram with the unconcern of the Hindu goddess she worships" (Sidhwa 3).

In "The Last Tonga Ride" the child narrator enjoys the company of a tonga-driver, Bansi Lal. He feels rejuvenated and much more important on being called *dost* (friend) by him and enjoys his raised status: "He did not call me '*chota sahib*', or '*baba*', 'but dost' and this made me feel much more important. Not every small boy could boast of a tonga driver for his friend!" (CF 446) The boy loves the thrill of free tonga ride with Bansi. He accompanies him even though being scolded by his granny and ayah.

In "A case for Inspector Lal" Bond introduces a kind inspector Keemat Lal. He is made up of such instrument which is unlikely to be found in his profession. He keeps the sentiment and life of a little girl Kusum above his promotion. He hides all the evidence against her to save and protect her from the cruel law that can put her in a remand home and may have crushed her gentle spirit. Kusum the poor, rustic, innocent and trusting girl of twelve or thirteen is implicated in a foul game of lust and betrayal. In order to defend herself, she has to hit her molester and accidentally who trapped her gets killed.

Rani, a lecherous woman calls Kusum to her house and offers her tea and sweets. Mr. Kapoor, a customer of Rani who was already there starts harassing Kusum. Scared by Kapoor's amorous advance, Kusum slips away and makes a rush for the door. But Rani catches her and pushes her back into the room. Kusum seizes an axe and in panic she brings the axe down across Rani's head. The act of the murder by Kusum is done in self-defence. She is not a murderer. Rani receives what she deserves. The Inspector Keemat Lal does nothing even after discovering the truth. He tells the narrator, "I did absolutely nothing. I couldn't have the girl put away in a remand home. It would have crushed her spirit" (CF 95). Keemat Lal remained quiet. The case was closed. It was put in the pending tray and so was his promotion which was solely dependent on his tracking the case of murder. He was disheartened on not getting the promotion. He closed the "file" of Kusum's case and of his promotion for ever. His success as a human being smiles upon his failure as a professional. That makes him regret, "I should never have been a policeman" (CF 96). The act of Keemat Lal may be against the rule of law but not the law of humanity. He wins our heart despite not being loyal to his duty. The readers sympathise with Kusum and Keemat Lal for their decisions and are touched by the hint of an emotional attachment between them, even if it is a merely paternal affection. A humane interest in the welfare of others on Keemat's part confirms the importance of love in Bond's work. Bond's "childlike trust in grown-ups" (RIM 251) helps him in creating a captivating character like Keemat Lal.

The story "A Guardian Angel" invokes the loving bond between an aunt and her six-year-old orphan nephew.

Aunt Mariam assures the child by her warmth, worldliness and carefree chatter when his mother passes away. The child enjoys on being called *ladla* (dear) by her. Mariam is an outcaste for her family because of bringing disgrace to it by becoming a mistress but for the child she is an angel. The child is unable to understand why his mother was cold and indifferent towards such a friendly and cheerful person, Aunt Mariam. It is only Mariam who comes to rescue the child with great readiness when his mother dies. Her tenderness and selfless approach fills the void in the life of the child. The boy characteristically recalls her personality. For him she was a "joyous, bubbling creature—a force of nature rather than a woman—and every time I think of her I am tempted to put down on paper some aspect of her conversation, or gestures, or her magnificent physique" (CF 55).

The story "Getting Granny's Glasses" focuses on the attachment between a grandmother and his grandson Mani. Mani offers to accompany his grandmother on a two day journey to Mussoorie where the nearest eye hospital is located, so that she can get a new pair of glasses. The atmosphere of this Himalayan region during monsoon is charmingly described as the two set off on their adventure. They walk through fields and forests, up and down mountains, see a river rushing swiftly, pass a mule-driver singing a romantic song and admire a flock of parrots and the hills. The glasses renew Granny's zest for life. She buys gifts for the whole family, including a bell for the cow. With her improved vision, Granny excitedly rediscovers the beauty of her surrounding but her greatest joy is seeing what a fine boy Mani has grown up to be.

Majority of adult characters of Bond are portrayed in positive vein. But still there are some characters like Mr. Harrison, the strict guardian of Rusty, drunkard Mr. Kapoor, indifferent towards the need of his son and caring wife, in *The Room on the Roof;* Mrs. Bhushan a nosey and overbearing lady in *Vagrants in the Valley;* Satish's mother a domineering and imposing lady in "The Woman on the

Platform No. 8." The adolescent characters are shown in clashes with adults. They defy the authority and break the conventional rules. Adolescence is a period in one's life when one becomes very sensitive and opposes restrictions, rules and codes of conduct which one cannot absorb. Rusty in *Room on the Roof* rebels against the restriction of his guardian Mr. Harrison. He defies the rigid social codes of the English which do not allow him to mix with the natives. Harrison beats him for playing *holi* with his friends. Rusty repulses the attack of his guardian, beats him on the rebound and runs away.

The adults in Bond's stories in general are supportive of children. They stand by them, guide them and nurture them with love. They do not obstruct their way rather remove stumbling blocks from their path. Bond enforces healthy relationship through his loving adults. His portrayal of adults differs from Narayan and Dickens. Swaminathan of *Swami and Friends* suffers the oppressive regime of adults embodied by male authorities: father, teachers, headmasters, doctors and the forest officer. Child heroes of Dickens - Oliver, Pip, Neil, David suffer the ruthless treatment meted out to them by the adults and society. The exploitation, the sad surroundings and miserable life make the process of growing up difficult for Dickens' children. Bond's child protagonist also has to face difficulties and vagaries of life. They successfully overcome it. Both Dickens and Bond had unhappy and insecure childhood. The trauma of unhappy childhood is revealed in Dickens through the suffering world of children. Contrary to Dickens, Bond creates happy-go-lucky life where children enjoy blissful presence of the elders.

The relationship of friendship is a very important tie in Bond's work. This binds his young persona with each other and with the world. Bond remains unsurpassed in his portrayal of friendship, captivating the young minds. The bond of friendship plays a vital role in shaping the personality of young boys. Particular emphasis is placed on the need for security in the life of adolescents.

Adolescence is a difficult phase of life when one is in emotional and psychological transition. According to Judith Rich Harris and Robert M. Libert, "Adolescence is the transitional period from the dependency of childhood to the independence and responsibility of being an adult. At this point in their lives, young people struggle with the fundamental problems: to redefine their relationships with their parents and other adults, and to establish themselves as individuals" (*The Child* 460). Biological changes in the body make them insecure and apprehensive and they look more to friends for support than parents. They want the friends to be loyal, trustworthy and a reliable source of support in any emotional crisis. Peers play a crucial role in the psychological and social development of most adolescents. They are more dependent upon peer relationship than the younger children because ties to parents become progressively looser as the adolescents gain greater independence. Narayan in his *Swami and Friends* exploited this theme. Swami the central figure is shown constantly with his friends whose boisterous company he enjoys, and from whom he cannot stay away for any length of time. Even when he is at home his mind is preoccupied with the thoughts of his friends.

Bond has exalted the importance of friends and friendship in the life of youngsters. He uses it creatively. It is portrayed as an easy, protective and lovable relationship of life. The young friends are open, intimate and honest and show great concern for one another. Bond highlights this healthy peer relationship. The adolescent narrator Rusty in *Room on the Roof* and *Vagrants in the Valley* is very lucky to have great friends like Somi, Kishen, Ranbir, Sudheer, Devinder, Hathi and even a mute vagrant Goonga. His friends infuse in him the zest for life. Such close friendship contributes to Rusty's growth by offering a climate for growth and self-knowledge. The orphan Rusty lives with his strict guardian, Mr. Harrison. He revolted against Mr. Harrison's dogmatism and rudeness. His clashes with his guardian ended in his vagrancy. But the cheerful and enthusiastic company of his friends not only consoles him but also rejuvenates his dull and miserable life. In the invigorating company of his friends, fo. the first time he feels secure and perks up after his father's death. Their unconditional love and support bloom flowers in the dreary desert of his life. The spicy *chaat*, the thrilling bicycle riding, the exciting mountaineering, the wild enjoyment of *holi*, fun of picnic and many other exciting things, he experiences in the company of his lovely friends. He shares his doubts as well as hopes with them. Friendship is projected here as a great source of enjoyment. Rusty's sorrows are lessened and joys are multiplied through his friends. In one of notes Bond says: "If you have one true friend you have more than your share" (RIM 174). It is the institution of friendship that gives Rusty an impetus to live in the alien society and freedom from his stern and insensitive guardian. Rusty wants to become a writer. His friends motivate him. Kishen is hopeful about Rusty's bright future. He says, "One day you'll be great, Rusty. A writer or an actor or a prime minister or something. May be a poet!" (RL 32)

Somi is the incarnation of friendship. Somi enters in Rusty's life as a ray of light. He meets him on one of his solitary walks where Somi offers him a bicycle ride. Rusty gets attracted to the warmth, hospitality and disarming charm of Somi and his friends. The generosity and warmth of his behaviour always assures Rusty. Somi impresses us by his devotion and selfless love for Rusty. It is his devotion for Rusty which makes Rusty remark: "our friendship would last a lifetime and that the beauty of it would always be with me" (RL 108). Sometimes the friends get involved in petty squabbles. But they quickly settle it in increasing emotional bond. Rusty and Somi argue to have coconut and cucumber respectively. Somi moves away leaving Rusty behind. Rusty repents for denying his friend's choice. Somi returns after five minutes with coconut for Rusty and cucumber for himself. The two friends relish their favourite items: without any further grudge. It conveys the message of real friendship that lies in surrendering the self without expecting anything in return. Friends are ready to sacrifice their dreams for the sake of friends. Rusty was ready to leave India for England to pursue the career of a writer and for better prospects available in England. He meets his friend Kishen. The negligence of his father turned Kishen to the world of petty crimes. Rusty drops the idea of going to England. He returns to Dehradun with Kishen. Both the friends are now ready to fight bravely the hardships of life. M.A. Jeyaraju says: "In the absence of a conventional home, the adolescents draw all their homely comfort from youthful comraderie" (Singh, *Creative Contours* 83).

Bond's young characters spread the message of love and understanding through the bond of friendship. They are quick in making friends but are devoted in retaining it. It is not a give and take relationship for them. It is pure and spontaneous. The great things are not needed to start it. It could be started just by sharing of small objects like a marble stone, a flower, a flute, a coin, giving a lift or an assurance to teach the lessons of swimming. In the story "A Rupee Goes a Long Way" Ranji befriends Koki by giving her pretty necklace of bright coloured stones. In "Angry River" Kishen gives Sita a flute while parting from her. Sita hesitates to take it. He says: "Please keep it for me," "I will come for it one day," "It is a good flute!" (CO 121) In "Fight" Anil and Vijay fought for the right to bathe first in the pool. They had reached an impasse. No one was ready to leave the pool. Anil's expertise in swimming suddenly solved the matter. Vijay asked to teach him the tricks of diving. For that he would offer Anil to have meals with him. He would make him a real *pahalwan* (wrestler) for this. The agreement was done between the two strangers that turned them into friends: "They looked at each other with honest, unflinching eyes, and in that moment love and understanding were born" (CF 309). Now these two friends own the pool and who could dare to come there to disturb them.

Bond explores and presents a world where children are supreme. They enjoy the life and bravely face its ups and downs. He through his precocious and dynamic children portrays his vision of life: the challenges of life should be faced bravely. His children are epitome of his philosophy. His children make us believe that the world is a good place to live in. The difficulties and challenges of life have to be coped with. They by their unyielding spirit overcome the most formidable obstacles with little difficulty. Without grudge they help their family in earning livelihood.

Tembu in "The Tiger in the Tunnel," Jai in "The Eye of the Eagle," Sita in "Angry River," Bisnu in "Panther's Moon," Bisnu in "Dust on the Mountain," Kamal in the "The Coming of Kamal" happily bear their responsibilities and bravely face the hurdles and uncertainties of life. They display an unusual courage while tackling their harrowing circumstances. They by their capacity for hard work, by their positive aura and cheerful personality become a source of inspiration for the child readers. This glorified image of young persona fascinates the young audience. Tucker says: "...children like to find idealised reflections of their own good self-images in literature" (*The Child* 20). Bond avoids the approach of traditional Indian literature - the dull and direct way of preaching ethics. He provides the child reader a better understanding of life by projecting dynamic, brave and precocious children who bravely fight with their challenging circumstances. Nicholas Tucker has emphasised the need of stimuli for children:

> Children ... need stimulation in their literature to help them to move away from certain lazy, immature ways of thinking; a good author, consciously or unconsciously, provides this stimulation by writing about characters and situations in a way that is both fresh and convincing and which, in the light of a child's developing

> understanding, can also point the way forward towards greater insight. (*The Child* 2)

Twelve-year-old Tembu knows it well that "life had to go on, and a living had to be made" (PM 16) after his father, Baldeo's death. Baldeo was a watchman at the small wayside signal-stop. He was responsible to inspect a tunnel, whether it was clear of obstruction or not and signalling the train. His hand-worked signal stood before the entrance of the tunnel. A panther killed him when he was on duty. All the responsibilities now fell on Tembu. Three nights later after his father's death, Tembu was at the cutting, lighting the signal-lamp and waiting for the overland mail. The atmosphere was covered with darkness but he was not afraid. His father had killed the panther, "And besides, he had the axe with him, his father's axe, and he knew how to use it" (PM 16).

Like Tembu, Bisnu in the "Panther's Moon" too is a twelve-year-old fatherless child. There is no school in Bisnu's small village, Manjri. He studies in a school five miles away from his village. He covers the distance to his school on foot. There are other boys in Manjri village but Bisnu is the only one who goes to school. His mother will not fuss if he stays at home and works in the field. That is what other boys in the village do. But Bisnu goes to school. He goes because he wants to. He has set his heart on receiving a good schooling.

Bisnu stopped going to school because of the threat of a man-eater panther. It had terrorised the entire village. Bisnu's dog, Sheroo who accompanied him in his daily journey became the prey of the panther. Bisnu's fingers clutch the blood-stained collar which was all that was left of his dear dog. The next victim of the panther was Sanjay and then the postman Mela Ram. One day the panther chased Bisnu on his way to home from school. He bravely escaped its attack. To save himself from it, he climbed a spruce tree that showed his astuteness: "The branches of the Himalayan spruce are very brittle and snap easily beneath a heavy weight. They were strong enough to support Bisnu's light frame. It was unlikely they would take the weight of a full-grown panther" (CF 135). The panther gave its deep throated, rasping grunt to terrorise Bisnu and made him fall. He clanged firmly to the base of the spruce tree though he was trembling with fright. The cunning man-eater's all tricks failed to make the boy his prey. Bisnu again amazed us by his heroic deed and intelligence when he hit a spear on the Panther's rump who was scratching at his door: "With a roar of pain and rage, the man eater leapt down from the steps and disappeared into the darkness" (CF 141).

The encounter of Bisnu with the Panther shows his courage and prudence. It is by Bisnu's quick wit and determination that his neighbourhood gets rid of the beast. If Bisnu fights a panther to save himself and to rescue his sister, Jai another brave child hero like him, fights with an eagle in "The Eye of an Eagle". While Bisnu saves himself from the panther's clutches, Jai rescues his lamb from the clutches of the eagle. The simple courage these children are really captivating. Kamal and Sita are other characters who win our heart by their capacity to endure and survive.

Sita, heroine of the classic story "Angry River" startles us by her battle with the river in full spate. She lives on an island with her ageing grandparents and helps them in their work. In arranging knots, catching fish, milking goats, she helps her grandpa who feels "she could do all the things a boy could do, and sometimes she could do them better" (CO 87). She helps her grandmother in domestic chores. She sincerely takes care of her grandmother during her illness. The reader sympathises with this little heroine who struggles to forget her grief on her grandmother's death. She controls her tears on seeing grandpa's heartbreaking and gloomy look. She knows that the outlet of her sentiments can upset and weaken her grandpa. In her effort of suppressing her emotions for her aged grandparent, she has surpassed the great heroes:

> She wanted to cry—not for Grandmother, who could suffer no more, but for Grandfather, who looked so helpless and bewildered; she didn't want him to be unhappy. She forced back her tears, and took his gnarled and trembling hand, and led him down the crowded street. And she knew, then, that it would be on her shoulder that Grandfather would have to lean in the years to come. (CO 121-122)

Sita is left alone on the island when her grandfather takes his ailing wife to the hospital in the nearby district town of Shahganj. She bravely faces the angry river and the thunder booming down from the hills. As the river rises to flood levels and erodes the soil around the island, she carefully saves in an old tin trunk their few precious belongings. Worried about her own safety and the welfare of her grandparents, she prays to Indra, the god of thunder and to all other gods that her grandmother has taught her about. But they do not appear to listen to her pleas. A young boy on a country raft like lord Krishna appears miraculously and saves Sita. She finds her grandfather in Shahganj with the help of a kind farmer. She comes to know the death of her grandmother. Just as she has accepted the destructive form of the river earlier, she now accepts her grandmother's death as a natural phase in the wheel of life and realises that her old grandfather will now have to rely on her. Sita and her grandfather sadly return to the island when the water of the river recedes. The cycle of life is renewed. Together, Sita and her grandfather rebuild their lives, living afresh. They build another hut against the big rock, fish for food and plant a mango tree between the two protective rocks where a peepal tree had once flourished.

Kamal in the story "The Coming of Kamal" is an orphan who earns his own living. He has an assortment of things to sell in his tray of merchandizing as Laurie the child narrator notices and tells us what he sees in his tray: "In his tray were combs, buttons, and reels of thread, shoelaces and cheap perfumes" (HP 11). He lost his parents during the communal riots when the country was partitioned. He was sent to a refugee camp. Unable to bear the tough and imprisoned life, he ran away from there. He started making his own living. He spends the day selling things and the night by attending school. He does not have a home to live. He sleeps on somebody's veranda or in the *maidan*. But Kamal is not unhappy with his circumstances. He enjoys living a life of his own. Like Laurie the reader too gets impressed seeing him studying, sitting beneath the lamp on the pavement: "The noise from the road didn't appear to disturb him" (HP 15). Kamal failed despite working hard. But he did not lose his courage rather he consoled his distressed friend Laurie saying, "I'll have plenty of time now," "another year" (HP 20).

Bisnu from the story "Dust on the Mountain" is the man in the house. He has to bear the responsibilities of his family at a very tender age. He has to see that there is enough food for the family and for the oxen, for the big black dog and the hens. Bisnu is hopeful of the coming of the monsoon, then "there would be plenty of maize and rice to see the family through the next winter" (CO 131). He struggles with the old plough over his hard ground with little effect. As his luck would have it, the monsoon does not arrive. The crop fails. Now he has to do something to support his family. There is no money to be earned in his village. To find out some work, he decides to move to Mussoorie, a place unknown to him. After facing many difficulties on the way, he gets a job in a tea stall of a cinema in Mussoorie. Here, Bisnu's job is to help in preparing tea and *samosas*, serve these refreshments to the public during interval in the film and later wash up the dishes. Through Bishnu, Bond throws light on the plight of poor working children who become the victim of ruthless society. Bisnu has to bear the rudeness of customers:

> During shows, when Bisnu took the tea around, there was nearly always someone who would be rude and offensive. Once when he spilt some tea

> on a college student's shoes, he received a hard kick on the shin. He complained the tea-stall owner, but his employer said, "The customer is always right. You should have got out the way in time!" (CO 140)

Bisnu represents those poor Indian children who are backbone of their family and who have to work hard to support their family. Bond's humanistic bend carries these poor children to the height of life. Bond displays total acceptance for these unfortunate children. His sympathetic treatment of their plight and love for them offer the possibility of a human world where there is no place of cruelty of any kind. Bond finds slum children doing "all the living" amidst "grime and smoke" while the rich and privileged "fuss and fret through life" (Bond, "Slum Children at Play," *A Little Night*).

Unlike the traditional writers, Bond never tends to be didactic. His narration is unobtrusive and flowing smoothly unburdened with the direct preaching. He delineates life as he sees it. His readers are charmed by the heroic deeds and adjustable nature and attitudes of these children. The unyielding spirit of these run of the mill children promotes a better understanding of life. Prema Srinivasan writes, "Happy endings may not always be convincing, and children should face real issues in the books they read which would eventually help to build enough confidence to cope with them if the need arises" (*Children's Fiction in English* 112).

The children always want to extend the realm of their experience, by questioning about the things around them. They have countless questions about life. They love to inquire about each and every sight they see – questions that often put grown-ups in a tight spot. This inquisitiveness of children emanates from their innocence, their curiosity to know the world and their snoopy nature. Bond projects very vividly and forcibly this insatiable curiosity of children. The child in "The Room of the Many Colours" asks his father a number of questions. If his father answers one, he raises the other. The series of questions started from where the insect has come and the chain of questions finds no terminal till his father loses patience: "Where does the sea go?"; "Does it go to the end of the world?"; "Have you been around the world?"; "And my grandmother"; "Is India like England"; "What does "different" mean?"; "Will we always be in India?"; "... can we take Ayah with us?"; How long have we been here? ... (CF 230-31)

The children love to ask questions, but they prefer imaginative answers to logical one. It is because their mind is generally rich in imagination. They do not care for logic and reason as much as for enchantment and fancies. They build up their own picture of things as they want, not as they are being told. The child asks his father pointing to an insect "Where has it come from?" The father explains him, "It must have come down from the sky." Later on the father gives detailed description of the process of coming of an insect into life. The child does not find any interest in logical explanation. He enjoys the prospect of an insect falling from the sky: "Later, he told me how the insect really happened but I preferred his first explanation. It was more fun to have it dropping from the sky" (CF 229).

Children ask questions to expand the realm of their knowledge. They try their best to understand the strategies of the world but their inexperience in the worldly affairs make it difficult for them to comprehend it in a proper way. A nine year old British child narrator gets upset when his father tells that they have to move away from India in the story "My Father's Trees in Dehra." He has been living in India since his birth. He is unable to understand why his father decides to leave it. Being disturbed by the thought of leaving, he asks his father why they cannot stay in India, and why it would not be their land any more. The father says because they have to give India back to Indians. The answer of father confuses the child at the most. The Indians he knows are – the

Ayah, the cook, the gardener and their children. He is unable to figure out why these Indians whom he likes want.to get rid of them and want to send them to England.

A healthy and harmonious relationship is ready to welcome, provided that one puts off the veil of one's ego and petty selfishness. This message is characteristically conveyed by Bond's child protagonists. They are hardly bothered by the demarcations of caste, colour, creed, occupation or age. Commenting on this aspect of Bond's children, Meena Khorana writes: "Social distinctions among children are irrelevant in this mellow atmosphere: British and Indian, rich and poor, Christian and Hindu, brahmin and low-caste mingle as equals" (Singh, *Creative Contours* 150). Bond's young protagonists are kind and considerate about their friends and always ready to extend their helping hands to them. In "The Last Tonga Ride" the 'Sahib' child despite the grudges of the grandmother and Ayah, befriends a tonga-driver, Bansilal. In the story "Untouchable" the child narrator was instructed not to play with the sweeper boy because he was not clean and was just a servant boy. The child was alone in the red brick bungalow on the outskirts of the town, on the fringe of the jungle except for the sweeper boy who slept in the kitchen. He eventually befriends him one night when it begins to storm outside and felt safe and secure in his presence: "I sat down, my back against the wall; beside the untouchable, the outcaste....' The rainy season has started,' observed the sweeper-boy, turning to me. His smile played with the darkness, and then he laughed. And I laughed too, but feebly. But I was happy and safe" (CF 423).

The story "A Little World of Mud" presents the lonely British child who mixes with village children in spite of his grandmother's objection. He befriends the buffalo herder, Ramu who came from a family of bonded labourers. They spend their summer afternoons at a pond where Ramu gives him swimming lessons. Ramu tells him about the diversity of nature. Although Ramu is uneducated, is well-versed in Hindu mythology and the folklore surrounding the various animals and their predators. In "The Hidden Pool" Laurie the son of a British engineer, befriends Anil who is the son of a local cloth merchant and Kamal, an orphan child, a vendor of knick knacks and high school student. Their friendship is sealed forever and they cross cultural and economic barriers. In "A Job Well Done" the child narrator does not disclose the murder of his stepfather by his gardener, Dukhi. Both the child and Dukhi plot to keep the murder a secret. Bond says about the sociable and amicable nature of children: "... the children of all classes of people—play together. It is only when they are older that they become conscious of the barriers of class and caste" (DNF 355).

One of the appealing features of Bond's writing for children is his delineation of external peculiarities and appearances of children. He gives us a very vivid and precise picture of the externals: the face, the gesture and the dress. It is by the capacity of his vivid description, he evokes the images of children. The description gives us better perspective and deep insight into the child character. Koki is a fun loving dynamic girl. She loves to play cricket and running in the field. She trains her beetles for big race. It is her beetle Rajkumari that wins the race. The very depiction of Koki in "The Big Race" makes clear her boyish attitude. On the day of beetle race at dawn Koki hears tapping on the window pane. She immediately sits up:

> She was ten years old. Her hair fell about her shoulders in a disorderly fashion and her dark eyes were slightly ringed, but she was wide awake and listening....Koki got out of bed and tiptoed across to the window and unlatched it. Ranji was standing outside, looking somewhat disgruntled....Koki put a finger to her lips, for she did not want her parents and grandmother to wake up....Koki turned from the window and went to the dressing table. She combed her hair carelessly and tied it roughly in

> a ribbon. She was excited and in a hurry, and slept in her dress, which was very crushed. Now she was ready to leave. (CO 220-21)

Describing Kamal who is an orphan and earns his livelihood, Bond writes in "The Coming of Kamal": "He was a little taller than Anil, but thinner. He wore a red sports shirt, khaki shorts, and strong Peshawari sandals. A tray hung from his shoulders, filled with an assortment of goods" (HP 11). About Binya the immortal child heroine of "The Blue Umbrella" Bond illustrates: "Like most mountain girls, Binya was quite sturdy, fair of skin, with pink cheeks and dark eyes and her black hair tied in a pigtail. She wore pretty glass bangles on her wrists, and a necklace of glass beads" (CO 24).

Bond's fiction for children is woven around simple plots, cocooned around Indian milieu with an insight into child psychology. His fiction is abounding with the passages which characteristically reveal the thought processes and activities of children. The records of juvenile psychology in his literature enhance the knowledge about children. S.C. Dwivedi confirms, "He is superb while dealing with the psychology of children. It appears he lives permanently in their mental atmosphere as he depicts their inner and outer weather dearly" (Singh, *Creative Contours* 156-157). Children are agile in nature. Pointing out to the element of restlessness in children, Bond writes: "'Well, the animals also rest in the heat of the day. It is only the tribe of boys who cannot, or will not, rest'" (FSP 121). Bond gives an insight into the working of a child's mind. He meticulously studies children's psychology and their common activities and records them in his writings. He often hints what a child likes and what he does not. In "Time Stops at Shamli" the narrator meets a little girl. He was determined to befriend her so he was very careful while interacting with the little girl: "I did not smile at her because some children dislike adults who smile at them all the time" (CF 255). The statement made by the narrator brings forth the characteristic features of kids who do not like intimacy with strangers and smiling all the time.

The story "Home" remarkably presents the mindset of children. Mr. Kapoor scolded his son Suraj on his poor performance in studies. This made Suraj rebellious and he left his home with the thought of never ever returning. He had five rupees meant to be spent at the cinema, but now it would have to serve more urgent need like food. When unable to resist the desire to possess the big yellow toy Yo-Yo, he bought it for one rupee. It is difficult for a child to decide whether to spend money on a toy or on food. Suraj decided to stay with his friend Ranji till he got some work to support himself. His dreams got shattered when he found Ranji's house locked. The passer by an old gardener advised him to plan better before running away from home. Suraj at once decided to return with the thought that he would walk back into the house as if doing a favour to his parents. Suraj's running away and returning are very common phenomena, children often do this on being scolded. In "The Coming of Kamal" he throws light on the mischievousness of children and their frolicsome nature: "The balloon man was having a trying time. He was surrounded by a swarm of children who were more anxious to burst his balloons than to buy any" (HP 14). Suraj in the story "The Tunnel" gets fascinated by the sound and power of train. To see how it passes from the tunnel, he goes to the watchman's post to see it.

Bond's presentation of children in his stories is unmistakably realistic. His optimistic fervour, his large humane heart and his trust in essential goodness of man generate better understanding of life. Bond believes that the earth is the most suitable and beautiful place to live, provided we strip our analytical approach and mundane outlook and have love and concern for others. Bond does it by creating children like Suresh a retard in "Most Beautiful," Deepak a thief in "The Thief," Madhu a waif in "The Story of Madhu," a sweeper boy in "Untouchable".

The ingenuousness and naïveté of Arun changes the experienced thief Deepak, hardly fifteen-year-old. Deepak employs himself as a servant of Arun with the purpose to rob him with the first opportunity. But he fails to do so as he says: "He was the most trusting person I had ever met. And that was why I couldn't make up my mind to rob him" (CF 31). Deepak feels that it is easy to rob a greedy man because he deserves to be robbed. It is easy to rob a rich man because he can afford to be robbed. But it is difficult to rob a poor man, even one who really does not care if he is robbed. A rich man or a greedy man or a careful man would not keep his money under a pillow or mattress, he would lock it up in a safe place. Arun had put his money where it would be a child's play for Deepak to remove it without his knowledge. Deepak knew it well that Arun would show neither anger nor panic after discovering the theft: "only a terrible sadness not for the loss of the money but for my having betrayed his trust" (CF 32). Arun is a freelancer so he does not get a regular pay. Once he was paid a tidy sum of money for a story. Deepak steals that money and runs away. It was the affectionate nature of Arun and his trust in Deepak that brings Deepak back. He keeps back the money from where he has stolen it. Arun does not say anything despite getting the clue of his theft. He pretends that he does not know that there was an attempt to remove the money from its place. He rewards Deepak. Arun also offers to pay him a regular salary in the future and assures to teach him to write sentences, hence giving a vagrant, an opportunity to make something of him. This act of compassion and forgiveness has changed Deepak's habit of stealing for ever.

The story "Most Beautiful" pays homage to a physically challenged child. It explores the complexity of mind and struggles of a mentally handicapped child who has to put up with the cruelty of boys in the bazaar and the indifference of his father. The story evokes positive concern for an unfortunate twelve-year-old retard, Suresh. Bond portrays the struggle of this mentally and physically challenged child who wishes to be accepted in the society. The story highlights Suresh's craving to lead a normal life and the tortures that he has to undergo for being a retard. The story opens in a bazaar where the narrator finds a group of schoolboys tormenting and taunting a deformed handicapped boy. The boy was desperately trying to free himself by putting forth "a torrent of illegible gibberish abuses" at them. The hooligans continued to throw stones and mud at the boy. The narrator pities the poor chap and rescues him from the mischievous boys. He takes the boy to his mother. The narrator becomes the mentor and friend of Suresh who is ugly by normal standards: "His legs were thick, short and bowed. He had a small chest but his arms were long, making him rather ape-like in his attitude. His forehead and cheeks were pitted with the scars of small-pox" (CF 281). The narrator spends time with him. Gradually the abnormalities of Suresh become the norm for him: "The more I saw Suresh, the less conscious was I of his deformities. For me, he was fast becoming the norm; while the children of the bazaar seemed abnormal in their very similarity to each other" (CF 284).

The readers too develop love and sympathy for Suresh and forgive him when he kills his pet goat in a fit of anger. Bond here brings forth very characteristically the working of the brain of a retard: "His resentment against the animal began to show when others started admiring it. He suspected that they found it better-looking than its owner. I remember finding him squatting in front of a low mirror, holding the kid in his arms, and studying their reflections in the glass" (CF 285).

The incident of the kid-goat killing shows that Suresh is acutely conscious of his deformities, that the animal is valued by people and not he as a person. By portraying a child like Suresh, Bond successfully brings out the underlying theme that it is not appearance but perception which makes a thing beautiful or ugly: "And that was the last I saw of Suresh, lying alone on the crowded platform, alone in the great grey darkness of the world, crooked and bent and twisted—the most beautiful boy in the world" (CF 287). Bond's love for the disadvantaged in society is expressed through the character of Suresh. Even in a person like Suresh Bond finds beauty. His eyes see 'truth in beauty and beauty in truth.' For his compassion towards the miserable in the world, Bond may be placed with great humanists like Mahatma Gandhi and Swami Vivekananda.

Bond, therefore, remains a children's writer of everlasting value. He always aims to give good story - so loved by young children. Extolling Bond's art, Namita Gokhale says: "Bond's work has survived the vagaries of generations of readers. The simplicity, universality and lack of pretension in his writings make them especially accessible to young minds" (*Days of Innocence* xiv). The pastoral idyllic atmosphere of his short stories and novels, the "tender and poetic" (Alkazi, *The Book Review* 15) style of his writing, realistic description, deep concern and sympathy for children, their empathetic treatment and first person narrative are the hallmark of his creativity. The city bred children enjoy the adventure and tension free life of Bond's young characters. Modern children crave for the luxury of space and closeness to nature in which Bond's children are born and brought up. The experience of growing up, the recurring theme in many of his stories, and the child-centred perceptive of his writings won for him loyal and ever-expanding admiring readers. He is at his inventive best when spinning yarns for children from the middle and lower class. He deals mainly with the adventures and activities of boys. The girl characters rarely reveal 'girl sentiments.' They too become boyish in temperament and activities. The restricted area of Bond's theme and setting do not lose charm but make his picture vivid and forcible with heightened sensitivity. His immense love for suffering children - denied of parent's love, good upbringing, comfort and opportunities in life - makes him the conscience keeper of society and human civilisation. Bond has opened a new territory of children's dreams and fears, faith and wisdom, and soul searching for the adults in Indian English fiction. Bond has truly understood children and could see life again with their eyes. Bond through his fiction keeps it alive as he puts forth: "When I was young, I dreamt of power and fame; / And now I'm old, I dream of being a boy again" (RL vii).

4

Nature's Plenty: Loving Not the Man Less but Nature More

There is a pleasure in the pathless woods,
There is rapture on the lonely shore,
There is a society where none intrudes,
By the deep Sea, and music in its roar:
I love not Man the less, but nature more ...

Lord Byron

The lines beautifully encapsulate Ruskin Bond's deep association with the natural world that has sustained and inspired him over the years. The kaleidoscopic portrayals of nature in Bond's oeuvre enamours the heart and stirs the whole being of those who experience it. He invokes the serenity and splendour of nature that enraptures by the warmth of captivating scenes, picturesque descriptions, lively images, bewitching wit, encyclopaedic knowledge, exalting cheerfulness and originality of expression. The devotion to nature is ever present in his work and runs through it like a vein of gold. It is difficult to escape the magic which his 'nature-religion' exerts. For over a half century, Bond has celebrated the wonder and beauty of nature as few other contemporary writers have done. Nature loving heart of Bond could not find solace in the hubbub of crowded city life. Bond says: "In an odd way, it was my reaction to city life that led to my taking a greater interest in the natural world" (LIL 18).

Bond possesses an impeccable understanding of nature. Like a true devotee of nature, he finds ample delight in exploring its myriad vistas. His response to nature is personal and unique. His meticulously drawn natural phenomena are marked by accurateness. His heart warming relationship with nature and the stimulating magnificence of the dominant images of the hills, trees of the Himalayas and varied big or small animals are perceptible through every leaf that covers his work. Throwing light on Bond's heartfelt commitment to nature, Niranjan Mohanty writes:

> Bond's adherence to the world of flora and fauna and of hills, insects and the animals is a result of his commitment to the place he was born into. The woods, the hills, and the flocks of birds, insects, and the trees - all draw his attention with such impassioned intensity that at once he feels an inner urge to lose his own identity in them. (Singh, *Creative Contours* 46)

His inclination to the world of nature has much to do with his long rooting to Mussoorie, a place of beauty and reading of Henry David Thoreau, Richard Jefferies, H.E. Bates "who lived close to nature and made it part of their creative work"(BN vii). Bond's childlike curiosity extends itself to a complex animistic understanding of the genius loci of the Himalayan foothills. He speaks to Nilima Pathak on communing with nature:

> For me nature is very personal. That's because I have lived very close to it up in the mountains for the last 35 years. But even before that I was quite in kinship with forests and the general flora of the country. In India, and particularly in the Hindu religion, there's a very strong element of nature.

> In my case, I feel since I've lived so close to it, the influence shows in my work. Many of my books and stories have for the last many years had the strong element of the natural world. (Pathak, "Bonded to nature")

Bond passionately radiates his fiction with evoking images of landscapes, hilly terrains, water spots, mountain cascades, the rippling and gurgling brooks, trees - maple, sal, deodar, oak, peepal, banyan; flowering plants - petunia, marigold, bougainvillea, dandelion, primrose; host of birds - magpie, skylark, robin, thrush, sparrow, woodpecker, kingfisher, pheasant, crow and medley of animals. These diverse phenomenons of nature and its manifestations are not set in contrast with each other but in concordance and the euphony creates an ecstatic state. Commenting on Bond's rapport with nature, M.K. Naik writes:

> ... special feature of Bond's stories is his acute responsiveness to nature, 'the great affinity between trees and men.' It is not simply a matter of nature description as a narrative technique, but a genuine feeling for the natural world which has somewhat of a Wordsworthian quality about it. (Naik, *History of Indian* 250)

The hills and forests, the rivers and the ravines and numerous other forms of nature appear as an inseparable entity of Bond's consciousness. Like William Wordsworth, Bond too is a true devotee and worshipper of nature. He always experiences ecstasy amidst it. He reawakens our sense towards the natural exquisiteness around us and familiarizes us with its intricacies which one tends to ignore because of hectic and self-centred life. He explores the serene and scenic beauties. Nature has become a religion for him, as he tells Nilima Pathak, "I'm not a religious person but if I were to say I have a religion then I would say I'm a nature worshipper" (Pathak, "Bonded to nature"). Nature for him is a perennial source of joy and faith in life. His fiction promotes freshening and recharging power of nature. Enumerating the bliss of nature, he often states in his work that the company of trees rejuvenates him and makes him feel younger and "prevent him from going nuts" (Pathak, "Bonded to nature"). The sight of flowers refreshes him, the song of whistling thrush inspires him, the rustling of leaves and tinkling of rivers becalm his anguished mind, the presence of small birds adds sweetness to his life and soothing hues of various phenomena of nature heal his grief-stricken soul. The lively presence of nature with its serenity overpowers him with a sense of completeness and energizes in turn to pursue his art:

> ... its amazing how a little digging and friendly dialogue with the good earth can help reactivate us when we grow sluggish. Whenever I'm stuck in the middle of a story or an essay, I go into my tiny hillside garden and get down to the serious business of transplanting or weeding or pruning or just plucking off dead blooms, and in no time at all I'm struck with a notion of how to proceed with the stalled story, reluctant essay, or unresolved poem. (RIM 225)

Bond faithfully records the natural life around him: the small blooming bud in the crumbling of wall or by the road side; the fragrance of the wet earth after the first monsoon; the bed-spread of the wild dahlias over the hillside; misty or cloudy hillocks; dew-drops like pearls hanging loosely off tiny twig; birds chirping in the valley, far from the humdrum of common place; throaty chuckles of red billed blue magpies through the pines; reclining of an emerald green grasshopper on a petal and stretching its legs in the sunshine; a geckos protruding out from the crevice of a rock; a massive swarm of clumsy termites beneath the street lamp; the spiders spinning cobwebs in trees and bushes; the chorus of insects at twilight outside his window; the spreading branches of ancient banyan trees that curved to the ground and took root again, forming a maze of arches; a new moon, in a deep purple sky; straying of a bat into a room whose presence makes a night less lonely. There are innumerable images of the natural phenomenon. Nature in its entirety appeals Bond. Even the tiniest and ignored aspects of nature electrify him more than any majestic buildings or sculptures. This may dishearten the marble lover. He remarkably articulates:

> If someone were to ask me to choose between writing an essay on the Taj Mahal or on the last rose of the summer, I'd take the rose—even if it was down to its last petal. Beautiful, cold, white marble leaves me—well, just a little cold....Roses are warm and fragrant, and almost every flower I know, wild or cultivated, has its own unique quality, whether it be subtle fragrance or arresting colour or liveliness of design. (Bond, *Funny Side* 30)

Bond believes that nature is a stirring force that quickens every object and creature to act, to respond, to grow and to die. For pantheistic Bond anything that vibrates with life is beautiful. He is of the opinion that the beautiful and lovely face of nature - birds, flowers, fountains, butterflies and flowing rivers not only delight us but spiritually awaken us. Unlike Wordsworth, he is not confined only to the creative and beautiful aspects of nature. He knows nature is not always birdsong and dew-drenched daffodils. He is aware of the fact that the very benevolent and beautiful face of nature sometimes becomes 'red in tooth and claw.' It is whenever man takes nature for granted or misuses its generosity; it turns against and unleashes the forces that disturb life - earthquake, tidal wave, typhoon, flood, forest fire and drought. When the pent-up forces of nature are released, there is little that human can do about it, except try to survive. All these violent elements of nature in Bond's view "come to remind us that we are not, after all, the masters of the universe.

We might trample upon our natural heritage and do our best to destroy it, but the forces of nature are greater than man's. Nature will always have the last word" (BN 248). In some stories like "Angry River," "Flames in the Forest" and "Nature's Fury" Bond reveals the devastating aspect of flood, fire and earthquake respectively. His analytical mind is aware of nature's power of taking, albeit he advocates his childlike trust in nature's power of giving. He believes the life-force-nature remains kind to man if man sensitively handles it. In his "Introduction" to *Ruskin Bond's Book of Nature,* Bond highlights the law of change. Sometimes man has to suffer the fury of nature. But after showing its fury nature settles down again and resumes its generous ways:

> For it is all about renewal—seasons and the weather, sunlight and darkness, the urgency of growth, the fertility of the seed and the egg. Governments rise and fall, machines rust away, great buildings crumble, but mountains still stand, rivers flow to the sea and the earth is clothed with grass and verdure. Nature gives. And takes away. And gives again. (ix)

The salient feature of Bond's treatment of nature is its uniformity. The gentle soul of Bond experiences strange and captivating beauty and sensation in every aspect of nature - trivial or significant, grand or tiny, useful or useless, beautiful or ugly. He asserts that every particle of nature has its own value and own role to play in the intricate web of the Almighty's design. The fervour of his mercury never comes down while sketching and colouring the canvas of his fiction with beautiful rose or ignored marigold; magnificent banyan or slender grass or a small poppy; majestic tiger or sluggish buffalo; cheerful *myna* or venomous scorpion; clever chameleon or stupid hornbill; musical cicada or croaking frog. For example, Bond celebrates the marigold while in general the loveliness of rose, the fragrance of jasmine and the serenity of lily occupy most of the space in nature writing. Despite the fact that marigold is the most used flower in worship and decoration; it fails to fire the imagination of the writers in India. All the admiration goes for rose and lily. But Bond bugles his conch for marigold: "which flower is most redolent of India, of the heat and light and colour of India? Not for me the lotus or the water-lily, but the single marigold, fresh, golden, dew-drenched, kissed by the morning sun" (RIM 124). For Bond the huge banyan is as much important as the tiny grass. For Walt Whitman, "a leaf of grass is no less than the journey work of stars" (Whitman, "Song of Myself"), for Bond, "... grass is obviously a good thing, providing a home for crickets and ladybirds and other small creatures. It wouldn't be much fun living on a planet where grass could not grow" (BN 44).

Bond's fervid adoration for nature comes into view from every composition and provides a feast to the devotee of nature. He passionately observes the various elements of nature: concrete and abstract, hidden or open and startles his readers by its faithful documentation. This portrayal often gushes forth spontaneously like a fountain. He, like many of his characters, feels blissful and gladdened—running with winds, smiling with flowers, conversing with trees, swimming in the forest pools, taking nap under shady trees, riding bicycle down the precipitous hills, exploring rivers and mountain paths and wondering at the tenacity of spring. His infinite passion for nature sees no limit. In a sense he breathes through her and lives for her. It is recurring and predominant ambience of his stories. He brings nature to the point of making it a part of the story, of the character, its effect on the people or people's approach towards it. In his macabre, he uses it to create eerie and deadly atmosphere, in his children's stories to weave the free spirit of children and their innocent world, in his travelogue to highlight the beauty and view of the place and his other writings he uses it to form the background. He also uses nature as a tool to express the euphoric or troubled state of his characters' mind. The rain imagery used in *The Room on the Roof* could be cited to reveal the changing phases in the life of the hero Rusty and the setting of the story. The rain is used as a symbol of exhilaration and tedium and unification and separation throughout the novel.

Rain imagery in the beginning of the novel is presented as sensuous, refreshing and intoxicating. The novel starts "with the light spring rain rode on the wind, into the trees, down the road" that brings an exhilarating freshness to the air and smile to the eyes of Rusty, an adolescent orphan. Rusty is walking on the road to enjoy the freedom from the rigid attitude of his unsympathetic guardian, Mr. Harrison and the suffocating atmosphere of his house. The rain gives an opportunity to Rusty to meet friendly Somi and a lift onto his cycle. The meeting with Somi has brought a great change, happiness and awareness in his life. Rusty, an English child, with Somi enters the forbidden Indian bazaars and relishes spicy *chaat*, an act thoroughly unbearable by Harrison. In Harrison's regime mixing with Indians is not allowed. Harrison believes that a British boy should keep himself away from the uncultured and uncivilised Indians. Rusty meets his friends and plays *holi* with them despite Harrison's warning. Angry Harrison thrashes him. When unable to bear any more the callousness and flogging of his guardian, Rusty rebels and leaves the house. The loneliness and darkness of the night make homeless Rusty scared. He feels everything around him is dark and silent. He is brooding over the upcoming hardships but in no case he is ready to join his guardian. The sudden arrival of rain has changed the atmosphere. The rain water refreshes him and washes down the colour of *holi* from his body and the pangs of sorrow from his heart.

Somi has arranged tuition for Rusty in Kapoor's house where he is appointed to give English lessons to a brat, Kishen. In turn he is given food and shelter. Rusty enjoys the new life in Kapoor's house. The caring and protective company of Mrs. Meena Kapoor brings a happy change in dull and dreary life of Rusty. The smooth course of Rusty's happy life receives a jolt when his beloved, Meena dies in a car accident. The downpour comes the day before the telegram announcing Meena's death. The premonitions of upcoming doom have been felt all along. The rain imagery very characteristically brings it out:

> The tense sky shuddered. The blanket of black cloud groaned aloud and the air, which had been still and sultry, trembled with electricity. Then the thunder gave a great clap, and all at once the hailstones came clattering down on the corrugated iron roof....The storm continued all night....The rain had stopped by morning, but the sky was still overcast and threatening. (CF 626-27)

The feeling of impotence and futility overpowered Rusty. He contemplates the insignificance of life. He longs for something to happen. Everyday passes in the same way – "days are passing dry and dusty and nights lonely and sad." Again it is the rain that has come to break the monotony of summer and feeling of boredom from his life. Rusty wants to experience to the full the novelty of the first shower. The rain has made everything smell fresh and good:

> He threw off his clothes and ran naked on to the roof, and the wind sprang up and whipped the water across his body so that he writhed in ecstasy. The rain was more intoxicating than the alcohol, and it was with difficulty that he restrained himself from shouting and dancing in mad abandon. The force and freshness of the rain brought tremendous relief, washed way the stagnation that had been settling on him, poisoning mind and body. (CF 641)

Trees occupy an important place in his nature writing. He loves to write about the grand banyan, the sacred peepal, the stately deodar, the fragrant pine and the valuable sal. He invokes the grandeur and splendour of trees and also brings awareness towards its various usages. He recounts an entire story about the divine association of various trees. His pantheism emerges from his belief that "every human needs a tree of his own" (RIM 151). He looks forward to positive response from his readers: "Even if you do not worship the tree-spirit, you can love the tree" (RIM 151). In his *Ruskin Bond's Book of Nature* he gives detailed description of trees, its usage, effect on people, association with daily chores of life and the myths associated with it. He pays tribute to the trees for shaping his whole being. His lonely and stressful life brightens up by the benign presence of trees. He says as long as he is "aware of their presence" he can "try to avoid the trivial and the banal" (BN 121). He evokes them by calling "the guardians of my conscience" (BN 121). He also accepts the fact that trees are his best critics and he lives and works under "the generous but highly principled supervision of the trees" (BN 121). He spans the horizon of our knowledge by enumerating the account of the structure of trees, its roots, branches, flowers, leaves. Bond's Indian susceptibility is discernible in his loving portrayal of peepal the most sacred and worshipped tree in India. Bond loves and invokes peepal, not for its association with holiness but for its splendid shape and oxygen giving quality. The heart-shaped leaves of peepal are highly sensitive to the slightest breeze and would flip gently when the clouds stand still while other trees witness the least movement in the air. People love to sit beneath it in hot days. There is a peepal tree in every Indian village and it is common to see a farmer, tired at the end of an afternoon's toil in the fields, being lulled to sleep by the rustling of its leaves. About the structure of its leaves, Bond says:

> No other tree has a leaf which tapers to such a perfect point as the peepal. When it rains, you can

> see the water drip from the points. Water runs off more easily from a point than a blunt end, and the sooner a leaf dries the better it is for the tree. The leaf is beautiful, and has been likened to the perfect male physique. From the stalk (the human neck) the edges of the leaf run squarely out on either side (the shoulders) and then curve round inwards to end in a finely pointed tail (the waist), so that the suggestion is of a square, broad torso upon a narrow waist—a body such as we see in pictures of Krishna. (BN 134)

Bond always gets fascinated by the grandeur and huge size of banyan. He feels banyan is not only the biggest tree but also the friendliest of all. He likes its hospitality. The large innumerable branches of banyan provide shelter to variety of animals: "Apart from boys and girls, it attracts a large number of visitors—birds, squirrels, insects, flying foxes—and many of these interesting creatures actually live in the tree which is full of dark, private corners suitable for variety of tenants" (BN 131). The tree is to Bond like a big family or a boarding house, "in which a number of different families live next door to each other without interfering very much in each other's business" (BN 131). The other trees, about which Bond talks affectionately, are oak and deodar. The trees are considered sacred and are worshipped by Indians in different ceremonies and festivals which is a common practice in India. Bond brings forth these aspects as well in his writing.

The remarkable feature of Bond's presentation of nature is its personification. The personification emerges in the scenes when nature too reciprocates his love. The following lines beautifully record the corresponding love between trees and Bond, through visual and aural evocation of nature:

> When the trees saw me, they made as if to turn in my direction. A puff of wind came across the valley from the distant snows. A long-tailed blue

> magpie took alarm and flew noisily out of an oak tree. The cicadas were suddenly silent. But the trees remembered me. They bowed gently in the breeze and beckoned me nearer, welcoming me home. Three pines, a straggling oak, and a wild cherry. I went among them, acknowledged their welcome with a touch of my hand against their trunks--the cherry's smooth and polished; the pine's patterned and whorled; the oak's rough, gnarled, full of experience. (DNF 62)

Like trees the animals also reciprocate his genuine feelings by trusting him. His unflinching love for animals makes them fearless in his presence. They are not scared of him rather get used to his presence: "As I had not come to take anything from the forest, the birds and animals soon grew accustomed to my presence or possibly they recognized my footsteps. After some time, my approach did not disturb them" (TSS 172).

Bond has grown oneness with the environment around him. His senses are highly receptive to the vibrations in nature. His snapshots of nature marked by evocative imageries are captured in action: like scuttling of lizards; singing of crickets; cooing of pigeons; the squeaking of squirrels; droning of the bees; whistling of thrushes; swooping down of a blue jay to catch grasshoppers; wading of buffaloes in slush and mud; dancing of poplar leaves in the breeze; humming and rustling of wind in the pine and deodars; creaking of branches; gurgling of fountains; "tumbling, turning and twisting of moving currents over rocks;" "blowing of burning, choking, stinging dust and clutching and clinging to everything it touches;" "coiling of big black rumbling clouds during the arrival of monsoon;" pouring down of rain and drumming on the corrugated tin roofs; "the sound made by dry and thirsty earth, as it sucks at a sprinkling of water" (RIM 108). Like Shelley, Bond records phenomena of nature in action. But it is the mild aspects of nature that capture Bond's attention.

The delineation of flora and fauna is marked by beautiful visualised imageries that reveal Bond's art in perfection. It flows smoothly out of his pen as if he is painting his canvas with vibrant strokes of joyous and innocent colours. His images evoke our emotions and sensory impressions. He beautifully recaptures - the struggle of the sun on a winter morning to penetrate the banks of cloud, mist or drizzle, during dawn, the colour of sky gets changed from ultramarine to a clear shade, of lavender and then rising of "gloriously naked sun." His characters enjoy the thrill created by the monsoon rain that brings relief from the scorching sun, cleans the dust from the sky and the earth and throws them into the state of ecstasy. He beautifully captures the scene of the first rain of summer:

> When the monsoon brings to northern India the first rains of summer, the parched earth opens its pores and quenches its thirst with a hiss of ecstasy. After baking in the sun for the last few months, the land looks cracked, dusty and tired. Now, almost overnight, new grass springs up, there is renewal everywhere, and the damp earth releases a fragrance sweeter than any devised by man. (RIM 105)

Bond's imageries and sensuousness are not overshadowed by any symbolic representation of nature. They sprout out as a result of his adoration for and commitment to nature. He does not crush the spontaneity of nature imageries by associating it with double layer of meaning or a display of his erudition. Beautiful and sensational vibes of nature stirs him that he loves to share with his readers. His nature imageries provide feast to all five senses and his evoking synesthesia startles us - rich pungent colour of crushed neem pods; generous shade and spreading branches of banyan tree; awe inspiring feeling aroused by erect and dignified deodar; wild dahlias - red, yellow and magenta rearing their heads from the rocky crevices; gathering of stormy clouds over the purple mountains; cheerful whistling of purple plumaged thrush. The plethora of concrete details and impeccable descriptions are marked by his minute observations: "... the smell of pine needles, the silver of oak-leaves and the red of maple, the call of the Himalayan cuckoo, and the mist, like a wet face-cloth, pressing against the hills" (RIM 93). Bond creates an authentic picture using a wide range of simple and straightforward imageries: "The hill was covered with lush green ferns, the trees were entangled in creepers, and a great wild dahlia would suddenly rear its golden head from the leaves and ferns" (RIM 82).

Sensuousness is one of the important characteristics of Bond's narrative art. There is always a sense of déjà vu. One can visualise the images which he artistically creates. In this respect Bond is communicating with John Keats, particularly for pictorial effect. Like him Bond too portrays the natural world through the series of beautiful crafted pictures. The difference is traceable not in matter but in the manner of projection. Keats is poetical and Bond prosaic. Keats' pictures are executed with few words; Bond does it with elaborate descriptions.

Bond feels that God speaks to us through nature. Nature is the best source to establish a communication with God. This grand and beautiful universe with its sparkling natural phenomena is a gift to mankind from God. Bond thanks God for His creation. Admiring the Almighty, he writes: "And I would thank my God for leaves and grass and the smell of things, the smell of mint and myrtle and bruised clover, and the touch of things, the touch of grass and air and sky, and the touch of the sky's blueness" (RIM 96-97). His thoughts here echo Gerard Manley Hopkins' "Pied Beauty":

> Glory be to God for dappled things –
> For skies of couple-colour as a brindled cow;
> For rose-moles in all stipple upon trout that swim;
> Fresh-fire coal chestnut-falls; finches' wings;

> Landscape plotted and pieced – fold, fallow, and plough;
> And all trades, their gear and tackle and trim.

Bond is of the view that beauty of nature has the capacity to bring closer even the strangers and bind them in the bond of friendship. This is shown through the relationship of Koki and the narrator child in "The Window," Miss Mackenzie and Anil in "The Prospect of Flowers" and the small girl and the young man in "The Coral Tree." Koki came to stay with her aunt in a nearby house of the child narrator. One day, she was invited by the child to his window. The child-spirit of Koki was overwhelmed viewing the scenes from the window. She also enjoyed the charm of the people forming a little world of their own while passing from there. The beauty of nature with its thrilling and magical effect turned the two strangers, Koki and the child into friends: "She said nothing but stared out of the window uncomprehendingly at first, and then with increasing interest. And after some time she turned round and smiled at me, and we were friends" (CF 15).

The colourful and lively aspects of nature have always bewitched children. Amidst nature, their emotion and imagination and free spirit find an outlet. They enliven by enticing forms of nature and find infinite pleasure in its company. The images of children - swimming and playing in the forest pools, running with the winds, smiling with the flowers, dancing in the rain, exploring the plenty of nature, desiring to possess a garden or zoo of their own, are focal points of Bond's literature. In the story "The Window" Bond describes about the frolicsome activities of children during rainy season. He tells about Koki when it rains, Koki "would run out on the roof, and shout and dance in the rain" and "naked children would be frisking about in the rain" (CF 16). In "All creatures Great and Small" the child narrator takes delight in experiencing nature on his own: "It became a habit with me to visit the pond on my own, in order to explore its banks and shallows. Taking off my shoes, I would wade into the muddy water up to my knees to pluck the water lilies that floated on the surface" (RBH 16). In "How Far the River?" the child covers seven miles all alone to reach the river hidden behind the thickly forested mountains. From the villagers, he comes to know about a river, of the fish in its waters, rocks, currents and waterfalls. The longing to touch the water of the river and to know it personally, overpowers the whole being of the child. One day, in the absence of his parents, he starts his excursion without being discouraged by the distance of the river. The child, like Lama in *Kim* by Kipling succeeds in viewing it and gets thrilled by its water. For Lama it was spiritual purification but for the child it was emotional tie with nature and its beauty.

Bond's protagonists express his concern for nature. They try to establish harmony with nature and hence develop a touching relationship with it. Like Bond, his child characters too reveal a desire to possess nature. They show this affinity by conserving and preserving it. The children in the story "The Window" have thought to create a garden of their own on the roof and have planned to grow all sorts of flowers. They spent two days carrying buckets of mud up the steps to the roof and laying out the flower beds. They planted few small plants and pumpkin seeds and felt proud of their adventure. In "The Cherry Tree," Rakesh has sown the seed of a cherry tree and takes care of it. He waters it regularly even when it rains because "He wanted it to know that he was there" (NTD 136). Watering the plants by Bond's characters even though it rains is a recurring feature of his stories. This emphasises the importance of personal communication with nature. The story advocates Bond's belief that the presence of God and his power on earth could be sensed through trees. The majestic shape of the tree starts from a tiny seed into a sapling, into a plant and finally a tree: "'Just one small seed,' said Rakesh, and he touched the smooth bark of the tree that had grown. He ran his hand along the trunk of the tree and put his finger to the tip of a leaf. 'I wonder,' he whispered. 'Is this what it feels to be God?'(NTD 137) The magnificence of trees reminds Bond the presence of God on the earth. The tiny creatures' perfect body structure reminds him God's fine creation. In *Landour Days,* Bond describes a small fly and its superbly crafted structure: "The smallest insect in the world is a sort of fairy fly and its body is only a fifth of a millimetre long. One can only just see it with the naked eye. Almost like a speck of dust, yet it has perfect little wings and little combs on its legs for preening itself. That is perfection" (LD 7).

Bond sees an affinity between children and nature. Both of them are marked by innocence and purity. He believes that children are unadulterated specimen of living and kind nature. It becomes visible when Bond uses nature imageries to portray his child characters. In "The story of Madhu" the reader meets Madhu a nine-year-old poor girl. Her real parentage is unknown. She lives with an old lady who out of compassion brought her up as her own. Bond describes Madhu using nature imageries: "She was very slight and frail, like a flower growing in a rock, vulnerable to wind and rain....She was there every morning, chasing butterflies, stalking squirrels and mina, her voice brimming with laughter, her slight figure flitting about between the trees" (CF 100). The little girl in "The Coral Tree" is also described in a similar vein: "she was fresh and clean like the rain and the red earth" (CF 8).

Bond's literature off and on highlights the analogy between tree and man. He points out the similarity of evolution and decay in human beings and trees. Both trees and men grow much at the same pace, if are not hurt or starved or cut down. Both in youth are resplendent creatures and in declining years stoop a little. At the end of journey a man like a tree sheds his leaves with a sigh. "The Kitemaker" exclusively presents the affinity between trees and human beings. The old grandfather Mehmood is compared with a banyan tree and the young grandson Ali with a young mimosa plant: "Mehmood was like the banyan, his hands gnarled and twisted like the roots of the ancient tree. Ali was like the young mimosa planted at the end of the courtyard. In two years both he and the tree would acquire the strength and confidence of their early youth" (CF 77).

Bond, a true devotee of nature not only records it in its fullest form but also advocates its preservation and conservation. Bond seems to have been writing about saving our environment and concern for it long before ecology became an important aspect of our daily life. He has been writing about the steady decline of the forest cover due to growing industrialisation, urbanisation and about the ruthless destruction of the natural habitat of the creatures of the jungle. "The Tree Lover" and the "Prospect of Flowers" reveal Bond's concern for trees which deserve our love, care and protection. He pleads for favourable responses for trees. He quotes George Morris:

> Woodman, spare that tree!
> Touch not a single bough!
> In youth it sheltered me,
> And I'll protect it now. (BN 133)

Bond expresses his anguish for rapid disappearance of the forest and animal wealth through many of his stories. If he heartily welcomes the exploration of nature, he severely criticizes its exploitation. He puts up in his fiction environmental consciousness and reminds us of our dependence on the earth and its resources. In "Dust on the Mountain" he shows how the "trunk of a scraggy old oak tree" saved the life of a truck driver Pritam Singh. Pritam likes the idea of Bisnu when he says that he wants to go back to his land and to grow things on the land and then to blast things out of it. Growing things reminds Pritam of growing trees because it is a tree which saved his life: "There is something to be said for growing things," said Pritam. "But for that tree, the truck would have finished up at the foot of the mountain, and I wouldn't be here, all bandaged up and talking to you. It was the tree that saved me. Remember that, boy" (CO 153).

Bond believes nature is a part of community not a commodity to be used and thrown. In a subtle way he proposes that humans should be responsible towards it. He writes with a strong eco-consciousness. Summarizing the views of eco-critics, Peter Barry writes: "...nature really exists, out there beyond ourselves, not needing to be ironised as a concept by enclosure within knowing inverted commas, but actually present as an entity which affects us, and which we can affect, perhaps fatally, if we *mistreat* (italics mine) it" (Barry, *Beginning Theory* 252). Like Maneka Gandhi and Sunder Lal Bahuguna, he speaks for the cause of animals and plants. He appeals for gentle behaviour towards animals. He tries to awaken the feeling and awareness of his readers towards the trees. He believes the life giving trees could be saved only by the effort of every individual: "In the long run, it is the 'common man,' and not the scientist or conservationist, who can best give protection to the birds and animals living around him" (DNF 178). In "My Father's Trees in Dehra" he laments the ruthless felling of trees: "If people keep cutting trees, instead of planting them, there'll soon be no forests left at all, and the world will be just one vast desert" (CF 119). He feels environmental crises are a result of humanity's disconnection from the natural world, brought about not only by increasing technology but also by particularisation, that is, a mentality of specialisation that fails to recognize the interconnectedness of all things.

In "Kitemaker" Bond bemoans the ravages of "development" which has turned once a lively city into a congested metropolis with no space for innocent activities. He feels traumatised on seeing ruthless killing of animals and felling of trees which has brought many species of flora and fauna on the verge of extinction. In some of his stories, he makes a dig at the unwise decision of the authorities to cut trees and build roads and buildings in those places. In "Death of Trees," he writes with a tinge of irony: "The peace and quiet of the Maplewood hillside disappeared for ever one winter. The powers that be decided to build another new road into the mountains, and the PWD saw fit to take it right past the cottage, about six feet from the large window which had overlooked the forest" (Bond, *Our Trees Still* 93). Bisnu in "Dust on the Mountain" feels restless on his way to Mussoorie while journeying by bus. The treeless land disheartens this hill boy who was born and brought up amidst nature. He asks himself, "Why are there no trees here?" The fellow old passenger mourns with him and tells him that the negligence and greediness of man is the cause of the gradual erosion of the beauty of the hills: "There were trees here once ... but the contractors took the deodars for furniture and houses. And the pines were tapped to death for resin. And the oaks were stripped of their leaves to feed the cattle ... and the bushes that remained were finished off by the goats!" (CO 135)

Bisnu becomes the spokesperson of Bond's concern for the depletion of forests and the disappearance of greenery. Bisnu gets horrified anticipating the turning of Green Mountain of his homeland into desert. Bisnu watches in awe as shrubs and small trees are flung into the air because of the blast on the mountain for making the roads. It always frightens him - not so much the sight of the rocks bursting as under, as the trees being flung aside and destroyed. He remembers the trees at home - the walnuts, the chestnuts, the pines. He wonders if one day they would suffer the same fate and whether the mountains would all become a desert like this particular range: "No trees, no grass, no water—only the choking dust of mine and quarries" (CO 149). The grandfather in "All Creatures Great and Small" not only protects all kind of animals but also talks about their rights. He "couldn't understand the pleasure some people obtained from killing the creatures of our forests" (CO 195). The grandfather in *Rusty the Boy from the Hills* shares the same view. He urges for gentle behaviour towards animals. He says: "'It is also important that we respect them'....We must acknowledge their rights. Everywhere birds and animals are finding it more difficult to survive, because we are trying to destroy both them and their forests. They have to keep moving as the trees disappear" (RBH 19).

Bond's nature writing shines with a wide range of animals vibrating with life. His lively presentation of humorous antics of animals engulfs the readers in its captivating charm. His genuine projection of animals marked by humanistic bend makes our perspective better about them. The succeeding thoughts of Walt Whitman about animals noticeably summarize Bond's approach to animals "I think I could turn and live with animals, they are so placid and self-contain'd, / I stand and look at them long and long" (Whitman "Song of Myself").

Bond, like a master chef, has used all those ingredients and flavours while creating mouth watering delicacies which can stimulate the taste bud of his young readers. Portrayal of fauna is one such recipe that exhilarates the young audience and easily grips their attention. About the use of animals in children's literature, Prema Srinivasan says: "Animal fantasy is most endearing category of children's fiction, for it lends itself to a cheerful and lively approach. In Indian fiction as well as early Western folklore, the humanized animal has a long tradition behind it" (*Children's Fiction* 95). The animal world has always fascinated the children and they identify themselves more readily with the animal characters than human. Emphasising this aspect, Ira Saxsena points out in her essay "Fiction": "... Children at this age identify themselves more readily with animal characters and because emotional relationship with animals is easier to handle than with human beings, the use of animal figure strengthens the realistic appeal of a story" (Menon, *Children's Literature* 122). Stories of animals and pets make children feel at home. Tucker observes that animal life in reality as well as in fiction appeals to the young. It is because "like children themselves, animals can also be small, vulnerable and inarticulate, as well as open and quite artless in their appetites and needs" (Tucker, *The Child* 100). This is why the writers who have child readers in mind create the bewitching world of animals. *The Panchtantra, Jatak Katha, Aesop's Fables, The Hitopadesa,* and the characters created by Walt Disney are all-time favourites of children because of the animal portrayal.

Bond's depiction of variegated animals: from a tiger to a frog, from an eagle to an insect, from a python to a lizard enchants with its vivacity. Unwavering love and persistent commitment for all kinds of animals is the distinctive feature of Bond's presentation of animals. He dazzles us by the panorama of colourful birds, awe-inspiring tigers, mischievous monkeys, humanized reptiles, murmuring crickets, whistling thrushes, croaking frogs and so on. Bond's deftness has sculptured these animals into beautiful carvings and his vivid descriptions vivify them. His conceited pythons, wicked and revengeful monkeys, boastful and bullying crows, demanding crocodiles, gracious and majestic tigers, crazy and faithful dogs, gossipy rosy pastors, quarrelsome *mynas,* cheerful *bulbuls,* noisy coppersmiths, cheeky sparrows and many more grip our attention and create an everlasting impression. The appeal of tiny creatures like squirrels, butterflies, caterpillars, beetles, fairy flies, termites, hoopoe etc. is equally irresistible. He invokes his relationship not only with diurnal animals but also with the nocturnal life of owls, foxes and nightjars. This world is depicted with rare gusto as walking leopards in forest, staring owl on trees, sounds produced by fluttering of bats wings during the silence of night.

Children have always been attracted by the animal story, even when there are hidden layers of meaning as in allegories, parables and fables. They get fascinated by animal lore as long as the created world is an approachable one. The animal story is popular with a wide age group.

The kids get fascinated more towards humanised animals who talk and act like them. But older children expect animals to be presented in a more realistic manner. Bond has used both the techniques - realism and romance while depicting animals. In "Grandfather's Private Zoo" and in his macabre stories, the element of fantasy takes over. It is realism which mainly dominates his animal portrayal as in *Panther's Moon and Other Stories*. The story "Eyes of the Cat" is eerie as the girl Kiran takes revenge on an ill-tempered teacher by killing her when on full moon day she turns into a leopard. In "The Monkeys," the author gets horrified seeing the killing of Miss Fairchild by monkeys and the futile effort of her dogs to save her from them. But when he goes to save the lady, he finds nothing - the shrieking lady, monkeys and dogs all disappeared like ghosts. Later on he comes to know that Miss Fairchild had died fifteen years ago. The way Miss Fairchild was murdered by the monkeys was the same as the one he witnessed at night from his window.

Bond's surpasses traditional literature in his profiling of animals - *The Panchatantra, Hitopadesha, Jatak Tales* and *Aesop's Fable*. These literatures are marked by moralistic tone, edifying approach and constrained projection. Animals projected here are often of the stock kind and have fairly constant characteristics: the lion is strong but dull of wit, the jackal crafty, the heron stupid, the cat hypocrite, the fox vile, the donkey foolish and the dog faithful. Each animal is invested with certain human qualities and endowed with the gift of human speech and action. Bond's literary world is different - free from such stock projections. He excels in presenting variety of animals marked by authenticity. His anthropomorphic animals and birds are able to capture the imagination of young children.

There seems to be two main objectives of Bond behind the projection of animals: firstly to entertain his young readers and secondly to bring awareness for these fine specimens of God. His projection differs from the writers like Kipling and Anna Sewell. Kipling through animals passes comment on the human world. Sewell arouses our compassion for them by exhibiting the miserable condition of animals. Sewell in her most famous work *Black Beauty* advocates concern for horses. In *The Jungle Books,* Kipling presents a variety of animals and critiques through them the complex social structure of human life and the cruelties of existence. Bond keeps himself away from the double layered interpretation. His animals are for the sake of children - stem out from the pen of an animal lover.

Bond like Salim Ali talks about peculiar habits and habitats of birds and lovingly delineates the bird of cities as well as of jungle. He feels sorry for the wild birds that for life depend upon the forests. The disappearance of forests played havoc with their life. They are disappearing simply because the forests are disappearing. Only those birds can survive who have learnt to live with and off humans. Crows, mynas and sparrows do this to perfection. So they continue to thrive as our cities grow. Bond like Jim Corbett colours his canvas with majestic tigers. But his is not *Shikar* literature like Corbett who was a sport hunter. Bond has always opposed hunting done for pleasure. Bond is praised for arousing love for tiger the magnificent beast of Indian jungles. But Corbett was blamed for exaggerating the danger that tigers posed to people and indirectly legitimizing the culture of hunting. Bond has shown love and concern even for ferocious animals. For him they are not dangerous as they are thought to be. It is only when some bullet wounds them and they are unable to hunt, they attack herds or when their habitat is ruthlessly destroyed by men they enter human settlement for prey. Ramu's grandfather in "Tiger, Tiger, Burning Bright" expresses Bond's love for the national animal of India. He says: "The tiger is very soul of India, and when the last tiger has gone, so will the soul of the country" (PM 127). Bond enjoys observing the living creature in their natural habitat. He is averse to the idea of killing animals for pleasure and using its stuffed head for decoration. In *Time Stops at Shamli,* he condemns mounted stag's head: "... how could anyone with a true love of the beautiful care for the stuffed head of an animal, grotesquely mounted, with no resemblance to its living aspect?" (TSS 39) Through the presence of the majestic tigers Bond exposes the vanity and the false ego of man about his being the most beautiful creation of God. In *Book of Nature,* he says that man kills tiger because they "coveted his beauty—his stripes, and the gold of his body, his fine teeth, his whiskers, and his noble head" (BN 211). Human beings are foolish boasting his triumph over the king of jungle by hanging tiger's skin on the wall or with his head stuffed and mounted and the pieces of glass replacing his fierce eyes.

Bond tries to arouse love for the animals through his appealing portrayals. He meticulously gives the detailed account of animal behaviour in his tongue-in-cheek style. With Bond, the readers too laugh at the funny antics of animals that generally one let pass or ignore because of the hectic and preoccupied life. When one comes across them in Bond's stories, one gets enthralled by them. In *Funny Side Up,* Bond writes about the nuisance maker monkeys who pester people. Living in North India, sometime or the other one must be pestered by these uninvited guests. Bond says he could tolerate them while doing "bhangra" on his roof, but resent them when they start invading his rooms and spoiling his important things. One day he got shocked seeing a very large Rhesus monkey sitting on the toilet-seat. The stubborn monkey was like a bully not ready to vacate the throne when politely requested, so Bond slammed the door very loudly to scare him. Another day a female monkey irritates him by lifting his telephone receiver as if she has to make an STD call. But when Bond interrupted her she was so resentful of this intrusion that she made off with his telephone directory and tore it to shreds, scattering pages along the road (Bond, *Funny Side Up* 13). In the story "Thus Spake Crow" the crow advises the freelancer narrator how to deal with this crafty world which does not understand the simple man.

He suggests him some pragmatic tips to achieve success.

The lively activities and eccentricities of these animals delight us for its vivid description. Even a chameleon, a creature often feared and despised by adults and children alike, is lovingly portrayed in the story "Henry: a Chameleon." Bond's lively narration creates an indelible impression on our psyche. Bond does not create a make belief world for his animals; he rather depicts them in their environment. The portrayal of Tutu and Toto the two vexatious baby monkeys in grand father's menagerie is fine example of Bond's affectionate humour. The funny activities of these monkeys make us an ardent lover of monkeys after going through the stories from "All Creatures Great and Small." Bond invests human sentiments and reactions to these monkeys which make it easier for children to relate to them and their frolics. Describing Toto, Bond writes:

> Toto was really a cute little monkey. His bright eyes sparkled with mischief beneath deep-set eyebrows, and his teeth, a pearly white, were often on display in a smile that frightened the life out of elderly Anglo-Indian ladies. His hands were not those of a Tallulah Bankhead (Grandfather's only favourite actress), but were shrivelled and dried-up as though they had been pickled in the sun for many years. (Bond, RBH 4)

The evocative description about Toto made him alive. But we enjoy more the company of Tutu. Her funny performances create boisterous laughter and amuse both children and the adults. Tutu is a little girl monkey. She insists on shaking hands with all those who visit the house. One day she is found scratching her armpits using Uncle Ken's hairbrush, much to annoy him but to amuse the readers. In the jeweller shop, she is found trying on a pretty necklace. When everyone runs to catch her:

> ... she used the heads and shoulders of people as springboards and so made rapid headway through

> the bazaar....She tried to make her escape speedier by leaping on to the back of a passing scooterist. The scooter swerved into a fruit stall and comes to a standstill under a heap of bananas, while the scooterist found himself in the arms of an indignant fruitseller. Tutu peeled a banana and ate part of it before deciding to move on. (RBH 46)

Aunt Ruby is a frequent taker of bath. This meets with Tutu's approval - so much so, that one day, when Aunt Ruby finished shampooing her hair she looked up through lather of bubbles and soapsuds to see Tutu sitting opposite her in the bath tub following her example. Slapstick comedy is created through these monkeys.

Like his monkeys, his crows in "A Crow for All Seasons" amuse us. The fun, forage and pecking pranks of the two crows: Speedy and Slow have been described with admirable wit and insight into human nature. The humour is here created with intellectual wit. The use of slang, colloquial language and inimitable style of Bond make the boasting of the narrator crow more lively and catchy. Bond generally uses sophisticated language. Here he uses a coarse language which goes well with a loafer kind of crow. Through the projection of this boastful crow, Bond wants to comment on the futility and silliness of man's false ego. The story starts with the aphorism needed to be followed by a crow: "Early to bed and early to rise makes a crow healthy, wealthy and wise. They say it's true for humans too. I'm not so sure about that. But for crows it's a must" (PM 84). The crow boasts about the superiority of his race saying "a crow's IQ is way above that of all other birds. And it's higher than a dog's, I bet" (PM 86). He feels human beings are funny. Inconstancy while favouring someone is a peculiar trait of human beings. They can love someone one day and can hate the same person the other day. The haughtiness of the crow crosses the limits and amuses the readers when he feels irritated at man's using napkins for wiping the mouth which is nothing but nonsense, used by particularly well-to-do sort. Once, he is appreciated for his whistling by a boy. Flattered by the admiration and in the state of ecstasy, the crow starts singing his favourite song, a rare composition of his own. When the song gets over, he bows and preens himself for the applause. But the crow gets a bottle opener flying at him by Junior Sahib. The insult irritates him. He says: "Well, I ask you! What can one say about humans? I do my best to defend them from all kind of criticism, and this is what I get for my pains" (PM 91).

The crow shows his unyielding spirit. He picks up the bottle opener and adds it to his collection of odds and ends. Like a human being, this crow also has some rare hobbies and passion for collecting things. The leisure pursuit and obsession of this crow is no less than found in the human world. He makes us laugh when he discloses his secret hobby of collecting tooth brushes:

> My own preference is for toothbrushes. They're just a hobby, really, like stamp-collecting with humans. I have a small but select collection which I keep in a hole in the garden wall. Don't ask me how many I've got—crows don't believe there's any point in counting beyond two—but I know there's more than one, that there's a whole lot of them in fact, because there isn't anyone living on this road who hasn't lost a toothbrush to me at some time or another. (PM 84-85)

The crow even surpasses ordinary human beings in his collection of things. The artistic disposition of the crow's sentiment entertains the reader. He likes to have different stuffs in his menu: "I don't eat rubbish and throw-aways--all the time. Just occasionally I like a ripe guava or the soft flesh of a papaya. And sometimes I like the odd beetle as a *hors d' oeuvre*" (PM 85). Ungratefulness on the part of man irritates him. It is he who helps them in keeping down the population of fruit-eating beetles, even helps in recycling their refuse but gets nothing in return except their contempt. The crow also makes us aware how the evils rampant in human society can spoil the family dog Tiger who unsuccessfully tries to be manlike. The family has doted on Tiger so much that he pretends he is very great. The crow finds nothing special in him as it comments: "one of his ancestors was the great Khan's watchdog—but, as often happens in famous families, animal or human, there is a falling off in quality over a period of time, and this huge fellow—Tiger, they call him—is a case in point" (PM 85).

This personified bigheaded crow amuses us by his tall talk and the haughty narcissistic python in the story "All Creatures Great and Small" startles us. The python has become enamoured with its own reflection and spends the rest of the days in a narcissistic daze and also has grown conceited observing the attention it receives. The grandfather made a plan to trap it. He prepared a large cage with a mirror at one end. Like the child narrator, the readers too are taken aback seeing a snake fall in love with its own image. The child found the python spending its days curled up in a narcissistic haze with a dreamy look in its eyes: "[he] was relaxing in front of the mirror with something resembling a smile on his face—if you can imagine a python smiling ... he was in raptures over his handsome reflection" (RBH 15).

In "Cricket for Crocodile," Bond introduces a haughty and demanding crocodile, Nakoo. He is respectively addressed by children as "Nakoo ji" or "Nakoo Sir." Mr. Nakoo gets annoyed by the noise made by the cricketers. The noise frightens away "the water birds and other creatures required for an interesting menu" (CO 4) of Nakoo. His anger finds no limits when a "juicy bank manager" (CO 4), a nice change in his daily menu of frogs, eels and herons are alerted by the noise made by the cricketers. He tries to reclaim his territory by relaxing in the warm sun on the smooth cricket pitch until one of the player hits him with a fast ball. He sulks and withdraws into the river, waiting to take revenge.

Bond's empathetic treatment of animals, the ignored species of the world brings awareness towards them. His portrayal of animal is free from favouritism. He shows the same gusto and fervour while projecting different kinds of animals - a tiger or a scorpion, a frog or a *myna*. His search for the 'life force' throbbing in each - big or small, loved or despised, attractive or venomous never slackens. He benignantly presents his communion with animals - furred or feathered, fierce or friendly, diurnal or nocturnal. Bond pleads for favourable response towards this overlooked and exploited fine creation of God that we tend to gloss over because of our feverish and frenzied life. Bond's eco-sensitivity pervades in his animal projection. He feels man and animal both are integral part of this universe and depend on each other. A crow's honest confessions in "Crow for All Seasons," "how much we depend on humans" reveals the law of interdependence. Glorifying the importance of animals in our life, Bond says in *Tales of the Open Road*: "... the greater the distance we put between our world and the world of animals, the less human we become" (47).

Bond's treatment of animals differs from the traditional Indian view both in choice and manner. There are rarely cow, goat, cat, parrot, deer which are often used in the Indian myths and stories. They are rather python, chameleon, crow, monkey, eagle, jackal, hornbill, scorpion and frog. In India animals are reared and worshiped because of their association with daily life. Bond does not idealize animals yet he does not deny their importance. They have soul like human beings and have right to live. The concept of pet animals is common in the western culture. The family tie is weak in European countries compared to India. The search for freedom and space drift them away from the family matrix. They compensate their need of company through animals - dog, cat that are devoted and faithful to the master who provides them food and shelter. Bond exploits the tradition of pet animals. But his range is wide and uncommon. The grandfather in "All Creatures Great and Small" and "Grandfather's Zoo" raises monkey, parrot, python, chameleon, lion, elephant, cassowary bird and owl. Deepa Agarwal observes Anglo-Indian sensibility in Bond's animal stories. Pointing the difference between Indian and Western approach, Deepa writes: "While Hindu may venerate cows and worship snakes, the Indian attitude to animals remains quite different - animals are not considered pets, but either loyal helpers or sacred objects, or both" (Agarwal, *Book Bird* 32-34). Bond is not much interested in anthropomorphising animals or writing animal fantasies rather he celebrates them as individual creatures that have feelings and rights on the earth. He rarely refers his animals in the neuter gender. He generally uses he/she pronoun for them. He does not treat them with indifference but with respect and sympathy. He has given them identity and dignity through his understanding. Bond elevates his beasts and birds as heroes and heroines. He does not consider them inferior to man in any way. They constitute a vital part of the life. Bond has also chosen very interesting names for his animals that at once catch our attention: Timothy (the tiger); Henry (the chameleon), Tutu and Toto (the monkeys), Nakoo (the crocodile), Caesar, Speedy and Slow (the crows), Rajkumari, 2001, Moocha (the beetles), Pari (the goat), Popeye (the parrot), Chip, Sheroo, Motu (the dogs); Dickens (the myna); Harold (the hornbill) and so on as such, he humanizes them.

Bond's animal world always dazzles with detailed description and evocative treatment. He is able to authenticate them because of his deeper understanding and appreciation for them. Bond describes very often animals that are being abandoned or are in helpless condition. The characters in the stories, especially children rehabilitate them. Harold, the hornbill tumbles out of his nest and is rescued from the predatory cat by the grandfather. Henry, the chameleon is saved from being stoned to death by ignorant people of town. The grandfather bought a miserable looking monkey from a street entertainer. Pari, the goat is adopted by Mukesh because she follows him to his home and does not appear capable of surviving on her own. Bond has portrayed children who reveal great love for animals. They feel affinity with animals and readily come forward to rescue animals in peril. They do their best to protect them from various dangers: man made or nature made. Ramu in "Big Cat Tales" tries to save a tiger from the hunters. He ties bits and pieces of old clothing on small trees and bushes where the hunters were waiting for the tiger to come. Ramu knew the wily old king of the jungle, the tiger "would keep well away from the bait if he saw the bits of clothing—for where there were men's clothes, there would be men" (BN 227).

Bond's animal portrayal is not confined to one kind of animal species, there is a wide spectrum marked by sensuousness - a mongoose scurrying across the grass with an egg in its mouth; termites and white ants emerging from their lairs out of every hole, crevice and crack, fluttering about heavily on this the first and last flight of their lives; the lizards plying out their sticky pink tongues and devouring insects swiftly and for hours cramming their stomachs knowing that such a feast would not be theirs again; swooping of flying foxes silently out of the trees during the dusk; croaking and hopping of frogs in slush; bears found stealing pumpkin and so on. He enriches his animal world by graphically highlighting the peculiar habits of animals. In "The Elephant and Cassowary Bird," Bond tells about the nature of elephant. The tribe of elephant is "noted for its ability never to forget" (BN 11). Bond loves to observe the animal world and for his young readers he executes it with minute details. The facts blended with interesting imagination capturing the attention and bringing them close. Bond beautifully narrates the fighting of animals, their daily activities and their struggles for survival. The picture of the battle between a cobra and a mongoose in "Garden Adventures" is presented vividly. The children through the description get a deep insight into animal life:

> Hissing defiance, his forked tongue darting in and out, the cobra raised three of his six feet off the ground, and spread his broad, spectacled hood....The cobra stood on the defensive, swaying slowly from side to side, trying to mesmerize the mongoose into making a false move. The mongoose knew the power of his opponent's glassy, twinkling eyes, and refused to meet them. Instead, he fixed his gaze at a point just below the cobra's hood, and opened the attack. (BN 5-6)

Bond is unable to understand the strange pleasure man derives by killing innocent animals. The false pride of man has brought many species on the verge of extinction. Bond exalts animals for their fearlessness. Death an inevitable and uncertain phenomenon of life can take man or animal any time in its grip. The life of wild animals is always under threat. They could be killed at any time. They are not afraid of death though they live in permanent fear:

> It is only man, with his imagination and his fear of the hereafter, who is afraid of dying. In the jungle it is different. Sudden death appears at intervals. Wild creatures do not have to think about it, and so the sudden killing of one of their number by some predator of the forest is only a fleeting incident, soon forgotten by the survivors. (BN 218)

The uncorrupted and peaceful world of nature is set in contrast with the corrupted human world. In "The Tunnel" the watchman Kishen Singh who inspects the tunnel for passing train, feels safer in the jungle. On being asked by Ranji "Will it be safe?" to stay in jungle at night, he says: "It is safer in the jungle than in the town. No rascals out here. Only last week, I went into the town,

I had my pocket picked! Leopards don't pick pockets" (CF 312).

The entire corpus of Bond is a magnificent document of his profound association with nature and his questing of spirit through it. Like Rousseau, he propagates the idea 'return to nature.' His oneness with nature and his devotion to its beauty and tranquillity earned him an enduring place in the pantheon of the great Romantics. Bond shared the common romantic belief that so long man is in nature's lap; he enjoys freshness of mind, spiritual insight and security. Joy is his constant companion if he is the dedicated priest of nature. Like Keats Bond is eager to express her through senses and reawakens our sense to the natural beauty around us. Like William Blake, he observes the silent miracles of nature and celebrates it in its fullest form and like Wordsworth he extols the divinity of nature and views its world with spiritual reverence. Bond perceives 'Mother Nature' as infinite power and longs for observing her divine splendour in the objects of the world which he considers being his imitations. He too like Wordsworth feels that the nature can impart great lessons which all sages cannot do:

> One impulse from a vernal wood
> May teach you more of man,
> Of moral evil and of good,
> Than all the sages can. (William Wordsworth, "The Tables Turned")

The fictionalizing animal world, palpitating view of forest, of garden and glorified world of trees in Bond's literature have brought the young readers close to the natural world. The minute detail with which he invokes this world entails young children invaluable lessons in ecology. The affinity of child characters with nature and their effort in trying to understand the law of nature give them an insight into the wild life. In an age of environmental destruction, Bond's writing sensitizes towards the need for humanistic understanding of our relationships with the natural world. The magical aura of Himalayan flora and fauna presented as a persistent source of inspiration, joy, self realization and a means of survival in his writing. His nature writing promotes the idea: "Live close to nature and you will never feel lonely" (BN 30). Bond has grown oneness with the environment and desires the same from the readers: "When we walk close to nature, we come to a better understanding of life; for, it is from the natural world that we first emerged and to which we still belong" (BN 60).

5

Representing the Indian Reality

> I was hoping that there was still room in this world for a simple storyteller, one who strives to give pleasure to both child and adult; not by hiding our scars but by showing that we can be beautiful in spite of them.
>
> For me, all are significant: the lighted compartment with its farmers, shopkeepers, artisans, clerks and occasional pickpockets; and the lonely wayside stop, with its uncorrupted lamplighter.
>
> Ruskin Bond *Lamp Is Lit, Book of Nature*

The real world Ruskin Bond inhabits is transcribed in his fiction. His stories are firmly rooted to the Indian soil and are redolent of its culture. He has expounded the various facets of India with a regard for verisimilitude. Bond captures the attention and imagination of his readers, with his inherent ability to create lifelike characters, tangible events of everyday life and precise details of realistic settings. His stories float as gently as lily pads on the surface of Indian life yet suggest the depth beneath. It is not only the theme, the plot, the characterization but also Bond's art of story-telling that exquisitely creates the Indian reality.

Fiction as a creative process is an expression of the most intimate awareness of the society from where it originates. Since fiction represents life, realism becomes an important component of story-telling. The term realism can be described in two ways - firstly, it means projection of things as they really are or as they appear to be. Secondly, it means the art of making the unreal appear as real. The goal of realism is to treat the whole of life. This means including all social classes, the humdrum details, the crises and the savoury and the unsavoury aspects of human existence. Prose fiction on the large scale exploits the techniques of realism and is uniquely capable of revealing the truth of life. Very often, the novel presents detailed reportage of the physical minutiae of everyday life, the cataloguing of people into social types or species and radical analyses of the economic basis of society:

> [Realism] ... rest[s] on the assumption that the novel imitates reality and that reality is more or less stable and commonly accessible. But it is possible to conceive of the relationship between art and reality in terms of imaginative creation rather than imitation. The writer may be said to imagine, to invent a fictional world which is more than a copy of the real one. Such a shift in conceptual metaphors produces attitudes to the novel, and perhaps even novels, with quite different priorities from those of the realist tradition. The emphasis move from accuracy of representation to aspects of form - narrative structuring, symbolic patterning, linguistic complexity and so on. (Childs, *Routledge Dictionary* 198)

M.H. Abrams asserts "realist fiction is written so as to give the effect that it represents life and the social world as its seems to the common reader, evoking the sense that its characters might in fact exist, and that such things might well happen" (Abrams, *Glossary of Literary* 174). For subject matter a realist prefers "the commonplace and the everyday over rarer aspects of life—but they must render their materials in ways that make them seem to their readers the very stuff of ordinary experience" (Ibid).

Realism is a cardinal feature of Bond's literature. His recognition in the literary world rests on the authentic evocation and fascinating delineation of Indian milieu. He selects out of the kaleidoscopic events of the society the few related ones that have caught his fancy. He writes straight from the heart to create a captivating story. His believable characters and situations are free from any complicated expression. The setting, theme and characterization of his stories tinted with various hues that reflect one or the other aspect of Indian experience marked by accuracy and completeness. Murari Prasad comments on the element of realism in Bond, "He catches alive a slice of intensely felt and brilliantly perceived life in a small town marooned in time, people stepped in old social mores, their ordinary workaday world, objects of gross terror and hidden pleasures by sensitive evocation of life around hills and mountains" (Singh, *Creative Contours* 111).

Bond's portrayal of scenes and situations represent two different aspects of Indian life: the serene Indian mountains and the hubbub of Indian bazaars. The diverse features of Garhwal hills, the noise and confusion, taste and smells, beauty and squalor and the frantic activities of bazaar, of the railway platforms, of the roads are the important settings which Bond works out in his stories. His deftness and craftsmanship while executing the concerned pictures waver at no place. He is at ease while depicting the different phases of Indian life - negative and positive, gloomy and idyllic. He shuns from presenting the unattainable utopian or repulsive dystopian world. He does not wish to dwell in the world of fantasy.

Bond's writings have the undeniable stamp of authenticity because of his keen observation and genuineness of depiction. He takes us with him to the tantalising Indian bazaars, narrow roads and alleys, railway platforms - burgeoning with a throng of rustling people; alive with cries of vendors and the smell of cattle and ripening dung; where jugglers and fortune tellers are using all tricks to allure naïve customer; where children can be seen playing *gully-dunda, kabaddi* and *hopscotch;* where cows are found moving leisurely through the crowd or sitting in the middle of the road, nosing around for paper and stale, discarded vegetables; where eardrum is about to collapse with the blare of loudspeakers and horns; where beggars are lying on the roadside, naked and emaciated half-humans, some skeletons, some covered with soars; where vendors and hawkers are selling varieties of stuffs and where people especially children are found relishing *jalebies, gol-guppas, tikkees* and other mouth-watering delicacies. Like Rusty in *The Room on the Roof,* Bond too gets bemused by all these miscellaneous facets of Indian bazaars as says Rusty: "The bazaar and India and life itself began with a rush of noise and confusion" (Bond, *Rusty Runs Away* 131). Bond's curiosity brings him to these places and forces him to write about them off and on.

The railway system of India is one of the biggest in the world and is the biggest service sector of India. Indian picture cannot be completed without mentioning it. A realist who is writing about India cannot ignore its effect and importance in Indian setting. The teeming and varied life of Indian trains and platforms and its ambience always fascinated the writers from Jules Verne in the 1870's to Rudyard Kipling, Khushwant Singh, Satyajit Ray and other modern writers in more recent times. Kipling's description of a railway journey in *Kim* is just as relevant today as it was at the beginning of the 20th century. Bond gets fascinated by the very image of trains and platforms and invokes it repeatedly in his fiction. He is drawn by the noise, the cacophony and the unique culture that a railway station seems to spontaneously generate and sustain. Bond writes about its magic spell: "There is nothing like an Indian railway station anywhere else in the world. We are not a melting pot of races and religions; we are a mosaic of all these things. A mosaic that is best observed from the trains that pull the glittering pieces together" (LD 93). It is specially Bond's child characters who get enthralled viewing a train. Ranji in "The Tunnel" came to a jungle to watch a roaring steam-engine coming out of the tunnel. Ranji enjoyed the beauty and power of the train. When Ranji heard the whistle of the engine, he knew the train was coming and moved to see it: "A second or two later, the steam-engine shot out of the tunnel, snorting and puffing like some green, black and gold dragon, some beautiful monster out of Ranji's dreams. Showering sparks right and left; it roared a challenge to the jungle" (CF 310). The train as an innovation captures the imagination of the writers. The sense of discovery and wonder associated with trains is beautifully brought out in the classic poem: "To a Locomotive in Winter" by Walt Whitman, "I Like to See It Lap the Miles" by Emily Dickinson and "The Express" by Stephen Spender. If for Bond's Ranji it is a "beautiful dragon of his dreams" (CF 314), for Whitman it is the "emblem of motion and power—pulse of the continent" and "Fierce-throated beauty," for Dickinson it is an iron horse that neighs like Boanerges and for Spender "The Express" is a queen issuing a "plain manifesto" to her subjects and "like a comet through flame," it "moves entranced wrapt in her music."

Bond has spent a great deal of time travelling by trains, mostly to and from the boarding school. In the "Introduction" of *The Penguin Book of Indian Railway Stories* he unveils his love for railway platforms and the time spent on them when he was a boy. The odd incidents during those period remained tucked in his memory. He recollects them in his stories when he started writing. He paints a realistic picture of whatever he observes. The sights and smells of a typical Indian railway station and the trains have been presented with ardent interest in several of his short stories like: "The Night Train at Deoli," "The Woman on Platform No.8," "The Eyes Have It," "Going Home," "Time Stops at Shamli," "Masterji," "Sita and the River" and "The Tunnel." The distinctive flavour of the Indian life comes alive through his skilful portrayal of the scenes at the station. The description of hawkers, vendors, the nervous ticket collector, passengers moving with bedding rolls, platforms clamoured by the arrival and departure of trains, crowded third-class compartments present a lively description of an Indian railway station. The introductory lines from "Going Home" brilliantly capture the scene in a third-class railway compartment:

> The train came panting through the forest and into the flat brown plain. The engine whistled piercingly, and a few cows moved off the track. In a swaying third-class compartment two men played cards; a woman held a baby to an exposed breast; a Sikh labourer, wearing brief pants, lay asleep on an upper bunk, snoring fitfully; an elderly unshaven man chewed the last of his pan and spat the red juice out of the window. (CF 316)

Bond's description is so real that one is almost transported to a railway station. Vijay and Sita in "Sita and River" were waiting for a train. They found the platform full of bed rolls lying here and there. There were hundred other people waiting for the Shahganj train and were ready to leap onto the train as soon as it arrived and reserved a room for their family. Here, Bond deftly churns out a platform scene and evokes the smells, sounds and odour of a small-town railway station without missing on a single detail. There could not have been a more accurate picture of the din and bustle at an Indian railway station. Bond's eye for little details could be noted here:

> Moving among the piles of bedding and luggage were coolies, vendors of magazines, sweetmeats, tea, and betel-leaf preparation; also stray dogs, stray people and sometimes a stray station-master. The cries of the vendors mingled with the general clamour of the station and the shunting of a steam engine in the yard. 'Tea hot tea! 'Fresh limes!'

> Sweets, papads, hot stuff, cold drinks, mangoes, toothpowder, photos of film stars, bananas, balloons, wooden toys! The platform had become a bazaar. What a blessing for those vendors that trains ran late and that people had to wait, and waiting, drank milky tea, bought toys for children, cracked peanut shells, munched bananas and chose little presents for the friends or relations on whom they were going to descend very shortly. (CF 181)

In Kipling's *Kim* the Lama and Kim travel by train from Lahore to Umbala as the train roars into the railway station, the platform is described, "The sleepers sprang to life, and the station filled with clamour and shouting, cries of water and sweetmeat vendor, shouts of native policeman, and shrill yells of women gathering up their baskets, their families and their husbands" (Kipling, *Kim* 38).

The character is one of the ways open to Bond to grasp at reality. He presents the snapshots of Indian milieu through his art of characterization. His flesh and blood characters are drawn from authentic Indian backdrop which helps him in creating the genuine replica of lower and lower middle class life. His characterization is so effectively done that the characters take on a life of their own. Bond's lifelike characters provide intensity to his portraitures and exemplify his insight into human psyche. Basil Hograth observes, "In whatever category your novel may be placed it will stand or fall by the reality of its characterization" (*Technique* 91).The truthful reproduction of his characters under certain circumstances provides realistic bend to his narration. He has filled his opus with men and women who are as real to us as the people around us. His character gallery abounds with variety of characters: man and woman, young and old, fair and foul, sinner and saint, rich and poor, simple and complex, autobiographical and fictional. They are firmly rooted to the ground and never lose their credibility. They act and behave as their role demands. If his child protagonist throws tantrums, the teens aspire for love and romance.

If the old becomes nostalgic for the bygone days, the youth plans for prospective future.

The complete realization of a character by the novelist requires a harmony between the creator and creation. Bond's literature celebrates this harmony. Bond does not sit on an ivory tower while creating the personae of his stories; rather he puts himself under the skin of his characters and with vibrating strokes colour them. He comes down to their level and equally participates in the ups and downs of their erratic life. His ordinary folks do not make the headlines; nevertheless, they are remarkable for their quiet heroism, their endearing idiosyncrasies and their heart-warming ability to find happiness and contentment in everyday struggle. He is the creator of unsung heroes and heroines mapped out from the neglected strata of life – hawkers, barbers, rickshaw-pullers, truck-drivers, prostitutes, shirking servants, eccentrics, thieves, loafers, retards and crazy aunts and uncles.

The world of Ruskin Bond is inhabited by ordinary folks. Bond excels in transfiguring the 'ordinary life' of 'ordinary people' into profoundly emblematic. His undemanding common characters are faceless who could be lost any time in a vast country of more than one billion people. Bond has often hinted this happening when people get lost: "for in the great human mass that is India, hundreds of people disappear every day and are never heard of again" (CF 73). But they endure and survive in Bond's writings. Bond discovers meaning and pattern in the unassuming life of the humble people who are fascinating despite being commoners. Praising mule drivers, Bond writes that they are simply "handsome men in tattered clothes, sitting on a bench in the shade of the tree, drinking tea from brass tumblers" (RIM 16). In "The Civilized Wilderness," Bond addresses a hill lady as a "handsome woman although her ears, weighed down by heavy silver earrings, have lost their natural shape" (BN 50). Commenting on the humbleness of Bond's ordinary folk, Murari Prasad says, "Bond is not concerned with something kinky, extraordinary or unusual, but with the ordinary life, old values and quiet heroism of people living in villages and small towns straddling mountains and hills" (Singh, *Creative Contours* 118).

Bond's characterization reveals the magnanimity of his soul. It is his love for his *homo fictus* that illumines them. He perceives humanity even in his eccentrics, aggressors and amorous characters. He looks at their flaws and frivolities with amused tolerance and indulgence. His empathetic treatment makes the degenerate and decadent endearing and interesting. Nowhere, he seems to be writing with an idea to rectify the conditions of the world or the mindset of its people. He portrays humanity in its entirety with ungrudging acceptance. Bond celebrates not the rich but the poor and their capacity to fight with their harrowing circumstances. He glorifies the unyielding spirit of the poor. The stoicism and resilience of the poor are noteworthy in the face of death: "Death moves about at random, without discriminating between the innocent and the evil, the poor and the rich. The only difference is that the poor usually handle it better" (TIIL 32). Bond's characters remain happy and hopeful even when surrounded by darkness. S.C. Dwivedi writes: "His noble characters make us both society-oriented and individual oriented. They touch our hearts and awaken out conscience suggesting to break our narrow-minded cocoons of individuality and selfishness" (Singh, *Creative Contours* 160).

For Bond, every man and woman is the image of god. His characters, wicked or bizarre, innocent or crooked, dull or clever are drawn with extraordinary truthfulness and tenderness. They make the earth very colourful place to live. Bond believes that there cannot be watertight demarcation between good and bad, sinful and virtuous, ugly and beautiful and right and wrong. The need is just to penetrate beneath, the ugly will look beautiful and the sinful virtuous. Bond's insight and sympathetic treatment make his crooks, snobs, retards, thieves, drivers and prostitutes endearing and enduring. Bond has successfully created characters who may be best termed as 'pleasing crooks' and 'forgivable knave.' They may forge, murder, misuse a corpse, have extra-marital affairs, feign to be crippled, break the law yet cannot be despised and denounced. They are to be appreciated for their zest for life. It is these characters who with their varied feelings - love, joy, lust, hate, disappointment, bereavement and exhilaration colour the tapestry of Bond's literature. His vignettes of life present a variety of characters like an experienced thief, Deepak in "The Thief," Sudheer, a loafer in *Vagrants in the Valley*, Suresh, a grotesque retard in "Most Beautiful," Thanh, a hypocrite in "Tribute to a Dear Friend," Sunil, an impostor in "Death of a Familiar," Dilawar Singh, an exploiter of a chance corpse in "Dead Man's Gift," Kamla, a friendly and innocent prostitute and Suraj, an epileptic hawker who hopes to pass an examination in *Delhi Is Not Far*, Javed Khan, an aggressive Pathan and passionate lover in *A Flight of Pigeons*. Mr. Khushal, in "Masterji" an ever happy man as his name symbolically suggests, teaches Punjabi in the name of Hindi and issues false certificates for nominal charge to the students who have never got through on their own and failed two or three times. A dumb vagrant, Goonga in *The Vagrants in the* Valley who is pestered by hooligans. But the children in the story befriend him and offer him tea. Bond sees dignity and gentleness even in a killer Uncle Bill who kills by giving mild dosage of arsenic. Uncle Bill in "He Said it with Arsenic" is a born killer who tries to kill the narrator. But the narrator outsmarts him and makes him lie on the bed that Bill has made for him. The narrator asks Uncle Bill a question: "'Why did you drink the stuff? It was meant for me, of course.' He looked down at his shoes, then gave a little shrug and turned away. 'In the circumstances' he said, 'it seemed the only decent thing to do'" (TSS 129). Bond seizes up the character in a clincher "I'll say this for Uncle Bill: he was always the perfect gentleman" (TSS 129).

Bond lays emphasis upon the circumstances of a person for the evil he possesses. His humanism emerges from the thought: "...Man was born "good" or at least ethically neutral until corrupt philosophy and inequitable institutions perverted his will ..." (Philip, *Introduction to Jean* 15-16). He feels that it is not the genes of a person but the process of growing up that has made him what he is today: "We are creature of circumstances. If our genes have shaped our biological make-up, our environment has shaped the development of our nature" (Bond, *When Darkness Falls* vii). It is not punishment but acceptance is ordered in Bond's penal code. Bond's humanism is like that of the Christian Humanists, anthropocentric that means: "Instead of regarding man as a fallen, corrupt and sinful creation their idea of truth and excellence is based on human values and human experience" (Gray, *Dictionary of Literary* 100). His humanism is not political or social like that of Marxists, nor mystical like that of saints; it is completely humane and simple to follow. He puts faith in the creative vision and unconquerable spirit of man. The plot of his fiction emerges from the silent sympathies of human soul.

Behind the irresponsible and casual approach of a man is the over attention and indulgence which he receives from his family. Uncle Ken who appears in many of stories is a product of such indulgence. His eccentricity and stupidity make us laugh. He is one of the most interesting characters among several amusing and humorous characters of Bond. The misadventures of Ken are hilarious and Bond's ability to weave humour into the incidents is marvellous. One laughs at his oddity and sees through his laziness. But the portrait is neither bitter nor satirical rather marked by an underlying sympathy for someone who has not made anything of himself even though he is forty. Ken is a happy-go-lucky man, an overgrown boy though past forty and well spoilt by his doting sisters. Without being troubled for his expenses, Ken can spend the whole year by "zigzagging" through his sisters' homes.

Whenever his sister troubles him by asking to look for a job, he answers bluntly that there is no job in Dehradun. He had been through many jobs as private tutor, salesman, shop assistant, hotel manager (until he brought about the close of the hotel), cricket coach, tourist guide but all the jobs ended in fiasco. Either he himself quits the jobs after getting bored or gets fired for his negligence or silliness. He is a failure in worldly sense. He is not interested in straight walking. He believes the only way to know a place well is to walk in a truly haphazard way. The trouble is that he uses the zigzag method even when he has a train to catch. His love for zigzag walking never makes him reach anywhere on time. He cannot stand small boys and get nervous in their presence and by their never-ending questions; his tuneless and ceaseless whistle exasperates everyone; he always makes mess of the given task. Still everyone hopes that he will improve as he grows up.

The indifferent attitude of Ken often irritates the child narrator. He wishes that Ken should not be his uncle. He does not like the ungratefulness of Ken who flinches from praising the delicacies cooked by granny and complains of her for being repetitive as he says: "Although Uncle Ken has tremendous appetite, and ate just as much as I did, he never praised Granny's dishes. I think this is why I was annoyed with him at times, and why sometime I enjoyed making him feel nervous" (FSP 73). Aunt has prepared a lotion when Ken complains her that he is losing his hair and his bald patch is increasing in size. She soaks some gherkins in brandy for a week. She gives the bottle to Ken with instructions to rub a little into his scalp in the mornings and evenings. The next day, Aunt gets surprised to find only gherkins in the bottle. Ken has drunk all the brandy. One day everyone was surprised to see Ken running. A lazy person like Ken who even does not like to move is running. The smoke of Ken's cigar disturbs the wild bees of the trees beneath which he is smoking. The bees attack him. He runs and jumps into the pond to save him from bees.

Ken gets a job of a guide for showing the sights around Dehradun. Once he has to take a party of six Americans tourists to the hot sulphur springs. He could not remember even the straight route of hardly ten miles and returned home after three days with "dusty and torn clothes, sunken cheeks and burnt forehead." Despite so many shortcomings in his personality and the consequent failures, the fervour of Bond's sympathy for Ken never wavers. Here lies Bond's greatness as a creative artist who makes a good-for-nothing fellow so interesting and gripping. The world of Bond is of sunshine and laughter, a happy warm and compassionate humanity, under whose shade eccentric individuals revel in their absurdities. The frivolities and weaknesses of his characters are never annoying.

Javed Khan, the fiery Rohilla Pathan in *A Flight of Pigeons* is another such mixed bag - apparently a detestable character who wins our heart by the end of the story. Neither Mariam the dynamic lady, nor Ruth the charming heroine, nor Khan Begum the submissive wife of Javed Khan remains in our memory. But it is the aggressive and repulsive Javed Khan who leaves an indelible impression. The charm of Javed lies in the sympathetic approach of his creator. The novella *A Flight of Pigeons* is set in Shahjahanpur during the revolt of 1857. Javed one of the biggest ruffians in the city has a reputation for agreeing to undertake any exploit of a dangerous nature provided the rewards are high. He is involved in setting the bungalow of Anglo-Indians on fire and plundering their property. He has set fire to the Rosa Factory and destroyed 70,000 gallows of rum. He has abducted Anglo-Indian ladies Ruth Labadoor and her mother on the point of his sword and makes them captive.

Ruth Labadoor, the narrator of the story has taken shelter in Lala Ramjimal's house with her family to escape the sad fate of his father and other members of her community who were plundered and killed by the sepoys. From here the family hopes to escape to their relatives in Bareilly. But their plans go awry when Javed Khan seizes them and brings them to his house. Arrogantly he asks his wife Khan-Begum her views about his hostages Ruth Labadoor and her mother: "What do you think of my *Firangans*? Didn't I say I would not rest until I found them? A lesser man would have given up the search long ago!" (AFP 43) He shocks everyone when he blatantly expresses his love and passion for Ruth. Long before the revolt, he was captivated by the mesmerizing beauty of Ruth. Since the day he saw her, he wanted to posses her. He says to Kothiwali:

> 'How can I make you understand the fascination this girl exerted over me when she was in her father's house! The very first time I saw her, I was struck by her beauty. She shone like Zohra, the morning star. Looking at her now I realize the truth of the saying that a flower never looks so beautiful as when it is on its parent stem. Break it, and it withers in the hand. (AFP 45-46)

Javed's desire to marry Ruth upsets everyone but none can dare to oppose him. The demon of anger always slumbers in his heart and it takes little to rouse it. He is driven into frenzy whenever Ruth's mother Mariam defers the matter of Javed and Ruth's marriage. He loses control and vents his rage and frustration to anyone who falls on his way by misfortune. Everyone in the house was apprehensive wondering what would happen next. He severely lashes with his horse whip Saifulla, his half-brother, Rupia the very old servant woman and the boy who dares to play flute in the Pathan settlement. Saifulla and Rupia are badly beaten and wounded. Even Khan-begum was not spare from his rage: "She knew he was in a bad temper and had no wish to feel his whip again; so she did what he told her ..." (AFP 113).

The readers sympathise with the fiery Javed Khan despite his outrageous behaviour. He brings Ruth and Mariam with good intention to his house. He comes to know that a ruffian has intended to carry Ruth off with bad intentions and would have done so, had he not brought her to his house. He protected Ruth and her family from being murdered. As a gentleman, he waits for the consent of Ruth's mother for marrying her. It is due to Javed, Mariam could protect her family against any possible disgrace. He keeps his word and never tries to exploit the plight of the helpless creatures. He helps them to reach the British camp when Shahjahanpur was attacked by the British army. Behind the veil of fiery temperament is hidden the noble heart of Javed that makes him a hero in the eyes of Ruth: "He was very wild and muddle-headed, and often cruel, but he was also very handsome and gallant, and there was in him a streak of nobility which he did his best to conceal" (AFP 133).

In "Vagrants in the Valley" Bond introduces a mean fellow Sudheer known as "Lufunga" (CF 710) that means a loafer. He is a "420" (CF 711), a criminal who practises crime as a fine art. He is a connoisseur of women. He gambles, tells lies, befools other by his glib tongue, steals money of a Seth for whom he works, strolls leisurely down the bazaar road and never fails to play pranks on others. He disguises himself as a Sadhu to escape the police. He even flatters dancing girls Mrinalini and Hastini and extracts money from them by making them rivals for his love. He himself is aware of the fact that his looks give people the impression of his crookedness. He says to Rusty that the people "take only one look at me and then feel their pockets to see if anything is missing!" (CF 710-11) He manages to gain the confidence of some well-to-do people and acts on their behalf in matters that are not always respectable. He has neither morals nor scruples. Devinder bewares Rusty of Sudheer saying: "He is the most charming and the most dangerous person in town" (CF 710).

Ram Singh, a villager becomes the victim of his lies and pranks. Ram Singh denies opening the door of his hut and taking Rusty and Sudheer inside at night. Sudheer tries to befool him: "We are road inspectors, servants of the government—so open up, my friend" (CF 725). Ram Singh questions, "How do I know you are not thieves?" (CF 726) but subsides hearing the blunt reply: "If we were thieves ... we would not stand here talking to you. We would have cut your throat and thrown you to the vultures, and carried off your beautiful daughter....My friend I will sleep in your house tonight. We are not going to sleep in the forest" (CF 726). Poor Ram Singh let the intruder in. Using his wit, Sudheer gets Ram Singh cook pumpkin and potato curry for them. Ram Singh was left alone after the death of his three wives and the moving away of his children to city. He requests Sudheer to look for him a suitable bride. Sudheer asks mockingly the shape of the nose, size of the head, colour of the skin of his would-be wife. Ram Singh gets impressed by Sudheer's ideas and suggestions but the readers are well aware of Sudheer's pranks behind his deceptively simple comments.

Despite being vile, a bluff and morally a loose character, Sudheer charms his friends and the readers. Bond believes that once the vice is dispelled the inherent goodness gets revealed. Such is the case of Sudheer. Bond's portrayal of crooks like Sudheer seems to coincide with the views of E.M. Foster. According to Foster, a character in a book seems real and acceptable because the novelist who is the creator as well as the narrator knows everything and can share the details with his readers:

> They [characters] are people whose secret lives are visible or might be visible; we are people whose secret lives are invisible. And that is why novels, even when they are about wicked people, can solace us: they suggest a more comprehensible and thus a more manageable human race, they give us the illusion of perspicacity and of power."(43)

Like Tom in Henry Fielding's *Tom Jones, a Foundling*, Sudheer too wins our love regardless of his pranks, mischief and wickedness. Bond like Fielding is largely interested in human behaviour and motives. He is not concerned much with their psychology. So he tends to be explanatory rather than exploratory. Our sympathy for Sudheer grows stronger as the story progresses. The reader feels sorry knowing his troubled childhood. He came originally from the Frontier: "where little value was placed on human life; and while still a boy, he had wandered, a homeless refugee, over the border into India. A smuggler adopted him, taught him something of trade, and introduced him to some of the best hands in the profession" (CF 715). Devinder has also full sympathy for Sudheer. He knows Sudheer robs only them "who could afford to be robbed" (CF 715) and the greedy "who deserved to be robbed" (CF 715). Devinder and Rusty the poor and credulous fellows are never duped by him. He is good to them.

Sudheer's earnest request to Rusty to become his friend moves the reader: "Come on. Be with me. The day I met you, I wanted you to be with me. I'm a crook, and don't have any real friends. I don't ask you to be a crook. I ask you to be my friend" (CF 722). He becomes the true friend of Rusty. He collects information about the whereabouts of Rusty's aunt and accompanies him on his visit to her. When Rusty becomes sad contemplating the prospect of his future, he consoles him. He urges him to forget the dead and forget the past. He requests him not to trouble his heart any longer: "I have enough for both of us, so let us live on it till it is finished, and let us be happy, Rusty, my friend, let us be happy'....'This is only the beginning'....The world is waiting for us" (CF 730). The lonely and orphaned Rusty feels relaxed in the invigorating and friendly company of Sudheer. He is ready to face almost anything with Sudheer by his side.

There is honesty in Sudheer's love for both Mrinalini and Hastini. He loves both of them and he cannot help it out. He frankly confesses his love for Hastini before Mrinalini: "I love her because she is so comfortable. I love you because you are so sweet. Can I help it if I love you both?" (CF 747) He even advises Mrinalini to be with

Hastini to overcome loneliness. Once Mrinalini rises above her false ego, she would understand Hastini better: "You do not know her yet. When you know her, you will love her!"(CF 747) The liveliness of Sudheer makes others to follow his example. Being intoxicated by the beauty of the full moon and a bottle of country made liquor, Sudheer starts dancing and hopping in the middle of the street. He defends his crazy behaviour saying it is an outlet of his happiness. This makes Ganpat follow him: "And he too began hopping about on the road, slapping himself on the buttocks" (CF 744).

More than liveliness the readers enjoy Sudheer's pranks. He asks Mrinalini if she permits him, he would kill her fussy mother without being violent, simply by frightening her to death or by pouncing on her from a dark alley, or letting off a fire cracker. He pacifies Mrinalini when she gets angry by his cruel ideas, saying his killing will be an act of kindness because her mother is trying her best to outlive all of them. Thus the multi facet personality of Sudheer makes him an 'endearing crook.' Like Rusty we can only love him but cannot understand him. Joseph Conrad has once said: "In truth every novelist must begin by creating for himself a world, great or little in which he can honestly believe" (Conrad, *Notes on Life* 6). Bond believes more in honesty of soul than deed. That is why even a reprobate like Sudheer makes an impact on us.

In "The Amorous Servant," Bond introduces an amorous servant Kundan Singh who makes the writer envious by his adventurous life and heroic death. An idler and freeloader, Kundan ate more than most people, borrowed money, gambled in the bazaars, drank raw country liquor and usually overslept in the morning. He had a dull and expressionless face, which confirmed his wickedness. He was a connoisseur of women and had illicit relationship with many, mostly the married ones. Once he was caught red-handed by the cuckold husband and settled the matter for a few rupees that too borrowed from his master. Then he fell for the butcher's daughter but when threatened with castration, he escaped. Later he worked for the owner of a small restaurant who had a young wife. The narrator visited the last place of Kundan's work. He found that the restaurant owner's child had a striking resemblance to Kundan. Before he could become feeble, shabby and insignificant, Kundan joined the army. He died in a heroic action on India's northern border. The heroic end of Kundan made the writer feel proud of him because it is something that a few are able to attain: "I could not help feeling rather proud of Kundan Singh. And a little envious. His youth had been free and easy, he had sown his wild oats and before he could become old and decrepit and useless, he had died a hero. That is something very few of us are able to achieve" (Bond, *When Darkness Falls* 69).

The good sense of Bond and his belief in humanity helps him to accept the course of life without grudges. Bond is aware of the fact that evil exists along with good. He thinks it is foolish to worry about evils one cannot prevent. Life is an imperfect affair at the best but it has to be lived. He is also aware that there are no exclusive categories of man. A mind cannot be honestly painted with one colour white or black. He is an apparent idealist who tries to see the best in everything and everyone. He perspicaciously analyses the psyche and soul of his negative 'homo fictus' and makes them more subtle than 'homo sapiens.' His acceptance of evil along with good makes his murderer, fraud, hoaxer, loafer, miscreant, connoisseur of women and wrongdoer tolerable and convincing. There is no hatred for Bond's negative characters who very often cross the code of conduct and norms of society. Bond accepts them with their frailties because he knows that human nature is not perfect. Bond's philosophy of "the acceptance of evil" coincides with the thoughts of the *Gita*. In chapter ten "Vibhuti-Yoga" telling about his divine exposition, Lord Krishna says that everything emanates from him and he is the primeval origin of all things. There is nothing in the world in the heart of which divine spark is not there. "And whatever is the seed of all beings, that also am I, O Arjuna. There is no being, whether moving or unmoving that can exist without me" (10/39), (Ranganathananda, *Universal Message*).

It is the beauty of fiction writing that the characters take the shape and life as the author wants and experiences. A painting has the sketch and colour of the painter, fiction has the characters and the theme of the author. Bond gives shape to his feelings in his writings. He absorbs and interacts with the life around and writes about social situations and events. His stories are populated from the daily life around us. "In daily life we do never understand each other; neither complete clairvoyance nor complete confessional exists" (Foster, *Aspects* 44). But when the reader comes across Bond's characters, he understands them and can feel their presence. Bond with careful details and vitality exposes the inner and outer life of his so called 'negative characters.' E.M. Foster writes:

> ... people in a novel can be understood completely by the reader, if the novelist wishes; their inner as well as their outer life can be exposed. And this is why they often seem more definite than characters in history or even our own friends; we have been told all about them that can be told; even if they are imperfect or unreal they do not contain any secrets, whereas our friends do and must, mutual secrecy being one of the conditions of life upon this globe. (44)

Bond believes neither in Shiva, nor in Buddha, nor in Jesus Christ, but in an ordinary man. His attempt in moving away from the world of evil in search of goodness, presents him before us like an ascetic who shakes off the pleasures of the world in search of peace. Bond in an interview expresses his approach to life and writing: "I know that there is evil in the world....but I've never known anyone completely evil and I've always found the better qualities of goodness and truth dominating. I do try to bring out the best in people, in human beings because it is there in almost each one of us" (Singh, *Creative Contours* 146).

It is precisely a simple toiler whom Bond praises in his work. His well-disposed treatment of his characters: a truck driver, an innocent villager, an old vendor, an insane or even a prostitute promotes a positive view for them. It is Bond's compassionate outlook that provides the real alchemy. In "The Last Truck Driver," he presents the simple, unsophisticated but hard life of a truck driver who is often accused for being rough and stubborn fellow and a rash driver. In *Landour Days*, he pays a tribute to the ubiquitous highway truck driver whose strenuous life is looked down upon. He describes him as the "knight errant or rather errant knight, of India's Via Apia" (LD 104). He drives all day and sometimes all night carrying the goods and produces for hundreds of miles, across state borders, through lawless tracts, at all seasons and in all weathers. But still he is underpaid, undervalued and often disparaged. Bond defends his hogging the middle of the road for which he is often blamed: "he is usually overloaded and if he veers too much to the left or right he is quite likely to topple over, burying himself and crew under bricks or gas cylinders or TV sets" (105). Bond pities for holding his life cheap that is modern India's lifeline: "He drinks, he swears, occasionally he picks up HIV, and frequently he is killed or badly injured. And we hate him for hogging the road. But we cannot do without him" (105).

Bond has contributed powerfully to the 'marginality discourse' even before the post-modernist trend of focusing on the issues of marginality has become a popular literary theme. Marginalization is a process by which a group or individual is denied access to important positions and symbols of economic, religious or political power within any society. "The marginalised encompasses the economic, social and political dimensions of poverty and exclusion" (*Short Oxford English* 1700). Bond felt deeply for the marginalised and downtrodden. He is forcibly articulating in favour of marginalized and endeavours to bring them from margin to the centre. Under his 'Midas touch' the commoner, the subjugated and those that look so drab become alive. His marginalised characters especially the old, poor and weak do not oppose the society but succumb to the occurrence of the events as it comes to them. The heroes of Mulk Raj Anand, Munoo the coolie, Bakha the untouchable, Bikhu the chamar, Lal Singh of 'The Trilogy' suffer because they refuse to conform. But Bond's characters are complacent. They take the course of life as it befalls them. He writes about their simple joys of losing, finding and again losing but still being content. The complacency with life and its struggle is a characteristic trait of Bond's characters.

A poor fellow, Daya Ram in "Going Home" jingles his money to cheer a child in sulky mood while travelling by train but the mischievous kid threw his money bag out of the window. Somehow Daya Ram managed to pull the train. He got his money back after great toil. The people on the way had duped him and deprived him of his hard earned and saved money. Daya Ram was very much puzzled by the course of events befallen him: "He was not angry or resentful, but he was a little hurt. He knew he had been tricked, but he couldn't understand why" (CF 321). The uneasiness of his mind and day's misfortune was overcome by chatting with a fellow passenger: "Daya Ram had a bidi. He gave it to the other man and lit it for him. Soon they were talking about crops and rainfall and their respective families, and although a faint uneasiness still hovered at the back of his mind, Daya Ram had almost forgotten the day's misfortunes" (CF 321). There is heroism in Daya's conformity with his situation.

The conflict between tradition and modernity, rural and urban life, old and young are common phenomena in Indian society. Bond too in his fiction explores this aspect of Indian life. He finds the children and the old often become the victims of these clashes. He portrays the utter alienation and negligence experienced by the old. They are caught in the whirlpool of changing time. They are like peels thrown to rust in today's competitive and fast-paced society which has no time, or feeling to brood over the things and people of bygone days. The old who are moving slowly through the autumn of their lives find themselves caught in the vortex of changing time. Mehmood a skilful kite-maker in "The Kite Maker," Hassan a champion wrestler in "The Garland on his Brow," an old lonely lady Miss Mackenizie a ravishing beauty in her youth in "Prospect of Flowers," old vendor in "The Box Man," Mr. Pettigrew an old withering man who with a bottle of whisky sustains his still, lonely evenings in "Vagrants in the Valley" are some old characters who have made a mark in their young age. Today they desperately miss their prime. Through the portrayal of these old characters, Bond evokes the theme of passing time, their yearning for the irrecoverable and the inexorable past and their craving for company. The trauma of existence gets revealed through Pettigrew. He says to Rusty: "Full sixty hot summers have besieged my brow. I'm growing old so slowly. I wish there could be some action to make the process more interesting. Not that I feel very active, but I'd like to have something happening around me" (CF 754).

The lyrical sketch of a kitemaker in the story "The Kitemaker" sensitively register the gradual erosion of old crafts, changing face of the city life and the sense of vacancy that envelops an old dying kitemaker. The fast-paced society has no time to share the memories of the old. The old Mehmood's deftness in kite making at his prime won for him respect and glory. Mehmood becomes nostalgic remembering those bygone happy days, when he was well-known throughout the city and his neighbours cared for him. Once he had fallen sick everyone in the locality came to enquire about his health. But today nobody cares for him. His art, like him, gets lost in the rapidly changing world which has engulfed both the leisurely hours and open spaces. The city once a lively place with kite flying at its height is now a congested city. Its rapidly expanding size has swallowed up the open grasslands. People do not want to buy his kites, adults disdain them and children prefer to spend their money on movie. The old man remembered the days when: "There was time, then, to spend an idle hour with a gay, dancing strip of paper. Now everyone hurried, hurried in a heat of hope, and delicate things like kites and daydreams, were trampled underfoot" (NTD 102).

The children brought up in a swiftly changing and competitive world hardly have any time to hear the memories of the old. Mehmood feels himself ignored and isolated like the banyan tree: "Both were taken for granted--permanent fixtures that were of no concern to the raucous, sweating mass of humanity that surrounded them. No longer did people gather under the banyan tree to discuss their problems and their plans: only in the summer months did a few seek shelter from the fierce sun" (NTD 103). His grandson Ali is a ray of hope and regeneration amidst the darkness of alienation and gloominess. Mehmood gladdens watching the small boy at play in the winter sunshine and growing under his eyes. He makes kites for him and encourages him to learn how to fly it.

Bond's sympathetic delineation of those who are now in their autumn and waiting for their fall gives a rare warmth and authenticity to his writings. In this thematic preoccupation appears the old man and woman of Anglo-Indian community as well who were left alone in India after independence. The complex nature of their relationship to India and their utter isolation is projected with rare understanding. It was easier for young and middle-aged to leave India and move to England for better prospects. But for these old people, it was not easy to cut the roots from the land of their birth. A sixty-year-old granny says to her grandson when he asks her if she would not go to England when other uncles and aunts are leaving India: "No, I've grown here. I'm like the trees.

I've taken root; I won't be going away--not until, like an old tree, I'm without any more leaves" (RBH 152). Bond with great understanding comprehends and portrays their loneliness and complex nature of their relationship with India and its landscape, through Miss Mackenzie, Mr. Pettigrew, Miss Kellener, Miss Deeds and Miss Rippley Bean. About them Bond writes, "They were the flotsam of the Empire, jettisoned by the very people who brought them into existence" (SWL 47).

Miss Mackenzie, an elderly spinster over eighty in "The Prospect of Flowers" lives alone in her cottage. A ravishing beauty in her twenties, Miss Mackenzie now shares her loneliness with her pet, a large black cat. She remembers with nostalgia the days when eggs were six *annas* a dozen and gin only two rupees a bottle. Sometimes a young boy visits her and she eagerly awaits him. She feels disappointed and lonely and grumbles at her poor black cat when the boy fails to turn up. One day, the child comes to say goodbye to her as he is leaving for home for the holidays. Harsh winter and her loneliness make Miss Mackenizie's life difficult. She passed away from the world unnoticed. In the *Room on the Roof* Mr. Pettigrew is like many other older Anglo-Indians staying on after independence because he loved India and because he could not start life anew in England.

Bond has immense sympathy and understanding for those who are neglected in society. He often questions the apathetic approach of today's commercialised world towards the suffering masses. The callous attitude is revealed through the short memory of people who quickly forget the achievements of a hero like Hassan who is reduced to a beggar. The opening epitaph of the story, "The Garland on his Brow" noticeably encapsulates the hero's plight:

> Fame has but a fleeting hold
> on the reins in our fast-paced society;
> so many of yesterday's
> heroes crumble. (Bond, RGL 79)

The magnificent champion wrestler of Dehradun, Hassan was the most impressive and engaging young man in his youth. He was an ideal for the narrator with his "rippling muscles, magnificent build, great wide shoulders and powerful legs." The Rani of Raunkpur was so impressed by his magnificently built strong body that she made him her personal bodyguard. Under Rani's tutelage, the simple Hassan felt secure and spent a comfortable life. But all luxury and security were snatched away from him when the Rani like any other mortal succumbed to death. Hassan with no other alternative ventured again in wrestling arena to face nothing but a humiliating defeat.

After four years, the narrator visited the place of his childhood days. He came across a beggar who had a straggling beard, a hunch, a cavernous chest and unsteady legs on which a number of purple sores were festering. It took time for the narrator to recognize the hero of his adolescent days, Hassan, the most magnificent wrestler in the entire district reduced to a pitiable beggar. For him it is a sad reflection of the passing of time:

> Fifty years ago a popular local wrestler would never have been allowed to fall into a state of poverty and neglect. He would have been fed by his old friends and stories would have been told of his legendary prowess. He would not have been forgotten. But those were more leisurely times, when the individual had his place in society, when a man was praised for his past achievement and his failures were tolerated and forgiven. But life had since become fast and cruel and unreflective, and people were too busy counting their gains to bother about the idols of their youth. (RGL 85-86)

Hassan's wretchedness and the terrible way of his committing suicide to hide his identity shock the reader. To save himself from the humiliation of recognition and living in this apathetic world, Hassan "crawled into the drain to die and had done so with his head in the culvert so the world would not witness his last unavailing struggle" (RGL 86). Even the narrator did not come forward to identify the body and thus saved dead Hassan from the final disgrace. Bond has no anxiety to be tugging at our sleeve or to be giving us a knowing look. He does not use his writing as a platform to preach. But his profound philosophy gushes forth spontaneously as in the case of Hassan. The tragedy of Hassan makes us realise the futility of man's fame and false ego for it. The following lines outstandingly convey the message: "The garlands wither on your brow; / Then boast no more your mighty deeds ..." (RGL 85).

Bond has created a rich gallery of unforgettable female characters. The woman's world comes alive with his perceptiveness and understanding. The woman appears in her varied moods, facets, shades and hues - from a girl child to an old crippled woman, from a modest lady to a vivacious mistress, from a devoted wife to a liberated woman. In whatever role she is, she has a persona in which there is new unitary out-look resulting from the fusion of the attitudes of the East and West. However, the credibility of the characters never loses. In each female character the innate womanliness emerges as a distinctive quality. They are not portrayed as glittering heroines. Their role is not to glorify the virtues of great Indian women as the Indian fictionists like Bhabani Bhattacharya and Kamala Markandaya often do. They are also not shown struggling in the family matrix or dangling between the role of a wife and a professional as one witnesses in Anita Desai and Shashi Deshpande. Bond's female characters strike us by their individuality. They are not shown as a victim of male predominance or domestic drudgery; at the same time they are happy to confine themselves to domestic chores. They break the shackles only up to that extent which do not disturb their power and security. They love to look after home and family. They are gifted with amazing common sense and power of observation. They appear in diverse roles: of a mother, a wife, a sweetheart or a tender girl. If she is a caring mother of a retard in the "Most Beautiful," she is an amorous mother of a beautiful princess who seduces the lover of her daughter in "A Handful of Nuts." If she is a devoted wife in "The Most Potent Medicine of All" who cut one of her breasts to make medicine to cure her husband's ailment, she is a wife in *Time Stops at Shamli* who does not flinch from having extramarital relationship or a merry widow in "Susanna's Seven Husbands" who kills her husbands whenever she gets tired of them. She is a traditional mother-in-law who feels jealous when the son takes the side of his wife in "Bhabiji's House;" she is a tigress mother in *A Flight of Pigeons* who saves her daughter from the amorous design of her captor; she is a liberated woman in "The Girl from Copenhagen" who without hesitation shares the same bed with a stranger boy and bids him good-bye without making any commitment to meet again. To classify all Bond's women characters into any number of water-tight compartments will be unjustifiable. Every woman possesses an individuality of her own albeit share amongst themselves certain common traits. No two of them are absolutely identical with each other in all respects. That is why they are true-to-life as no two individuals are thoroughly similar in real life.

The humanistic bend always glance through Bond's woman rendering. His altruism gets reflected in exposé of degraded and liaison woman. Even the prostitutes who as a norm are considered a blot on the society and looked down upon for their profession are described with love and concern. He finds in them child-like innocence. He says "Prostitution is degrading, but a prostitute can still keep her dignity" (DNF 404). In *Delhi Is not Far* he introduces a prostitute Kamla whose husband has given her father five acres of land for the favour of having a wife half of his age. She appeases men and extracts money from them. She makes herself attractive to others to please her husband. She is more skilled in love-making than any of her colleagues. Despite meeting so many men, she feels utter loneliness and craves for the company of genuine friends. She adopts two lonely underprivileged - the narrator and his epileptic friend Suraj as her brothers, during the festival of *Raksha Bandhan*. She tells them, "I want your protection, not your money ... I want to feel that I am not alone in the world" (DIF 376). The loneliness and rejection from the so called honoured society brought three of them closer. She visits them in the morning whenever she finds time to spare from her profession. She has sensed death in Suraj's eyes so she gives as much of herself as she can in so short time. Out of compassion she fulfils his desire to possess a woman. Shankhini is another such character from the *Strangers in the Night: Two Novellas*. The sensualist in the story found her smile passionate and childlike. Shankhini has been trained in the art of making love yet the sensualist finds an undercurrent of innocence beneath her false love-making process: "I think this was because she suffered from no feelings of guilt. She had been brought up to please men as though this was her sole duty in life. She had not known and did not seek any other kind of existence" (Bond, SN 104).

Women in Indian writing in English in general are either presented as a sex object or a pitiable creature tortured at every step in the patriarchal society. But Bond's presentation of women is not eclipsed by such presentation. His modest heart and compassionate soul of a child dominates over his male ego. Bond celebrates woman's capability and completeness. He finds her stronger than man. Motherhood gives women a sense of totality: "A woman may often have the comfort of a child feeding at her breast; men grow up insecure" (LIL xiii). Whenever Bond gets a chance he speaks in favour of woman:

> As with most insect musicians, the males do the performing, the females remain silent. This moved one chauvinistic Greek poet to exclaim: 'Happy the cicadas for they have voiceless wives!' To which

> I would respond by saying, 'Pity the female cicadas, for they have singing husbands!' (LD 53)

The widow in "The Night of Millennium" is a poor and discarded woman who lives in a cemetery with her brood of children. She does not resist proud Pasand's entry into her 'boudoir.' The poverty-stricken widow is in need of money for herself and for her children. So she let Pasand a rich, egoistical fellow to have his way on her. Pasand has no time for tender love play. He clumsily claws at her breasts. He tears at her already tattered clothes, pressed his mouth hungrily to her dry lips. The widow made no attempt to defy. She coolly surrenders. After having his way on the widow, he lays supine across the cold damp slab of a grave. His chauvinism was now satisfied. The widow leans over him and bit him on the cheek and neck: "He cried out in pain and astonishment, and tried to sit up. But a number of hands, small but strong, thrust him back against the tombstone. Small mouths, sharp teeth, pressed against his flesh. Muddy fingers tore at his clothes. Those young teeth bit—and bit again. His screams mingled with the cries of the jackals" (Bond, AFD 197). The widow with her brood of children feasted on the flesh of Pasand. Thus we witness the male power exhausted and doomed by an impoverished widow who lives in an abandon cemetery with her children.

Bond's women are more powerful than men in the game of seduction. They are shown crushing the false ego of men about their manhood. His depiction seems to differ from the traditional Indian norms. Free reciprocation of love can rarely be seen in the Indian text or society during the period Bond was weaving his stories. The case of seduction is also reverse in Bond's literature. It is not Bond's women who are found running from the evil eyes or clutches of man but it is man who got trapped in the amorous design of women. Women like the Rani of Magador in "A Handful of Nuts," the Rani in "The Garland on His Brow," Mullia and hill woman in *Strangers in the Night: Two Novellas* seduce and crush the virility of strong and young man. Meena Kapoor of *The Room on the Roof* and Sushila of "Time Stops at Shamli" despite being married readily reciprocate the advance of their lovers. Leela in the story "His Neighbour's Wife," alters her love swiftly from her husband to her bachelor friend.

The sensualist in *Strangers in the Night: Two Novellas* was used to be a ravisher. He is made to muse that women are meant for pleasure and men to seek it. His hunt for pleasure dramatically is ravished by an overpowering unlettered hill woman and his entire false ego melted. He denounces the world, takes shelter in a cave and becomes a recluse. The subtitle of novella "A Cautionary Tale" refers to the theme: the danger of playing with the sentiments of women. The sensualist had an insatiable appetite for sexual pleasure. He was expert in seducing women, extracting from a woman all that she had: "exhausting her, drawing on her hidden resources, feeding on her like a vampire, until she had nothing to give and was completely destroyed" (SN 91). After mastering the power of concentration, he used it to channelize his thoughts in such a way that he could gain a measure of mastery over the minds of others. He used his power to seduce his cousin Samyukta and crushed her innocent pride.

The mind of the sensualist was never on rest. He met a hill boy, Roop and for a change went with him to his village in the hills, thirty miles walking distance from the road. Roop's mother was a strong widow of thirty-five. Her voice was deep and resonant. She had strong hands and large heavy feet. The sensualist felt that she was far stronger than he, both mentally and physically. This single-minded woman had stripped him of his manhood and pretension. With an opportunity, she trounced him and like a vampire sucked his blood. He realised that he who had always imposed his will on others, now found himself squirming under the will of others:

> Always proud of my virility, I now felt as though I would be inadequate for this woman who did

> not flinch, but who took me in her powerful arms and pressed upon me until I gasped for breath and wanted to cry for help. She did not give me any rest. She worked on me with her hands until I was roused again, and then she mastered me with complacent efficiency. Nothing seemed to happen to her. She could not be satisfied. She was some kind of vampire, a succubus—I swear to it—and she was determined to drain me of my last ounce of manhood. (SN 132)

The sensualist realised the power of a hill woman. He felt helpless before the overpowering innocence of the mountain. She was not a scheming woman. She sought to appease a basic hunger and she did so without a civilised veneer, without the cover of sophisticated talk. This primitive woman crushed his entire false ego: "Had another man violated me, I would not have found it as humiliating as the experience of being violated by this unlettered woman with the heavy feet and long twisted ears. It was not only my manhood that she has stripped; it was my beloved ego" (SN 134).

Bond's women are derived from Indian setting yet in their temperament and in their liberated attitude they give away the fact that they are English. They are dynamic and at times are delineated more remarkably than their male counterparts. The western theory is more visible when he writes about the beloved who frankly responds the advance of her lover. Bond with masterly strokes brings about man-woman relationship with all its physicality. The love scenes flow naturally, nowhere it seems to be imposed for cheap popularity. Bond's pragmatic woman beautifully manages her relationship with her husband and with her lover. Sushila in "Time Stops at Shamli" is an unceasing friend of both - her husband and her lover. There is on rush of passion in Sushila and her lover but she holds back the run away frenzy. She appears to be calm, level-headed and perfectly down to earth. When her lover asks her if her marriage is a success, she replies: "Of course it is, as a marriage. I am not happy and I do not love him, but neither am I am so unhappy that I should hate him. Sometimes for our own sakes, we have to think of the happiness of others (CF 271). But still it is Indianness which dominates Bond's women. They may fall in love with someone but marries only the person of their parent's choice. They may get involved in extra marital relationship but do not ignore either duty towards husband or family. In "Love is a Sad Song," sixteen-year-old Sushila enjoys the physical proximity and company of her lover but she rejects his proposal of marriage. She accepts the man her family has chosen for her as husband and is perfectly resigned to her fate. The narrator meets her accidentally after few years. She is now married but childless. Her drunkard and rude husband has made her life lonely and insecure. She is extremely practical and mentally reconciled to the compromise that is her marriage. The author praises her practical approach saying: "You are too practical" (CF 271). She responds "If women were not practical, most marriages would be failures" (CF 271).

Bond's little girl heroines Sita, Binya, Puja, Kiran, Koki, Madhu are portrayed with liveliness and zest for life. They fill the atmosphere with their charm. They are explicit mélange of passion of adult heroine and child yearning. Binya of "Blue Umbrella" is passionate for her umbrella and never separates it from her. To recover it from a thief Rajaram, she puts her life in danger. But this little heroine willingly donates it to Ram Bharosa because she feels herself responsible for his ruinous condition. Kiran, hardly ten-year-old, in "Time Stops at Shamli" gets ready to make the narrator her second best friend when he moves the swing and plucks flowers for her. Her ruthless comment about the guests of the hotel amusingly shocks the narrator. He is scared imaging how she is going to summarize him. She dreams to visit the world and promises the narrator to meet him anywhere in the world. The volatile high spirit of Kiran takes the young narrator into his childhood days. Koki, portrayed in many stories is energetic and vivacious like boys. She helps Ranji in his practice of playing cricket. It was her stunning catch which made Ranji's team victorious. She roams alone in the dale without being scared of anything. The girl characters of Bond are more boyish in nature and free from stereotype portrayal.

Bond has spent major part of his life in Mussoorie, Dehradundun, Shimla and Delhi. He recreates ambience of these places in several of his stories "Coming Home to Dehra," "My Father's Trees in Dehra," "A Guardian Angel," *The Night Train at Deoli and Other Stories*. His convincing description of the Dilaram Bazaar, Allahabad Bank, Clock Tower of Dehradun, and Picture Palace, Kempte and Landour Bazaar of Mussoori make the two cities come alive. The setting of Bond's stories revolves around Musssoorie and Dehradun. His inadequate knowledge of rural or urban life on the plains may be the cause of this limited range. But perhaps there is a deeper cause for this partiality. One notes an apparent distrust of urban life. The association with Delhi and Haridwar that figure in *The Room on the Roof* are unfavourable. Meena Kapoor Rusty's beloved dies in a car accident which took place while travelling from Dehradun to Delhi. Even Haridwar forebodes no good. This is where an innocent boy like Kishen becomes a notorious thief. The touch of urban values, it implies, corrupts the normal simplicity of human beings.

India is a wonderful country with a civilization stretching across several millennia. The joint family has survived for centuries and at its best, much can be said about it. It has always provided rich fictional material because of the variety and complexity of human relationship that it offers. The joint family system is the oldest system of Indian society, though with various migrations rarely can be seen in the cities today. The setting and the theme of Bond's fiction is Indian and taken from the real life. In "Bhabiji's House" and "Chachi's Funeral" Bond has minutely observed the tensions in an Indian joint family, the shifting of emotions from hate to love, misunderstanding to understanding and in spite of vicissitudes, people's clinging together. Bond records in "Bhabiji's House" the amusing and vexing experience while staying with the joint family of his Punjabi friend Kamal. The head of this lively family is middle class Punjabi lady Bhabiji, a bossy matriarch. She is a practical lady who with tremendous confidence and enthusiasm presides over the lives of her three sons, a daughter, two daughters-in-law and fourteen grand children. It is her benevolent and sometimes malevolent autocracy under which her sons and their families live together as one unit. Bond gives interesting records of hubbub and hullabaloo of the family. The bickering, scolding and preaching form the external veneer of the household but the deep undercurrent of familial warmth goes at heart: their petty squabbles ending as quickly as being aroused. Bhabiji's taunts her daughters-in-law for not getting up early, for not bringing enough dowry and for complaining of headache whenever there is work. The participation of everyone equally in any celebration or quarrels and involvement of everyone in completing house chores happily or grudgingly are important features of this family. The description of a morning goes like this:

> By nine o'clock everyone who is still in the house is busy doing something. Shobha is washing clothes. Bhabiji has settled down on a cot with a huge pile of spinach, which she methodically cleans and chops up. Madhu ... is washing down the sitting room floor. Manju ... is engaged in the unwelcome chore of sweeping the front yard. She does this with a sulky look....She creates a drifting cloud of dust, and seems satisfied only when the dust settles on the clothes that have just been hung up to dry. She does not like sweeping because the boy next door can see her at it, and she wants to appear before him in a more glamorous light. (Bond, *Rusty Comes Home* 19-21)

Bond here hilariously points out the predicament of the Indian male who has to do a tough job of handling wife and mother who always pull him to their side. His endeavours to appease both the mother and the wife at a one go drastically fails. His dilemma is even greater than that of Shakespeare's Hamlet. He is unable to decide whom to please first the mother or the wife. Bhabiji's son Shiv is proud of his wife's militancy when it comes to taking on neighbours. Once she vanquished the woman next door after a verbal battle that lasted three hours. But in arguments or quarrels with Bhabiji, Shiv's wife always loses because Shiv favours his mother. Arun, the second son of Bhabiji is afraid of both his wife and his mother and simply makes him scarce when a quarrel develops. He tells his mother she is right and then to placate his wife Shobha he takes her to the movie. Shobha once gets upset by the taunts of Bhabiji. It is Arun who has to bear the burnt of his wife's outraged feelings when he returns home. The story on the surface startles but if verisimilitude is the test of great art Bond excels in it.

Realism is the core of Bond's writing. It is visible even when the reader comes across his paranormal and uncanny tales. There is hardly a touch of improbability in his stories. He refrains from high sounding abstractions. His ghosts, witches, *jinns* are as real as the people he writes about. He makes the supernatural appear entirely natural and therefore harder to ignore. They deserve admiration for their appropriate atmosphere, telling phrases and vivid descriptions. There is a 'willing suspension of disbelief' in these tales. He exploits the popular beliefs in his supernatural tales: the peepal tree as abode of ghosts, the spirit haunting the places they once knew and the *jinn* gets attracted by loose long hair. To authenticate it, he uses the imageries of dark bungalows, dark alleys, mist, thick wood, howling winds, spooky corners. The ghosts in his stories are not always frightening. They are not laboured as they come out of the belief of the simple people in the hills where lonely spots abound to be called the places haunted by ghosts. Thus Bond fabricated the world of fairies, *jinns, churails* and ghosts as a part of 'regional realism.'

The ghosts of Bond have emotions no less tangible than those of human beings. Some are sad, some violent and some even funny. At times, they are silent, vague figures, appearing for a while and then fading into the silence and darkness of the night yet they form an inseparable part of the story. The story "Trouble with Jinns" is built around Indian superstition that ghosts and other supernatural creatures have a fascination for long black hair. In fact grandmothers in villages and small towns often advise the young girls to keep their hair tied in a bun or a plait. This is because the old ladies believe that ghosts are always on the look out to possess the spirit of young girls via their long hair.

Bond's ghosts seem interesting and real because he humanises them. One such story is "The Haunted Bungalow" (AFD 15) where the nuisance of a mischievous *pret* disturbs the peaceful life of a family. The author's grandfather had given PWD permission to cut the peepal tree which was the abode of the mischievous *pret*. Having deprived of the tree the *pret* took up residence in the narrator's bungalow. Within days he made everyone realise his presence by his mischievous pranks. It was the grandmother who became the victim of his mischief. After searching a lot the grandmother found her lost spectacles "balanced precariously on the snout of a wild boar" (AFD 137). Grandfather found "all his prize sweet peas snipped off and lying on the ground" (AFD 137). Aunt Mabel a nervous excitable person was the right sort of prey for the pret. She had been hit on the nose by a grapefruit by him. The mischievous *pret* changed the calm house into topsy-turvy: "Vases fell off tables, pictures fell from walls. Parrot's feathers turned up in the teapot while the parrot himself let out indignant squawks in the middle of the night. Windows which had been closed would be found open and open windows closed" (AFD 138-39).

To get rid of the pret nuisance the family decided to move. The bullock-carts laden with furniture and heavy luggage were sent ahead. The family boarded the old Ford. Grandfather had taken the wheel. But to everyone's surprise the *pret* too was moving with them to their new abode. Everyone heard the chuckling of *pret* and his talking to himself: '*Chalo*—let's go!' It exclaimed gleefully. '*Naya ghar*—a new house! *Kya maza aiga*...what fun I'm going to have!'(AFD 141) The portrayal of the *pret* is done in such a way that the reader readily believes its existence and enjoys its pranks.

Bond sometimes makes a story spooky by conjuring it up with gothic elements. One such memorable story is "When Darkness Falls," about Markham, a war veteran condemned to a lifetime of loneliness by a tragic accident. His face was horribly deformed by a shell explosion in Burma. He returned to a hill station to stay in the cellar of the old Empire Hotel. He lived in that small room for many years. His ugly features forced him to shun the outside world. He had become an outcaste in his own eyes although he was a creature of circumstances. His incarcerated face had created a sense of fear in him to confront people. The proprietor's wife insisted on seeing him which Markham could not do so he struggled to hide his face. It resulted into an accident that ended both of them. Markham had become a nightmare whose appearance in dark nights horrified even the brave heart. His craving for human company and his lonely life arouses sympathy rather than horror for a creature of destiny like him.

The story "Susanna's Seven Husband" reveals the secrets of a widow and her black method of dispatching cumbersome mates to the next world. The first one was given belladonna in his drink. The next one died while cleaning his gun. The gun was loaded without his knowledge. Another was given arsenic during a cholera epidemic. Still another, a doctor, was bitten by a cobra. The indigo planter was given a strong drink and then molten lead was poured into his ears. And the one died defending Susanna against bandits that she herself had set against him. The narrator was bewared of the place where Susanna's ghost is still looking for a right husband. The remarkable narratives vivify Susanna's passion for search of novelty in husband.

Bond's imagination incorporates legends, mythology, history and details of everyday life. Bond, a keen observer, successfully captures the hard-to-pin down characteristics humdrum of Indian reality: a day in a joint family; a busy scene at the platform; an old vendor unable to carry the heavy load; a rash truck driver has an accident; a stray buffalo blocking the road; an adolescent unable to adjust in the domineering adult world; young children chasing the butterflies or bathing in the pool; the sleepless night in the months of May-June; the tantalizing smell of wet earth after the first rain; a blind man's effort of hiding his blindness from a young girl coincidentally who too is blind; the retard and destitute are being tormented by mischief-makers; a rumour resulting in the collapse of a bank; the people of the same sex moving on the road with hands joined; a barber as a good reporter of the village activities; the inquisitive nature of Indians who are ready to ask anything and everything from a stranger, either he likes it or not; the bus driver who carries on a heated political discussion instead of watching the road while driving; suffocating atmosphere and filthy environment in third-class railway compartment; a school boy walking many miles to reach school; a kite maker sitting under an old banyan tree and contemplating the glories of bygone days. Bond's minute observation of external scenes filtered through his nostalgic vision, his extraordinary perception of myriad colours and shades of Indian ambience and his effusive love for India radiate through every line and image of his writing. The vignettes of everyday life, characters, situations, dilemma and objects which he presents are firmly grounded to Indian ethos. He records and faithfully reflects them without idealization. Hence, Bond's magnificent evocation of real India in the hills and its treatment contribute toward making him one of the greatest story-tellers of present times.

6

Narrative Art: Telling a Good Story

> 'Love thy art, poor as it may be ...' I have never regretted following this precept; for, no matter how skilful one is with words, it is only drudgery to have to use them in the more mundane spheres of journalism. I have tried to use words creatively and lovingly. The gift for putting together words and sentences to make stories or poems or essays has carried me through life with a certain serenity and inner harmony which could not have come from any unloved vocation.
>
> Ruskin Bond, *The Lamp Is Lit*

It has rightly been said that the face mirrors the mind and the language the personality of a writer. It is through the language the individuality of a writer reverberates and essentiality is revealed as it does in the strokes of a painter's brush or in the marks of a sculptor's chisel. In other words, the style of an author is governed and modified by the attitude he bears towards his audience and the special delight he takes in the act of composition. It is the result and the final expression of his prevailing outlook on the totality of existence. Style "... is a means by which a human being gains contact with others; it is personality clothed in words, character embodied in speech. If handwriting reveals character, style reveals it still more" (Lucas, *Style* 49). Gustave Flaubert says, "Style is life! It is very life-blood of thought! E. Gibbons puts it, more briefly: "Style is the image of character" (Murray, *Autobiographies of E. Gibbon* 353). Bond's narrative art can be analysed in the light of the foregoing discussion. Bond's style unmistakably carries the mark of his graciousness. It is the 'dress of his modest thought' and cordial personality. It is marked by aptness of expression, clarity of vision and lucidity of notion which confirms more his modest disposition and accentuates the virtues he possesses and commands. Swapan Kumar Banerjee says, "The crystal clearness in his writing shows the child-like, pure heart he is gifted with" (Banerjee, *Garhwal Post*). His uncomplicated and transparent style never loses its charm like the serenity of the Himalayas. He writes with energy, enthusiasm and expertise. His narrative flair differs from book to book and adds an extra appeal to his creativity. The humble acceptance of Bond about his narrative art and thematic pattern emphasise his modesty:

> Among writers, I am not one of the big guns. I am not even a little gun. I'm just a pebble lying on the beach. But I like to think that I'm a smooth, round, colourful pebble, and that someone will pick me up, derive a little pleasure from holding me, and possibly even put me in his, or her, pocket. Could you be that wanderer by the sea? I shall nestle there, close to you. I shall try to make you feel better. And if you tire of me, you can always throw me back into the sea. Perhaps a kindly wave will wash me ashore again, and someone else will pick me up. (LIL xi)

Truth-Telling encompasses the theme (truth) and technique (the way it is told). The fictional world of Bond focuses the truth of day-to-day experiences. He churns his writing out of diurnal happenings capturing the essence of loving in its most crystallised form. The commonplace theme of Bond is elevated by the well-crafted narrative art and his desire to "tell a good story." The artistic value of his stories lies in his method of execution. Kempton has rightly observed, "a noble theme may sound merely pretentious under poor telling" (Son, *The Short Story* 33). Form and technique are the vital elements of fiction: "The way of telling is the mark of good fiction: scene, detail, dialogue all the elements that make an imaginative creation of life" (Slote, *Dimensions of Short* 514). Bond has achieved a perfect craftsmanship by paying attention to every detail and "working with loving care" (LIL 195). He is content to present his lofty thoughts through lucid narration and eloquent expression, unlike the clever word play and verbal pyrotechnics of many Indian English writers. He states forth his invigorating and refreshing ideas without using any demanding devices or ambiguous articulation. He does not believe in dissecting the knowledge of the readers by plunging them into the labyrinth of language and expression. He seems to go with the opinion of F.L. Lucas who says "... it is bad manners to give them [readers] needless trouble. Therefore clarity. It is bad manners to waste their time. Therefore brevity" (Lucas, *Style* 67). His explicit use of language with positive adornment enriches his style. About the clarity in style, Aristotle says in the *Rhetoric*: "Style to be good must be clear, as is proved by the fact that speech which fails to convey a plain meaning fail to do just what speech has to do" (Aristotle, *Rhetoric*). Bond's well-structured and comprehensive style is the result of his persistent efforts. He exerts his soul to write vividly and forcibly. He has often being questioned why his "style is so simple" (DNF xii). He says that his style is in fact "deceptively simple, for no two sentences are really alike. It is clarity that I am striving to attain, not simplicity...I've spent forty years trying to simplify my style and clarify my thoughts!...I have always tried to achieve a prose that is easy and conversational (DNF xii). He even challenges the critic: "And those who think this is simple should try it for themselves" (DNF xii).

The words of F. L. Lucas go in favour of Bond's lucid narrative: "... This is all affection - fiddling with phrases and trifling with cadences! It is easier to criticise but to achieve clarity is the difficult task: "just as 'common sense' is far from common, simple English can prove in practice far from simple to attain" (Lucas, *Style* 17). David Lodge has also pointed out "style is not a decorative embellishment upon subject matter, but the very medium in which the subject is turned into art" (Lodge, *Language of Fiction* 31). The apparent simplicity in Bond's writing is crystallisation and culmination of his art. The simplicity is also symbolic of the milieu and characters in his stories. Almost all his characters are drawn from hilly regions and rustic life living in the foothills or mid-hills of the Himalayas. Bond's language aptly goes with the character portrayed. The language used by the characters never seems to violate their social class, status and age. It never loses the ground of reality. Praising his style Namita Gokhale says: "The simplicity of Bond's writing style has the hallmark of a great writer. The unpretentious, underplayed quality of his work, its control and mastery, helps the reader to effortlessly navigate the meandering flow of ideas and events" (Gokhale, *India Today*). Rajnish Wattas in an interview asks Bond, "Your lucid style has endeared you to many readers but it hasn't quite given you that place in the "hall of fame" as has been given to internationally acclaimed writers dealing with more complex themes. What is the reason for this?" (Wattas, *Tribune*) Bond says: "This is because I haven't been published very much abroad. For that reason I wouldn't particularly be very well known there. You have to be published in England or America to be reviewed by critics and also for your books to appear in the bookshops. It's a very strange system; unless a book is published there it is hard to find it in the bookshops" (Wattas, *Tribune*).

Bond weaves magic with the sheer simplicity of his words. The use of his effective diction is marked by harmony. The dictum "By thy words thou shalt be justified and by thy words thou shalt be condemned" (Matthew, *The Bible*) well goes for Bond's art. Bond's adherence to the accepted patterns and selection of words coincide with Jonathan Swift: "Proper words in proper places make the true definition of a style" (Jonathan, Swift). Words seem to flow from Bond's pen with the ease of a mountain stream, sometimes rapid like a torrent and sometime languorous like a river. The harmony of the words as they go rushing and humming along their shingly bed holds time in a suspended spell. His rare command of words is discernible in his use of the right word at the right place. His choice of words adds charm to his style. About his rich vocabulary, Manish D. Bhatt writes, "He can produce maximum effect by the use of minimum words, so the reader understands the meaning of each and every word without labour" (212). In "The Leopard" through the use of two phrases "a beautiful leopard" and "specimen," Bond highlights his love for the creatures of jungle and the attitude of ruthless hunters towards them. After killing the leopard, in great good humour the haughty hunters ask Bond: "Isn't he a fine specimen?"(CF 152) Bond answers: "He was a beautiful leopard" (CF 152). The words "specimen" and "beautiful" speak volumes. It reveals their mindset - Bond's love for soul and the hunters' passion for matter. Sometimes the very name of the characters become suggestive and denotes the meaning. The name of the main character Keemat Lal that means 'something valuable and rarely found stone' in "A Case for Inspector Lal" rightly conveys the sense. Keemat Lal loses his promotion for saving an innocent girl, Kusum, from the strict law that may have crushed her gentle spirit for the crime she has committed in self-defence. Keemat Lal gets nothing from the worldly law but he becomes 'valuable' in the eyes of readers for his gesture of kindness.

Bond's language has virile force and a mastery which

conveys the maximum of meaning in the fewest and simplest words. He has mastered the language and never seems to falter for expression. It is to the ease, the refinement and the exquisite naturalness of his prose that Indian English writing owes. His work has never seen departure from the Standard English. English is the language of Bond's emotional make-up as well as intellectual make-up. His is not the case of 'Indianisation of English.' He does not fuss like Raja Rao: 'one has to convey in a language that is not one's own the spirit is one's own.' For Bond the spirit and the language both are his own. Bond's love for India and expertise in language resulted his everlasting and enriching contribution to Indian literature in English.

Bond elegantly infuses the tempo of Indian life and culture into English expression. He uses words from Hindi to add flavour to his writing. This goes well with the thoughts of H. Hoijer, who says that the interaction of language and other aspects of culture are so close that no part of the culture of a particular group can properly be studied in isolation from the linguistic symbols in use (*Language in Culture* 455-66). Bond's direct rendering of the vernacular expressions add local colour to his characters and story-line. The general use of Hindi words (code-mixing, code switching and hybridisation) captures the rhythm of vernacular in English and becomes integral with total pattern. The expression is not imposed rather it sprouts out spontaneously with the demand of story. Sometimes Bond gives the meaning of these words otherwise he directly employs them. The following words of Hindi are used in the story "A Handful of Nuts": "Seeda-sada," "Khatmals," "Dast," "Kachi," "Big nasha," "Writer saḥib," "Filmi," "Beedi," "Tongawallah," "Maidaan," "ullu-ka-patha," "rakshasni" (Bond, *Strangers in the Night*). The casual use of these words indicates Bond's proficiency in Hindi and insight into Indian culture.

Bond has moved more to the Indian bazaars, railway platforms, trains, road sides and mountain sides and captures the ambience of these places in his stories. He rarely enters into the Indian houses. But whenever he enters, he has to depend upon vernacular expression and words. His culturally specific vocabulary and context-sensitive topics make the pictures lively and genuine. In *A Flight of Pigeons,* he talks about the life of English women in Hindu and Muslim houses. His direct and frequent use of Hindustani words in demanding context grip the attention of reader: "dolie," "chatty," "missy-baba," "dulhan," "Angrezans," "Padri-Sahib," "Lalin," "Memsahib," "lado," "chachi," wallah," "Khan-begum," "beti," "churail," "dhobi," "hai, hai," "bhai." Here he has amply exploited not only Hindi words but also expressions as well that provide distinctive identity to his language. He has translated Indian expressions into English. The Indian reader enjoys the handling of English in such an interesting way: "Drown yourself in a handful of water," "held me on his knee," "no one comes into this house except over my dead body," "go your way," "he would not lift his hand against women," "don't weep child" (this expression is used twice as is done in Hindi common parlance), "they will receive nothing but kindness from my hand," "it is the talk of the mohalla," "fire ranging in your wife's bosom," "in the name of Allah," "upon my head" (whenever a character gets angry he uses it. It is used three times in the text.); "you must take me for a pumpkin." The use of Hindi words and Hindi expressions authenticate Bond's characterization. Bond seems to agree with David Lodge who says: "... reality is structured by the novelists not only in the particular characters, events, and objects in which he represents it, but initially in the words and arrangements of words with which he creates these characters, events and objects" (19).

Bond has created a certain texture and tone through language that defines theme and meaning. The most charming quality of his language is its simplicity and explicitness. His occasional use of Latin and French phrases and terms are comprehensible. It is because he puts them into a detail narrative. His lexical innovation is also very fascinating: "the strangest" (RGL 99), "Cinderfella" (RIM 25), "disgustipating" (SN 63), "Scooterist" (RBH 46). Bond rarely uses sentences of complicated grammatical construction with such dependent and subordinate clauses, as make the sense difficult to follow. His pithily expressed concise and short sentence helps to comprehend meaning in its fullest sense. His rare use of long sentence is made comprehensible by use of the dash. Here is a paragraph from the story "The Woman on Platform No. 8" where the use of dashes provides the breath:

> Trolleys rolled past me, and I was conscious of the cries of the various vendors—the man who sold curds and lemon, the sweetmeat-seller, the newspaper boy—but I had lost interest in all that went on along the busy platform, and continued to stare across the railway tracks, feeling bored and a little lonely. (CF 3)

Accuracy and precision, the hallmark features of Bond's evocative style sprout from his minutely observed and vividly described scenes and settings and characterization. He observes things that others would fail to notice and makes them come alive through skilful handling of lucid prose. Like an efficient sculptor, he carves out colourful and expressive images by his exact description and picturesque delineation. The pictures that effloresce from his fiction garden are simple yet heartfelt. He says: "My forte is observation, recollection, and reflection" (TIIL 17). His fictional world gleams with realistic and graphic description of scene and background. He enlivens the atmosphere with vibrant and intense illustration before leading us towards the crux of story. This helps the reader to gauge the importance of the image portrayed.

"Sita and the River" revolves around the life of an epic heroine Sita and her heroic battle with the forces of nature. It is the fury of the river which plays a crucial role in moulding the events of her life. Bond explores changing relationship with the river, from a deep love and gratitude for its many boons, to awareness of its duality, to an understanding of its mystical nature. Sita lives on an island with her grandparents. The family depends upon the river for livelihood. But the life force the river becomes a destructive force when its flood submerges the island, uproots the shelter and carries Sita away. The story commences with the description of the river and hints its approaching role in the forthcoming events:

> In the middle of the river, the river that began in the mountains of the Himalayas and ended in the Bay of Bengal, there was a small island. The river swept round the island, sometimes clawing at its banks but never going right over it....More than twenty years had passed since the river had flooded the island and at that time no one had lived there. But then years ago a small hut had stood on it, a mud walled hut with a sloping thatched roof. (CF 153)

Sita was left alone on the island when the grandfather along with sick grandmother had gone to the hospital in Shahganj. Sita was not afraid of being left alone but she did not like the look and sound of the river. She was brought up listening to the sound of river but she had never noticed it. That night she noticed a change in its sound: "There was something like a moan, like a wind in the tops of tall trees, and a swift hiss as the water swept round the rocks and carried away pebbles. And sometimes there was a rumble as loose earth fell into the water" (CF 158). The river flooded the island, uprooted the only peepal tree and took Sita away with its waves. It was a village boy Vijay who rescued her. She returned with her grandfather to the island when the river water receded. Sita had by now experienced both the generator and destroyer aspect of nature, as she says: "Sometimes the river is angry and sometimes it is kind" (CF 186).

Explanatory narration of scenes and elegant illustration

of background occur in every story Bond pens down that make the most ordinary of things an exciting proposition. The real strength of Bond lies in his close attention to little details. His vivid and graphic description of background familiarises the readers with the setting and provides an insight into the story. The novella *A Flight of Pigeons* records the escape of Ruth and her family from the grip of ruthless sepoys who massacred Anglo Indian community of Shahjahanpur. The flight of Ruth starts from a small sturdily built cantonment church where she has gone with her father. The sepoys attack the Englishmen. Ruth's father is killed by them in the church. The premises of church witness the ruthless killing of innocent and helpless Englishmen and the narrow escape of Ruth. Bond minutely describes the church and its vicinity which is going to witness the horror of massacre. The acquaintance with the structure of church and its premises intensifies the horror more when the reader sees the Englishman running to save themselves from the cruel clutches of ruffians:

> St Mary's, the little church in Shahjahanpur, was situated on the southern boundary of the cantonment, near an ancient mango-grove. There were three entrances: one to the south, facing a large compound known as Buller's; another to the west, below the steeple; and the vestry door opening to the north. A narrow staircase led up to the steeple. To the east there were open fields sloping down to the river, cultivated with melon; to the west, lay an open plain bounded by the city; while the parade ground stretched away to the north until it reached the barracks of the sepoys. (AFP 5)

Bond through his interesting narrative illustrates a world of interesting shape and size, of form and design, of rhythm and order. He records the life truthfully and artistically. He often depicts the familiar situations and scenes with which the reader is well aware but it is his close observation, fidelity to detail and total involvement which infuse charm to his delineation. Here is a scene from the railway compartment. There could not have been a more accurate picture of the din and bustle inside the railway compartment. The narrator is journeying with his friend Suraj in the third class compartment. The variety is striking here:

> We slept fitfully that night, continually shifting our positions on the hard bench of the third-class compartment; Suraj with his head against my shoulder, I with my feet on my bedding roll. Above us, a Sikh farmer slept vigorously, his healthy snores reverberating through the compartment. A woman with her brood of four or five children occupied the bunk opposite; they had knocked over their earthen surahi, smashing it and flooding the compartment. Two young men in the corner played cards and exchanged lewd jokes. No general companionship was at all evident, but whenever the train drew into a station everyone cooperated in trying to prevent people on the outside from entering the already crowded compartment; and if someone did manage to get in--usually by crawling through a window--he would fall in with the same policy of keeping others out. (DNF 409-10)

The minute observation of scenes and its invocation bring Bond closer to Anglo-Indian writers - Rudyard Kipling, E.M. Foster. An Indian writer rarely observes and records the common happenings around as does an English writer. The Indian writers simply ignore it because of being too accustomed to it. When a non-Indian writer comes across it, he gets fascinated by it and automatically he represents it through his writings.

The vivid descriptions of scenes provide an understanding of the situation and condition of the protagonist. In *The Room on the Roof* Mr. Harrison thrashed Rusty when he defied him and visited the bazaar. Rusty ran away. With no other place to move, he came to bazaar. The noise and hubbub of bazaar tempted him in the morning. But it is now deserted and forlorn. The depiction of the scene explicitly focuses the condition of lonely and dismayed Rusty:

> The smart shops and restaurants were closed. In the bazaar, oil lamps hung outside each doorway; people were asleep on the steps and platforms of shopfronts, some huddled in blankets, others rolled tight into themselves. The road, which during the day was a busy, noisy crush of people and animals, was quiet and deserted. Only a lean dog still sniffed in the gutter. A woman sang in a room high above the street—a plaintive, tremulous song—and in the far distance a jackal cried to the moon. (CF 573)

Rusty sees the reflection of his own ruinous condition in the lean dog, in sad song of the woman and in the cry of jackal. The fear and the anxiety of Rusty are characteristically revealed through the setting of scene. Rusty is lonely and homeless yet he is hopeful for tomorrow. He knows that he is alone only for today; tomorrow his friends are going to accompany him and help him. Rusty longs to remove the roofs of the buildings and wants to feel the presence of people inside. He knows the street is empty but the houses are not: "But the empty, lifeless street was very deceptive if the roofs could have been removed from just a handful of buildings, it would be seen that life had not really stopped but, beautiful and ugly, persisted through the night" (CF 573). The pictorial description provided by Bond set the tone and mood of the story. This could be witnessed especially in his tales of macabre. The moving trees, the rustling of leaves, the howling of wolves, the torrent winds, the heavy rain, the flashing of light, the forlorn bungalow, the old graveyard, the gothic scenes and encounter with supernatural elements anticipate the spooky stories or mysterious plot.

Bond's outstanding power of observation and

description can also be discerned in his remarkable art of characterization. He describes the characters in his inimitable clarity of style. The exquisite presentation of the distinctive physiognomy of characters helps the reader to form an association with them. With his fine strokes, he paints the whole man - the exterior and interior. In order to convey the sense of individual identity, he vividly describes the appearance and attire, the action and activities and the manners of his characters. Miss Bun a baker's daughter in "Miss Bun and Others" brings *samosas* and patties for the narrator. She lessens the weight of his pocket by talking sweetly and offering expensive kisses. Description of the radiance and sensuousness of her features vividly hint the passionate nature of Miss Bun:

> She sits at the foot of my bed, absolutely radiant. Her raven-black hair lies loose on her shoulders, her eyelashes have been trimmed and blackened and so have her eyes, with kajal. Her eyes, so large and innocent—and calculating! There are pretty glass bangles on her wrists and she wears a pair of new slippers. Her kameez is new too—green silk, with gold-embroidered sleeves. (CF 518)

The profession, caste, age, attitude become alive itself from Bond's precise factual record and meticulous narrative of physique and features of characters. The simplicity of his style never foreshadows the fascination of his faithful description. He neither exaggerates nor undermines his characters. He presents them as they are found in any society. He introduces a character Sudheer in *Vagrants in the Valley* who is a loafer and practises crime as a fine, art. Sudheer tries to win favour with his crooked and captivating smile. The very description of Sudheer hints his profession. He was whistling when he came striding towards Rusty and Devinder: "He looked taller than Devinder, mainly because of his long legs. He wore a loose fitting bush-shirt that hung open in front. His face was long and pale, but he had quick, devilish eyes, and he smiled disarmingly" (CF 710). At times the external description speaks of itself, other times its relation to a trait is explicated. In "The Garlands on his Brow," Bond describes the physique of a stout wrestler, Hassan, his strong body, wide shoulders and powerful legs. Later the downfall of Hassan from a wrestler to a beggar and his committing suicide intensify the difference what he was and into what he became.

In "The Man Who Was Kipling" Bond beautifully records the facial expression of a man who accosted the narrator while sitting on a bench in the Indian Section of the Victoria and Albert Museum in London. The narrator noticed something familiar behind the "swarthy features," "heavy moustache" and "horn-rimmed spectacles" of this tall, stooping, elderly gentleman. The man in a soft pleasant voice asked the narrator "Do you recognize me" (CF 21). He told the narrator that he used to write books. He asked him about his favourite writers. When the narrator was mentioning the names, he noticed "a shadow, a sad shadow, passes across" (CF 21) his face. It seems that the man was groping for a particular name. The sad face of stranger glowed, the moment the narrator mentioned Kipling: "His face brightened up at once and the eye behind the thick-lensed spectacles suddenly came to life" (CF 21). The man with whom the narrator was interacting was the ghost of Kipling. He came to defend his writing that was accused for propagating 'white man's burden.'

Miss Deed in "Time Stops at Shamli" is an unmarried woman of about thirty-five. She is a teacher and caught in the sluggishness of Shamli from years. She got frustrated with her routine life. She is a short-tempered lady who pours her affection-cum-love on the narrator and the keeper of the hotel, Daya Ram. The little girl Kiran describes her as a funny creature. Before the reader meets this lady, Bond describes her in full length:

> She had on a skirt and blouse, which accentuated a firm, well-rounded figure, and she walked on high heels, with a rhythmical swaying of the hips.

> She had an uninteresting face, camouflaged with lipstick, rouge and powder—the powder so thick that is had become embedded in the natural lines of her face—but her figure compelled admiration. (TSS 43)

Bond's method of presenting fictional persona varies with the concerned character. When dealing with types, he sketches only the general features. Sometimes it is the description of surrounding that gives a clue to the status and profession of the characters. Aunt Mariam in "A Gurdian Angel" is a mistress. The condition of her room suggests it. Her beds "were usually left unmade, while clothes lay draped over chairs and tables. A large water-colour hung on a wall but Mariam's bodice and knickers were usually suspended from it and I cannot recall the subject of the painting. The dressing table was a fascinating place, crowded with all kinds of lotions, mascaras, paints, oils, and ointments" (CF 55).

Bond is a great master of humour and it is an integral part of his technique. It plays a vital role making his day-to-day observations and experiences appealing and spellbinding. It also confirms his English taste and English origin because it has been said that the Indians are less sensitive to humour. The tone in Indian writing in English is generally serious as Bond comments: "It's very hard to find a funny book. You know a humorous book ... writers take themselves too seriously only if they address some ... shattering theme—where everyone is suffering. You know; the lighter side of life is ignored" (Sharma, *Studies in Contemporary* 173) While answering to the question of Ruby Gupta "Do you think you have a typically British sense of humour—subtle and sophisticated?"(Ibid) Bond says:

> It could be that. Or may be just the fact that the influence on me of humorous writers. I used to read a lot of ... Some of my favourite books would still be *The Diary of a Nobody* where the sense of

> humour is at oneself. Or *Three Men in a Boat* where again the humour is self-inflicted humour....Which may be people in India....we don't laugh at ourselves—it's more laughing at others. I meet a lot of Indians—I mean a lot of Indians have a great sense of humour but it doesn't seem to be so much in the writers. Writers take themselves too seriously—part of their vanity. (Ibid)

Bond's humour stands for gentle mirth, the most important ingredient of which is sympathy and charity for its victim. In the broader sense humour includes 'fun' i.e. boisterous humour, 'wit' i.e. intellectual humour and 'satire' i.e. gentle and mirthful humour. Bond's humour is mostly of the genial type like the humour of Chaucer, Shakespeare, Lamb and Narayan. It possesses freshness of outlook and is marked by tolerance and forgiveness for its victims. It is tinged with a sense of pity though directed towards foibles and eccentricities of characters. Bond aims to make the world a better place simply by making us laugh with him, at him and at ourselves. Emphasising the importance of humour, Bond writes: "A sense of humour will help you to get through the worst of times. A little light laughter is the best kind of magic" (LD xiii).

The sparkling humour is generated through Bond's self deprecation, mischievous pranks of children, funny antics of animals, eccentricities of aunts and uncles and witty dialogues. He entails humour with a predominant aim to amuse the readers. At times the external description speaks for itself; other times its relation to a trait is explicated by the narrator. Imrat Lal and the bickering of his two wives in *A Flight of Pigeons* amuse by the use of witty dialogues. The language used by the character evokes comical scenes. Imrat Lal is short and stout and his first wife is tall and ugly. He has no children by her so he becomes intimate with a low-caste woman and has got two sons. The wrangling of the two ladies disturbs the peace of Imarat's mind. He runs away leaving his family behind to struggle. Having heard his whereabouts, the second wife writes a letter:

> 'O thou who hast vanished like mustard oil which, when absorbed by the skin, leaves only its odour behind; thou with the rotund form dancing before my eyes, and the owl's eyes which were wont to stare at me vacantly; wilt thou still snap thy fingers at me when this letter is evidence of my unceasing thought of thee? Why did you call me your *lado*, your loved one, when you had no love for me? And why have you left me to the taunts of that stick of a woman whom you in your perversity used to call a precious stone, your Ratna? Who has proved untrue, you or I? Why have you sported thus with my feelings? Drown yourself in a handful of water, or return and make my hated rival an ornament for your neck, or wear her effigy nine times round your arm as a charm against my longings for you.' (AFP 29)

The humour is very soul of his literature and like the soul permeates a living fabric which could never exist without its creative breath. In his children's literature it generates through insatiable inquisitiveness, prank and tall talk of young boys. The crazy activities of children abound with fun and mischief delights us. In *Hidden Pool* after experiencing the thrill of a long, tiring and perilous excursion the children Anil, Laurie, Kamal and Bisnu returned to the bungalow and were virtually dying of hunger that made them remark:

> 'I could eat a whole chicken,' said Kamal.
> 'I could eat two,' I said.
> 'I could eat a Snowman,' said Bisnu.
> 'And I could eat the chowkidar,' said Anil. (HP 70)

Bond's puckish sense of humour springs up while delineating the young boys who are generally mischievous by nature like the popular 'Dennis the menace' by Hank Ketcham. The humour spills out in "Life with Uncle Ken" through the prank and playfulness of the narrator child. He gets cheesed off by the carelessness of his uncle. Once Uncle Ken takes two large helpings and eats most of the stuffing of a roast duck, a mouth-watering dish for the child. This irritates the child. He empties his uncle's favourite apple sauce onto his plate to tease him: "Uncle Ken knew I loved the stuffing; and I knew he was crazy about Granny's apple sauce. So we were even" (RBH 139). Irritated by the behaviour of the child, Ken asks him when he is going to join his father, so that he can get rid of him and can enjoy all the delicacies alone. Rather than answering, the child promptly counter asks when he is getting another job, an exasperating subject for him. Ken a shirker by nature avoids talking about jobs. Granny once asks the child his views about his uncle. He says: "I wish he was someone else's uncle" (RBH 140). To hearten the child, Granny says that his uncle is not bad, he is just eccentric, means just a little crazy. The word "crazy" confuses the child because it is the name of his pet dog. So he says to Granny: "At least crazy runs round the house...I've never seen Uncle Ken running" (RBH 140). Uncle Ken does not want to join her sister's school because the demented children make him nervous. The child asks Granny the meaning of "demented." "It means crazy," says Granny. The child gets puzzled by the meaning of the word "demented." He asks: "So many words mean crazy....Why don't we just say crazy. We have a crazy dog and now Uncle Ken is crazy too" (RBH 145). The comment of the child makes Ken angry. Granny manages the situation by speaking in favour of Ken: "Your Uncle isn't crazy," "He's just lazy" (RBH 145). To this the child says "And eccentric" too. Ken asks "Who said I was eccentric" (RBH 145). The child lies Miss Leslie. To tease Ken the child deliberately takes the name of Miss Leslie. He knows Ken is fond of her and will never like to be called eccentric by her.

In *Friends in Small Places,* Bond humorously portrays a superintendent of police who is fond of writing verse and bores others by compelling them to listen to it. The constable Ghanshyam Singh who seeks his transfer to a better place requests the narrator to get his boss's poem published. The SP writes poetry and his subordinates have to listen and must say *Shabash* (ah, wonderful!) after every recitation. This comment should be enough for the quality of his poem: "... the SP has extracted confessions from a couple of thieves simply by making them stand for hours and listen to him reciting his poetry. I know our police have a reputation for torturing suspects, but I think this is carrying things a bit too far" (FSP 270-71). Bond's prose like polished silver is decorated with those luminous nuggets of humour which crop up unexpectedly. Bond's humour is gentle and laid-back humour. It brings spontaneously a chuckle. The 'funny side is always up' in his writings.

The eccentricities of characters woven with witty dialogue enrapture the reader. The reader curiously flips over the pages to know about the concerned character. The caricature of the rich and "baggy-eyed" Maharani of Magador in "A Handful of Nuts" is gloriously funny. The Rani is described as *Rakshani,* a witch and a dragon. She seduces the lover of her daughter Indu and messed up his life by her amorous designs. The narrator is somehow eking out his livelihood through free-lancing. There is great difference between his and his beloved's status. His friend Sitaram advises him to pretend himself as Maharani's lover and this will help him in winning her daughter Indu's favour. The difference between soft, delicate, butterfly Indu and coarse, harsh, dragon Maharani horrifies him. He takes reader into confidence:

> Have you ever made love to a dragon—and a scaly one at that? How could a monster like the.Maharani have produced a beautiful, tender, vivacious, electrifying girl like Indu? It was like making a succulent dish from a pumpkin, a bitter gourd, and

> a spent cucumber. The Maharani had denied me the dish, but she was prepared to give me the ingredients. (SN 61)

The narrator finds himself entrapped in the amorous designs of Maharani who torments him to become her lover. The more he tries to free himself from her clutches, the more he gets entangled in her schemes. She brings him to her home and offers a drink. A shudder runs down his spine when he finds his "free hand encased in a fold of crocodile skin—her hand!" (SN 61) But she mistakes the shudder for a shiver of excitement, and starts playing with the lobe of his ear. Suddenly she cuddles up to him and he finds his escape difficult. He has never realised that "this badly-preserved Christmas pudding could be of an amorous disposition. I had always thought of middle-aged mothers as having gone beyond the pursuit of carnal pleasures. But not this one!" (SN 61) She asks him to call her darling or by her pet name Liz as in "lizard." She tries to set the nervous narrator at ease and requests him to recite one of his poems. He recites a limerick to please her. Being pleased by it, she takes a lump of barley-sugar from a box and asks him to open his mouth which he dutifully does:

> But instead of popping the sweet in, she planted her lips on mine, large lips like suction pumps, and thrust her long lizard-like tongue down my throat. Her crocodile fingers were all over me, and even if my buttons did not reach Mhow, they must have landed on Mussoorie.
>
> What can you do in such a situation? Not much, really. You just let the more active partner take over—in this case, the rich Maharani of Magador. She certainly knew how to get you worked up. After a hesitant start, all I had to do was imagine that I was another crocodile. I slid into her quivering orifice, and my virginity was at an end. (SN 62-63)

The piteous narrator confides to his friend Sitaram his misdemeanours and a hair-raising account of his seduction by the royalty. Rather being sympathetic for the narrator, Sitaram wittingly remarks: "Congratulations, *ullu ka pattha* ...you cannot escape her now. She'll suck you dry. A succubus, forsooth!" (SN 65) It is charm of Bond's style which designs a character like Maharani interesting. His gentle criticism laced with humour softens the blow and makes Maharani an acceptable and endearing character. The readers heartily laugh at her discomposure. The scene of seduction is designed in such a way that tickles our funny bone. Without being sarcastic it amuses the reader to its best and provides a charm and freshness to the story.

Bond a master artist aims to become clear in his expression so he gives detailed account of scenes and settings. Sometimes the eccentricities of the characters and the funny situations create boisterous laughter. Bond presents a scene of crowded platform in "Sita and the River." The effort of the people to get in or out the train even before the train had come to a stop presents slapstick comedy:

> For a few moments there was chaos. The crowd surged backwards and forwards. No one could get out. No one could get in! Fifty people were leaving the train, a hundred were catching it! No one wanted to give way. But every problem has a solution somewhere, provided one looks for it. And this particular problem was solved by a man climbing out of a window. Others followed his example. The pressure at the doors eased and people started squeezing into their compartments. (CF 181-182)

Besides this awareness of the comic, Bond also possesses in a large degree, a rare command of wit which appears very frequently in his epigrammatic statements and delightful dialogues. His epigram could be seen especially in his philosophical ideas. Passing comment on the futility of wealth, Bond writes in *The India I love*: "If death was a thing that money could buy / The rich they would live, and the poor they would die" (35).

Bond's style is marked by the subtlety of expression and visualization. The frequent use of auditory imageries adds a charm to it. It makes the graceful description pleasing. He creates sound imageries directly observing the various components of nature and man made world. The very sensitive ears of Bond never fail to hear both cacophony and symphony: the blares of the horns, the jingles of the tonga, the cow and the school bells, chunk-chunk of a night jar, hoo-hoo of the wind while moving in the branches of tall deodar, rattling and swishing of the rain on the corrugated tin roofs, the clip-clop of a pony carriage, the creaking of the wheels of a bullock cart over rough country roads, the sound made by the dry and thirsty earth, as it sucks at a sprinkling of water, sound produces by a child while drinking thirstily water running down his chin and throat, creaking of a door at its hinges, the warbling of the birds, the roaring and chattering of the animals, the whispering of the plants. The exhausting list of the aural imageries heightens the effect of Bond's invigorating style and racy language. Bond is of the opinion that these often ignored tunes of nature and of life have a healing power and capacity to change the dull and dreary mood. He eagerly records the impression that it creates on him:

> Gentle rain on a tin roof is one of my favourite sounds. And early in the morning, when the rain has stopped, there are other sounds I like to hear--a crow shaking the raindrops from his feathers and cawing rather disconsolately; babblers and bulbuls bustling in and out of bushes and long grass in search of worms and insects; the sweet, ascending thrill of the Himalayan whistling-thrush; dogs rushing through damp undergrowth. (RIM 108)

Bond also recaptures the sound produced by the blowing of wind and the flowing of the river: "The wind in the pines and deodars hums and moans, but in the chestnut it rustles and chatters and makes cheerful conversation" (LD 1). It is especially Bond's young readers who get fascinated by the euphonious sound imageries. Nicholas Tucker has also pointed out the importance of sound imageries in Children's literature: "....young readers can also be exceptionally sensitive to the sound and overtones of words, and good writers should always try to cater this response" (Tucker, *The Child* 13).

Images play a vital role in Bond's literature and secure an outstanding place for him in the array of visual artists. His appealing and sensuous images make the description forceful and effective. Illuminating images enlighten the understanding of the reader and denote the rich poetic sensibility to his writing. They are subtle and appropriate and emanate itself with the need of situation. The images deftly incorporate all kind of sense qualities: auditory, tactile, kinaesthetic, gustatory, thermal and olfactory and augment the power of language. Some recurrent images are: lizards scuttling on the wall and roofs; the mountain path dipped through oak, rhododendron and maple; the murmuring sounds of brooks and rivulets; the rustling of dry leaves and grass; the shadow of clouds on the Mussoorie hills; the chorus of insects at twilight outside his window; the beauty of first snowfall in the mountains; the slushy and muddy roads in rainy season; people found leisurely spending time, smoking hookah or chewing *paan* (beetle); the buzzing of the flies on the sweets; barefoot boys riding buffaloes or chewing on sticks of sugarcane; people relishing *jallebies, golgappas, tikkies* by the roadside vendor; stray dogs and cows moving in the alleyways; pot bellied shaped man. Bond's images cause a mental reproduction of sensations. The use of wide and speculative imageries is an invaluable resource of his language.

Bond's use of appropriate and vivid figure of speech is one of the rare charms of his style. It spills out spontaneously. He by his unique talent makes them very apt and suggestive. His similes are very simple, precise and effective. It is always marked by clarity and exactness and by the extraordinary quality of saying exactly what is supposed to be said. Describing Ruth in *A Flight of Pigeons* Bond writes: She is a pretty girl "with raven black hair and dark, lustrous eyes" (3); "She shone like Zohra, the morning star" (46); "She was like a rose touched by a breath of wind, a doe-like creature" (47); she was "like a frightened doe" (73).

Bond has almost exclusively confined himself to the form of short story 'chips from fiction workshop.' He is a devoted short story writer. It is used regularly unlike other male writers who use it during the lull of creativity in their life. It is his forte. He enjoys it because of its brevity and the free play it allows with themes, style and characterization. A.J. Merson has rightly pointed out that "much of short story today is due to the diversity and unexpectedness of the subjects" and that "manner as well as matter further reveals the individuality of the writer" (*Modern Short Stories* ix). Bond feels it is the best medium suited to his temperament. His stories are marked by restraint, reticence and moderation both in theme and style. His penchant for short story and novella, first person narrative, lucid language and digression free plot are characteristic traits of his writing that attract young readers. The concentration span of children in general is short. They prefer shorter fiction to longer one. The children enjoy the first person narrative because it gives them an idea that a child is narrating the story. The clarity of expression makes it easier for the children to grasp the plot. Because of the multilingual culture and three-language-formula of Indian Education System the Indian children many times fail to master English language at a very young age. They like to read the stories where they do not have to hassle with the language. The young Indian children become the ardent readers of Bond because of the simplicity of his language and exactness of expression.

The short story also confers Bond an opportunity to concentrate upon the various subjects. He has introduced a qualitative quantity of incidents and effects through short story: a blind man's imaginative perception of another blind young woman; a peanut seller selling nuts for years sitting at a place whose identity is never being noticed and who is all alone even being surrounded by the people; a poor villager returns home contemplating why he has been duped; a child covers miles alone to find the river hidden behind the mountain; the local politician giving free taxi rides to his voters; a narrow escape of a man from a house where two sisters committed suicide and the ghosts of the dead sisters kill the person who unfortunately arrives there; the ghost of a whistling boy who saves the narrator from danger; a servant taking care of the house of his master for years in hope of his returning; the petty quarrels followed by quick reconciliation in a joint family; a rumour caused by a sweeper's remark resulted in the collapse of a bank; a kite maker reflecting upon the changes that the time has brought; a strong wrestler's or a poor beggar's miserable plight; the woes of people who lost home and family during the riots of partition; problems faced by a freelancer in eking out his livelihood; a loving lady feeds a boy and wins the heart by her generosity; a youth becomes nostalgic visiting the place of his childhood days. The theme may be undoubtedly 'anything,' but its presentation carries the impression being of 'unified and whole.' Bond surpasses in presenting the music of life of the people around him in realistic manner within the limited range of the short story and the novella.

Bond's art is 'spontaneous overflow of powerful emotions.' The emotions are recollected from his life-experience. He belongs to the tradition of subjective writers who are adept in shaping the record of personal life into memorable and creative piece of art. The autobiographical nature of his fiction makes him an Indian Charles Lamb. With his meticulous deftness and craftsmanship, he shapes the events and incidents of his simple and single life into artistic force. He works the best from very close to his experience as James Joyce does in his *Portrait of the Artist,* Lawrence in *Sons and Lovers,* Samuel Butler in *The Way of All Flesh,* Wordsworth in the epic poem *The Prelude,* R.K. Naryan in *Swami and Friends.* Talking about the writer's attitude who explores their mind for their subjects Salman Rushdie says that he too follows the same trend: "I have never had a reader in mind. I have ideas, people, events, shapes, and I write 'for' those things, and hope that the completed work will be of interest to others" (Rushdie, *Imaginary Homelands* 19). In this sense Bond precedes Rushdie. He generally writes about the people who come into his orbit. In Bond's work it is difficult to guess where the autobiography ends and the story begins or the other way round. One gets a wonderful glimpse into the deepest recesses of his heart especially in three books: *Rain in the Mountains, Scenes from a Writer's Life, The Lamp Is Lit.* He is content to record the events of people, places and animals around him with whom he has daily communion. About his subjectivity, Bond writes: "I've been writing stories of one kind or another for nearly fifty years and, along the way, it has always been the people I've known and met who have given me these stories—friends, lovers, relatives, chance acquaintances, strangers, or other people's friends and relatives" (FSP vii).

The personal 'I' is prominent everywhere in Bond's literature. It becomes more persuasive with his first person narrative and imparts a certain credibility and genuineness to his stories. The narrator in most of the cases is a freelancer who struggles to make out his position in the literary world or an Anglo-Indian boy who gets fascinated by Indian nuances or a man meeting someone on the road. The person met could be anyone - a thief, a retard, an epileptic boy, a small girl, a recluse, a vendor and sometimes a ghost. The artist says James Joyce remains like God in this creation, within or behind, or beyond and above his handiwork. Bond remains silent yet eloquent, unseen yet ever present behind the subjects of his writings. Almost every story discloses some facts of his life. This self exposé is often clothed in a web of fancy. The reader can form more or less an accurate idea about him, his life and his character.

Mulk Raj Anand once said in his essay, "Why I Write": "Some people feel an inexplicable urge to communicate what they feel intensely to say it to others" (Sinha, *Indian Writing* 4). Bond is one among them who lays bare his heart and his experience through his work. In *Landour Days* he says: "I am a subjective writer, and much that I have written over the years has been drawn from personal experience" (xiii). The autobiographical streak is subtly covered in his narrative. But this world is not an exact replica of his life. He admits: "True, the autobiographical element is present in much of my work, but there is really more fiction in my fiction that the reader may realize...I have used the first person and taken the trouble to make the backgrounds and episodes convincing" (SWL xiii). Sometimes the self-revelation becomes repetitive but it never grows monotonous. It appeals us for ease with which he transcends us into his own world. Bond defends his excess subjective mode: "Perhaps there is too much of me in my stories....It is a weakness, I know. It can't be helped; I am that kind of a writer, that kind of a person....I can't write unless I am in love with my subject" (NTD 9).

One of the dominant themes of his narrative art is brooding nostalgia - longing for something that is lost. In *The Night Train at Deoli,* he *says*: "It is longing that has been experienced by all of us at various times in our lives unless one has become desensitized by power and money" (10). Nostalgia in Bond's writing is like a lingering fragrance pervading the entire ambience. M.K. Naik is also of the opinion, "Bond is at his best in evoking a mood of nostalgia for the vanished sights and scenes of boyhood, of the pathos of the inexorable march of time ..." (Naik *History of Indian* 250). Asserting its importance Bond says: "Nostalgia is an attempt to preserve that which was good in the past" (Bond, *When Darkness Falls* vii). Bond believes, "The past is always with us, for it feeds the present" (Bond, *Town Called* 202). Bond has a fund of memories of persons, sights and scenes which became part of his being. Bond's exclusivity as a writer rests on his knack of conjuring up the past. In stories like "The meeting Pool," "I can't Climb Trees Any More," and "My Father's Trees" the narrator visits a scene of his boyhood and feels the impact of the change both in the setting and the tune. These stories written in first person narration reveal the truth "Remembered passion grows sweeter with the passing of time" (Bond, *Night Train at Deoli* 210). Bond concentrates on the salient features and oddities of the various people; he is portraying and brings them out with dramatic effectiveness. Most of these people sketched were real persons associated with Bond, either in the past or in the present: "I have been writing stories of one kind or another for nearly fifty years, along the way, it has always been the people I've known and met who have given me these stories-friends, lovers, relatives, chance acquaintances, strangers, or often people's friends and relative" (FSP vii).

Bond's characterization is so well done that the characters take on a life of their own. They show his insight into the human mind and his psychological penetration. His stories owe their exalted position to two pre-eminent qualities - excellence of characterisation and harmonious development of plot. His evergreen characters are drawn from real life and are amazingly and indomitably alive. They act freely out of their own nature. They are brought into being by a happy combination of Bond's observation and invention. They are real not because they are like ourselves but because they are convincing. They are wonderfully energetic and vital despite being ordinary folks. The remarkable feature is their individuality and universality. They linger long in the memory once we have formed an acquaintance with them. He has emphasised the beauty of moral virtue which is to be found in all classes of people, irrespective of birth and education. He colours the canvas of his fiction with the joys and sorrows of common masses - their small gesture of kindness, their unyielding spirit and their struggle with their distressing circumstances. He captures the glimpses of everyday which one tends to ignore: the cobbler fanning himself using his lather, the drunken truck driver driving rashly and blowing the horn to scare the pedestrian or to prove his expertise in driving, the rickshaw man taking the long root to cheat the lady passengers, the sweeper boy murmuring the problem of being unpaid. He deals with the ordinary life of ordinary people in a gay compassionate manner that adds a charm to what he describes. Bond's authentic projection of theme and character agrees with David Lodge:

> ... life, not language, is the novelist's medium: that it is the way he manipulates and organizes and evaluates the life or, more precisely, the imitation - life of his fictions, that constitutes his literary activity; that his language is merely a transparent window through which the reader regards this life - the writer's responsibility being merely to keep the glass clean. (5)

Oscar Wilde says that "One's style is one's signature always" goes well with Bond's style. Bond has develcped his individual style of narration. His artistic excellence and art of story-telling is something unique. His narrative is marked with simplicity of tone and depth of meaning. He adds to his style classical discipline, a deeper poetic vision, a sense of discernment, an auditory imagination, a developed onomatopoeic sense and a fine sense of humour. He respects his vocation of writer and pays as much attention to his style as his content. His prose does not gain effect by a laboured artifice but with a floating rhythm and spontaneity of expression that signals the spontaneity of life itself. It is his special skill that makes his delightful and unsurpassable simple prose appears effortless. The author reads the complex psychology of his characters and describes it in his distinctive clarity of style. His hallmark literary style has always been a simple choice of words, woven together in a breathtaking manner, sentence after sentence, paragraph after paragraph. David Davidar extolling his narrative art says the style of Bond bears his distinctiveness: "deep yet uncluttered, evocative yet spare, gentle yet searching and still the writing flows as strong and as vibrant as it has ever been and that is something we continue to be grateful for" (Davidar, *Books Today*). The 'lamp of Bond's writing is lit' with his explicitly narrated stories, evocative characterization, well constructed plot, natural flow of vocabulary and above all his use of inimitable and lucid style.

7

Conclusion

> I have nearly always enjoyed myself in my writing. And if some of that enjoyment has been conveyed to the reader, then I have achieved what I set out to do, and no prizes are solicited.
>
> Ruskin Bond, *Time Stops at Shamli*

Ruskin Bond secures an outstanding place in the entire gamut of Indian English fiction. His devotion to the muse of writing makes him a sort of guardian angel of Indian English writing - scripting novels, stories, children's tales, literary columns in newspapers and editing anthologies. Bond's work in its entirety is exploration of the truth, meaning of life, understanding of his own self, the identity crisis of Anglo-Indian's in independent India, devotion to nature, integration of the outer space with the inner space while writing about children and adolescence and above all his belief in the noble virtues of mankind.

The gossamer like light and frothy stories of Bond are meticulously drawn from Himalayan and Dehradun region depicting its beautiful forest, cascading rivers, mesmerising scenery, undemanding simple folk, their trials and tribulations, faith and frustration and the romance of their day-to-day life. His fiction could be termed as local colour literature emphasizing the settings, customs, dialects and other features peculiar to the region. Bond's invocation of social and natural landscape of the region is like Thomas Hardy's Wessex and R.K. Narayan's Malgudi. Like Hardy, Bond gives great importance to the beauty and natural landscape around and like Narayan touches the human emotions and sentiments of this part of the country. Bond's intimacy with his locale has earned him comparison with Wordsworth. But Amit Chaudhuri feels this likeness inadequate. He says, "Bond is not an architect of overarching theoretical designs as Wordsworth was, a more apt analogy would be with John Clare, a kindred and similarly self-effacing 'spirit of place,' whose seemingly naïve vernacular had the ability to express the different, and tender, gradations of belonging" (Chaudhuri, *Vintage Book* 414). Bond's merit as an artist lies in investigating the unassuming events in the life of simple men and women and making them captivating and memorable with an artistic touch. The simplicity of mundane truth and its artistic telling deeply affect us. His stories unleash a world of gay abandon, a world of magic in realism filled with ingredients of faith, love, courage and joy. He has courage to write about the uncomplicated and composed things of life and raise the experience to the sublime. He taps the potential of divinity in all things great and small. His God is the God of small things. The heartfelt love of Bond for the 'quiet heroes' and the have-nots pulls at the reader's heartstrings. The common and familiar persona of Bond's fiction: the *dhaba* or the bookshop owner by the roadside, the mule, the rickshaw, the truck or the taxi driver, the destitute: from a sweeper to a vagabond, from a waif to a retard, from a T.B. patient to an epileptic boy, from an emaciated beggar to a stout wrestler, children from a mischief maker and happy-go-lucky to alienated adolescent, women from a ten year-old vivacious girl to an old kind lady, ordinary hill-folk who earn their living as humble farmers, street vendors, cattle-herders all these people that at first glance appear lacklustre come alive under his vibrant inventive stroke. The uneventful life of these ordinary men nowhere loses its appeal. Bond's sympathetic bend and trust illumine them. Bond has captured the nuances of their life through the remarkably created narrative pattern. He arduously works upon their language and their way of speaking and thereby presenting the true image. His narrative art celebrates their life and characteristically presents the unheard and unnoticed saga of their ignored existence. His stories aim to present life as it really is in its nobility as well as its banality. Simple yet deep sketches of these people are the hallmark trait of each of Bond's stories - depicting pain, poignant moments, desire, avarice, love, compassion and innocence. Some of the characters are so genuinely delineated that they interest the readers just for their plain humanness. The spark of life that his characters generate, captivate us for its authenticity.

The loving altruism of Bond, his deep insight into human nature, his tolerant attitude and warm sympathy for both wicked and virtuous secure for him a distinguishing place in the world of humanists. He unfurled his flag in favour of the marginalized especially the old, the retard, the deprived, the orphan, the poor children and the old Anglo-Indians. He foresees an imaginative drama of feelings and responses in the degenerated and ignored personages of society and in their seeming triviality. His characters like an innocent murderer Kusum in "A Case for Inspector Lal," a waif Madhu who died at a very young age in "The Story of Madhu," a retard neglected by his father because of his mental and physical deformity in "The Most Beautiful," a motherless brat Kishen turned to a thief in *Vagrants in the Valley* touch the chord of heart and haunt memory long after one has finished reading. Occasionally his eccentric uncles, mischievous boys and humorous description bring delight to his sometime serious vignettes of life. His characters are both believable and likeable. He is supremely gifted for he possesses an innate power to move the reader. His stories reveal some aspects of human nature and the joys and the sorrows of everyday living.

Bond's commitment to Indian muse is visible in his adoring invocation of Indian locale. His love for India and the things Indian, despite many opportunities he had to go and settle abroad, is a great testimony of his love for India. He writes passionately about Indian milieu and sensibility for the Indians and from the perspective of a genuine Indian. His British origin and his devotion for the literature of East and West and love for India enrich him with double inheritance. Endowed with remarkable openness, he is always ready to receive impression coming from all sides. His characters like him enjoy the every aspect of Indian life - its culture, festivals, monuments, hullabaloo of bazaars and feel nostalgic in any place other than India. Even the English ones enjoy the Indian flora and fauna and get well adjusted with Indian heat and dust. His portrayal is free from false exotica and from callous observation of Rudyard Kipling, E.M. Foster and John Masters. In his sincere and empathetic portrayal, Bond surpasses these writers whose insensitive projection of Indian ambience sometimes hurts the Indian sentiments. Without the feeling of superiority, Bond has entered the home, the locality and the heart of his Indian characters. His is the voice of an insider who keeps in the centre the basic Indian ethos. He is "as Indian as the dust of [northern] plains or the grass of a [Himalayan] mountain meadow" (Bond, *Room on the Roof* vii-ix). He gives his readers the true feel of Indian life he has seen and lived. His European blood seems to be fully naturalised with the Indian spirit.

Bond's social realism does not penetrate deep into Indian custom and thinking. He does not raise the strong voice for the reform of downtrodden as does Mulk Raj Aanad and Bhabani Bhattacharya. His writing is also untouched by India's rich philosophical legacy and the ancient Indian values of service, sacrifice and non-detachment. Bond, the timeless gentle-dreamer of Garhwal hills stands apart amidst, the media hyped 'exuberance' the bold new voices in Indian English writing such as Arundhati Roy, Vikram Seth, Allan Sealy. He is a self-declared introvert and his contribution has been to show humanity in a pretty good light. The dominant impact of his stories is a deeper understanding of the common masses. His faith in the elemental truthfulness of man, ungrudging acceptance of the evils and a world view in which the animate and the inanimate worlds have their own place, enlighten the perspective. He is the manufacturer of that massive treasure of stories that have embroiled the readers in their gentle, multi-layered magic by its romantic realism and strong optimism.

Bond writes with charm about everyday proceedings and rejects imaginative and idealised in favour of authentic presentation. His faithful recording and reflection of an actual way of life is distinguishing trademark of his truth-telling. The mundane background of his stories with which every Indian can connect takes the readers into times and minds of the characters. His stories revolve around serendipitous encounters which leave lasting impression. The stories narrate about a chance meeting of the narrator with a stranger and finding something that fascinates him about the stranger. In many cases the stranger is lost in the wilderness of the crowd. Anything could fascinate the narrator, from a coy smile of a little girl to the gentleness of a thief, from the wrestling bouts of a wrestler to the sensational meeting of a blind man with a blind girl, from the simplicity of an old lady to the vivaciousness of a young girl and from the exuberance of a innocent child to the malignity of an evil spirit.

Bond shares a unique relationship with nature and most of his writings celebrate his deep association with it. His pantheistic philosophy sees a spirit in trees, mountains, rivers, birds and animals. The exquisite portrayal of Himalayan landscape with its moods, its seasons, its flora and fauna is unparalleled of its kind. His pastoral vignettes are evocative, filled with bird-trills, the flash of butterfly wings and the smell of the wet earth after rain. Nature is always present in his works with all its colourful vibrating and soothing forms, sometimes in the background and sometimes actively participating in the course of the action. The solace in its peaceful embrace, its importance in our lonely and stressful life and aversion to the crowded man made world brought Bond closer to the world of nature. Like a child he loves to play beneath it, like a tired traveller he takes shelter under it and like a devotee he sings hymn in its praise. The murmuring sounds of brooks and rivulets, whispering sound of the wind, rustling of dry leaves and grass and the shadow of clouds on the ancient Mussoorie hills enchant his mind and soul's eye. These are, for him, watch towers. He marvels at nature's infinity. At times there is a sense of *déjà vu* while reading his work - there is morning-dew freshness and a timelessness of the hills permeating it. If Bond's humanism makes us to identify the beauty 'within,' his natural description of the beauty 'in the world around us,' and awakens our minds to old-world charms and snow-specked hills.

Bond's beautifully crafted stories speak directly to the reader as if he is right there, chatting with his audience, rather than spinning a tale on paper. They have a haunting quality that holds the reader's heart enthralled. His strategy as a story writer is a poetic one that charms without exception for its *cri de cœur*. His characters are lively embodiment of the magnanimity of his soul and reveal his insight into human psyche. He excels in shaping his wide experiences into delightfully readable stories. His short stories are well-finished and are integrated works of art. He can leave the reader numb in just a handful of words when he writes about solitude and suffering and his subtle sense of humour can equally be disarming. Ruskin Bond's readers appreciate the sensitive and thoughtful expression in his writings. The characteristic softness of his tone springs out of his deep belonging to life and things. He is a talented writer who has a skill to transform any mood or situations into an aesthetic experience. Extolling Bond's art, Swapan K. Banerjee writes:

> Not many artists had to face
> What he did.
> All along, he was ready to trade anything
> To safeguard his freedom to write.
> Very few writers attain freedom
> Through their works of art.
> He is certainly one of this 'few'
> Who dabble in art for soul's sake. (Banerjee, "Poetry," *The Asian Age*)

Through Bond's perception of life, understanding of children and capturing the ultimate truth - reality, this study has analysed threadbare the distinctive dimensions of Bond's creativity highlighting his artistic achievement. The first chapter "From Divided Loyalty to Double Inheritance: Making of the Writer" deals with the unusual background of Ruskin Bond which has great effect on his creativity. It presents a psycho-biographical approach to his life and work. Born in India during the Raj, despite having British parents, an elite British-style secondary education, Bond chose to spend his life in independent India rather than returning to Britain. It is in India where he feels at home. The biographical details firmly place him within Indian culture. The chapter throws light on Bond's life, his identity and the dominant autobiographical elements in his works. The perfection in his art is achieved by the artistic and pleasing blending of autobiographical and fictional elements. Sometimes it becomes difficult to guess where the autobiography ends and the story begins and vice versa. Semi-autobiographical and semi-fictional work of Bond gives the reader the feeling of oneness with the author himself, while he skilfully mesmerises us, not letting us sense the fiction in his writing. The chapter traces his journey from a detached observer of Indian life to an adaptor, from his assessment to assimilation, from divided loyalty to double inheritance. The chapter also shows his evolution as a writer and his significant contribution to Indian writing in English.

The second chapter "Personal Impressions: An Interview with Ruskin Bond" provides an inlet into Bond's personality and his creative art. The conversation with the author briefly and precisely presents thorough understanding of Bond's literary imagination.

The third chapter "Writing Children Writing Human" focuses the development of children's literature in India and Bond's remarkable contribution to it. Bond as a children's writer occupies the position of kingpin of children's writing in India for lucidity of his articulation, use of short-story and novella as art form, plot revolving around child protagonists and truthful and humane portrayal of young protagonists. With deep sensitivity, Bond conjures up the enchanting literary landscape of energetic and high-spirited children: their little squabbles, inquisitive nature, trouble on receiving poor report card, running away, adventure, eagerness while exploring the beauty of nature and their venture into the adult world with a caring adult beside them. Bond's children's writing remarkably achieves the traditional role of social and moral instructor though unknowingly. His fiction is a confluence of Indian and Western children's literature.

The fourth chapter "Nature's Plenty: Loving not the Man Less but Nature More" critically evaluates the pleasing world of flora and fauna and the use of it as a technique. The hill station of Dehra Dun and Garhwal region, its environment, mountains, hills, trees and rivers, subtly and ineffably, fill the nooks and crevices of one's consciousness while one goes through Bond's writings. He observes variegated phenomena of nature and sensuously and minutely records it in his literature. He presents the variety of bird and animal life and activities in and around the hills with great empathy. The chapter discusses his minute observation of nature like a taxonomist, authentic description of it like a realist, concern for it like an environmentalist, devotion to it like a dedicated worshipper and the presentation of varied moods of protagonists through its wild and mild aspects. The chapter also discusses the use of animal fantasy in children's stories of Bond.

The fifth chapter "Representing the Indian Reality" discusses the sensitive and sensible invocation of Indian milieu. Bond surpasses in presenting with photographic accuracy and uncanny insight the actual life of hills and towns, its topography, man and manners, customs and rituals and superstitions. His fiction is reproduction of life like photography. One feels that what he portrays is likely to have occurred in a certain setting in a certain period. It need not have actually happened as it is described word to word, but there is nothing in the book that precludes the chances of it ever happening. His corpus is free from off beaten theme of symbolic or metaphysical nuances, socio-economic or political upheavals, and psycho-socio issues. Its charm lies in its presentation of an "optimistic outlook" on life. The realistic and lively portrayal of Indian locale - from the hubbub of a railway platform to hullabaloo of the crowded third class railway compartment; from a busy bazaar imbued with clamour of the vendors, crying of the children, smell of the spicy *chaat*, blare of the horns and the loudspeakers, brimming buses, emaciated beggars, lazily moving cows and the serene forest make the perspective better. The chapter also deals with Bond's in-depth study of the marginalized with intense sensitivity. Bond's literature mirrors the life and like mirror it merely reflects but does not exaggerate or undermine the picture.

The sixth chapter "Narrative Art: Telling a Good Story" reflects upon the distinctive aspects of his narrative art. A creative wordsmith, Bond tries to make the reader understand the landscape and ethos through carefully mastered words. His language has virile force and a mastery which conveys the maximum of meaning in the fewest and simplest words. He keeps his readers enthralled by the enticing plot, lively characterization, evocative description, passionate delineation, humorous presentation, strict economy of narration and elegant simplicity of language. The plainness of Bond's language, brevity, manifested simplicity and masterly narrative art is result of his hard work. He emerges as the most consummate practitioner of narrative art projecting Indian reality and manifesting the outer space as well as the inner space through his lucid language. The seventh chapter, which is the conclusion of thesis sums up the points discussed in forgoing chapters.

Bond is endowed with all the features of a master story-teller: a deceptively effortless style, an eye for the extraordinary in seemingly humdrum lives, the extraordinary assortment of odd, eccentric yet charming characters, the special flavour of a particular locale, the panoramic view of Indian social landscape and natural landscape, sensitive blending of fiction with reality and a deep empathy with his characters. He pins his faith on each renewal of human life and nature which is a process of perpetual redemption. He is a philosopher with faith in humanity, always ready to tell a new little story, about a dreamy day, about a lovely yesterday, of a hot April and a hotter May. In ultimate analysis, Ruskin Bond emerges as a wizard with words, a humanist with a large heart, master narrator with ease, superb story-teller of truths and above all a human being who is to be loved as well as worshipped. Conveying his message of love for humanity the following words from Bond's "His Last Words" pay the true tribute to this great raconteur and living legend of our time:

> When I am no longer with you,
> I will still be in your midst.
> You have my laws, my words, my very essence.
> Beloved disciples,
> If you love my memory, love one another.

Bibliography

Abrams, M.H. *A Glossary of Literary Terms.* 6th ed. Bangalore: Prism Books, 1993.

Agarwal, Deepa. "Contemporary Indian Fiction in English: A Colonial Legacy." *Book Bird Winter* 34. 4, 1996: 32-34.

—. "Fifty Years of Children's Books." *The Book Review.* 21, November 1997: 26.

Aggarwal, Amita. *The Fictional World of Ruskin Bond.* New Delhi: Sarup and Sons, 2005.

Akmajian, Adrian. *Linguistics: An introduction to Language and Communication.* Prentice Hall of India: New Delhi, 2004.

Alkazi, Feisal. "Adapting Children's Literature to the Small Screen." *The Book Review.* 19, 11 November 1995: 15.

Alter, Tom. "The Perfect Bond." *The Metropolis.* 5 March 1994.

Aristotle. *Rhetoric.*Trans. W.R. Roberts. New York: Random House, Modern Library Edition, 1954.

Bandyopadhyay, Debashis. "The Past Unearthed: New Reading of. Ruskin Bond's Supernatural Tales." *Children's Literature Association.* Vol. 30.1(2005): 53-71. <muse.jhu.edu/demo/childrens_literature_association_quarterly/v030/30.1>

Banerjee, Swapan Kumar. "Poetry." *The Asian Age*. 21 October 2001.

—. "Exclusive Interview: Your Heart is Always Where You Grew Up." *Garhwal Post D ehradun*. 4. 33, 12-18 May 2000:1.

—. "Ruskin Bond." *Garhwal Post Dehradun*. 19-25 March 1999: 4.

Banerjee, Swapank. *Rusty and I*. A Collection of Interview, Review, Short Story, Profile, Poem and Letter.

Bansal, Richa. "Face to Face: Bonding in the Hills." *The Hindu*. 19 May 2002.

Barry, Peter. *Beginning Theory: An Introduction to Literary and Cultural Theory*. New Delhi: Viva Books private Limited, 2008.

Berger, Laura Standley, ed. *Twentieth-Century* Children's *Writers*. Detroit: St. James Press, 1994.

Bhargava, Rajul, ed. *Indian Writing in English: The Last Decade*. New Delhi: Rawat Publication, 2002.

Bhatnagar, K.C. *Realism in Major Indo-English Fiction*. Bareilly: Prakash Book, 1980.

Bhatt, Manish D. *Ruskin Bond as a Short Story writer: A Critical Study*. New Delhi: Sarup and Sons, 2008.

—. "Ruskin Bond as a Short Story Writer with Special Reference to *The Night Train at Deoli and Other Stories*." M. Phil Diss. Saurashtra University, Rajkot, 2003.

Bhattacharya, Arnab. "The Sahib Meets the Spirit of India." *The Telegraph Calcutta*. 20 December 2002.

Bhullar, Avtar Singh. *India Myth and Reality*. Delhi: Ajanta Publication, 1985.

Birch, David, and Michael O'Toole, ed. *Functions of Style*. Great Britain: Printer Publishers, 1988.

Birch, David, ed. *Style Structure and Criticism*. New Delhi: Bahri Publications, 1985.

Blishen, Edward, ed. *The Thorny Paradise: Writers on Writing for Children*. London: Kestrel Books, 1975.

Bond, Ruskin. *The Hidden Pool*. Illus. Ranjit Balmuchu. New Delhi: Puffin, 1966.

—. *Grandfather's Private Zoo*. Illus. Mario Miranda. Bombay: India Book House, 1967.

—. *The Wonderful World of Insects, Trees and Wild Flowers*. Bombay: India Book House Publishing Company, 1968.

—. *Tales Told at Twilight*. Bombay: IBH Publishing Company, 1970.

—. *It Isn't Time That's Passing: Poem 1970-71*. Calcutta: Writers Workshop, 1972.

—. *Lone Fox Dancing: Lyric Poems*. Calcutta: Writer Workshop, 1975.

—. *To Live in Magic: A Book of Nature Poems*. Illus. Suddhasattwa Basu. New Delhi: Thomson, 1985.

—. *The Adventures of Rama and Sita*. Illus. Valerie Little Wood. London: Julia Mac Rae, 1987.

—. *Beautiful Garhwal*. Dehradun: English Book Depot, 1988.

—. *The Night Train at Deoli and Other Stories*. New Delhi: Puffin, 1988.

—. *Time Stops at Shamli and Other Stories*. New Delhi: Puffin, 1989.

—. *Tales and Legends from India*. Illus. Sally Scott. New Delhi: Rupa, 1990.

—. *Panther's Moon and Other Stories*. Illus. Suddhasattwa Basu. New Delhi: Puffin, 1991.

—. *Mussoorie and Landour: Days of Wine and Roses*. Illus. Ganesh Saili. New Delhi: Lustre Press, 1992.

—. *The Room on the Roof and Vagrants in the Valley*. Delhi: Penguin, 1992.

—. *Strange Men, Strange Places*. New Delhi: Rupa, 1992.

—. *Ganga Descends*. Dehradun: English Book Depot, 1992.

—. *Rain in the Mountains: Notes from the Himalayas*. New Delhi: Penguin, 1993.

—. *Hanuman to the Rescue*. Cover Illus. Uday Shankar. New Delhi: Rupa, 1993.

—. ed. *The Penguin Book of Indian Ghost Stories*. New Delhi: Penguin, 1993.

—. *The Best of Ruskin Bond: Delhi is Not Far*. New Delhi: Penguin, 1994.

—. ed. *The Penguin Book of Indian Railway Stories*. New Delhi: Penguin, 1994.

—. *Children's Omnibus*. New Delhi: Rupa, 1995.

—. ed. *Ruskin Bond's Green Book*. New Delhi: Roli, 1995.

—. ed. *The Penguin Book of Classical Indian Love Stories and Lyrics*. New Delhi: Penguin, 1996.

—. *Strangers in the Night: Two Novellas*. New Delhi: Penguin, 1996.

—. *Collected Fiction*. New Delhi: Penguin, 1996.

—. *Scenes from a Writer's Life: A Memoir*. New Delhi: Penguin, 1997.

—. *The Lamp Is Lit: Leaves from a Journal*. New Delhi: Penguin, 1998.

—. *Our Trees Still Grow in Dehra*. New Delhi: Penguin, 1999.

—. *Treasury of Stories for Children*. Illus. Tapas Gupta. New Delhi: Puffin, 2000.

—. *Friends in Small Places: Ruskin Bond's Unforgettable People*. New Delhi: Penguin, 2000.

—. *Granny's Tree Climbing and Other Poems*. Illus. Tapas Guha. Gurgaon: Scholastic, 2000.

—. *When Darkness Falls and Other Stories*. New Delhi: Penguin, 2001.

—. *A Flight of Pigeons*. New Delhi: Penguin/Viking, 2002.

—. *Rusty the Boy from the Hills*. New Delhi: Puffin, 2002.

—. *Landour Days: A Writer's Journal*. New Delhi: Penguin, 2002.

—. *Rusty Runs Away*. New Delhi: Puffin, 2003.

—. *Rusty and the Leopard*. Illus. Tapas Gupta. New Delhi: Puffin, 2003.

—. *A Face in the Dark and Other Hauntings: Collected Stories of the Supernatural*. New Delhi: Penguin/Viking, 2004.

—. *Ruskin Bond's Book of Nature*. New Delhi: Penguin/ Viking, 2004.

—. *Rusty Comes Home*. Illus. Kallol Majumdar. New Delhi: Puffin, 2004.

—. *Rusty Goes to London*. Illus. Kalloi Majumdar. New Delhi: Puffin, 2004.

—. *The Road to Bazaar*. Illus. Valerie Little Wood. New Delhi: Rupa, 2004.

—. *The India I Love*. New Delhi: Rupa, 2004.

—. *A Little Night Music*. New Delhi: Rupa, 2004.

—. *Roads to Mussoorie*. New Delhi: Rupa, 2005.

—. *Funny Side Up*. New Delhi: Rupa, 2006.

—. *Book of Verse*. New Delhi: Penguin, 2007.

—. *The Parrot Who Wouldn't Talk and other Stories*. New Delhi: Puffin,2008.

—. *Book of Humour*. New Delhi: Penguin, 2008.

—. *A Town Called Dehra*. New Delhi: Penguin, 2008.

—. *Notes from a Small Room*. New Delhi: Penguin, 2009.

—. Mr.Oliver's Diary. New Delhi: Puffin, 2010.

Bradford, Richard. *Stylistics*. London and New York: Routledge, 1997.

Butts, Dennis, ed. *Good Writers for Young Readers*. England: Hart-Davis Educational, 1977.

Byrappa, K. T. Sunitha. "Bond with Memories." *Deccan Hearld*. 29 July 2001.

Byron, Lord. *Childe Harold's Pilgrimage*. Canto iv, cixxviii.

Chander, K.M. *What Ails Indian Writing in English? Commonwealth Language and Literature*. New Delhi: Bahri Publications, 1997.

Chandra, N. D. R. Chandra. *Modern Indian Writing in English: Critical Perceptions*. New Delhi: Sarup and Sons, 2004.

Chaudhuri, Amit, ed. The Vintage Book of Modern Indian Literature. New York: Vintage Books USA, 2004.

Chaudhuri, Rosinka. "Short story: Two Collections." *The Hindu*. 16 September 2001.

Childs, Peter and Roger Fowler. *The Routledge Dictionary of Literary Terms*.London: Routledge, Taylor and Francis Group, 2005.

Conrad, Joseph. *Notes on Life and Letters*. New York: Double Day Co. Garden City, 1926.

Crouch, Marcus. *Treasure Seekers and Borrowers*. Children's Books in Britain 1900-1960. London: The Library Association, 1962.

Cullinan, Bernice E. and Diane G. Person, eds. *The Continuum Encyclopedia of Children's Literature*. New York: A Ginger Book Continuum, 2004.

Das, Bijay Kumar. *Critical Essays on Post-Colonial Literature*. New Delhi: Atlantic, 2001.

Das, Manoj. "Children's Literature: Writer at the Crossroads." *The Hindu*. 3 November 2002.

Dasgupta, Amit, ed. *Telling Tales: Children's Literature in India*. New Delhi: New Age International P blishers Limited, 1995.

Davidar, David. "The Men with the Golden Pen." *Books Today*. April-June 2000: 4.

De, Rina. "Ideology and Meaning in Children's Literature." Diss. Jawaharlal Nehru University, 1998.

Dhawan, R.K. ed. *Indian Writing in the New Millennium*. New Delhi: Indian Association for English Studies, 2000.

Dhondy, Farrukh. "Indian Writing Now Is Totally Bogus." *Tehelka the People's Paper*. 22 April 2006.

Doubtfire, Dianne. *The Craft of Novel Writing*. London: Allison and Busby, 1978.

Dutta, Arup. "*Better Adventure Stories for children of the Higher Age Groups*." Writer and Illustrator vol.9.2, Jan-Mar: 45.

Ellis, Alec. *How to Find Out about Children's Literature*. London: Pergamon Press, 1968.

Engel, Susan. *The Stories Children Tell: Making Sense of the Narratives of Childhood*. USA: W.H. Freeman and Company, 1995.

Flaubert, Gustave. Letter to Louise Colet. 7 September 1853.

Foster, E.M. *Aspects of Novel*. New Delhi: Atlantic Publishers, 2001.

Garrard, Greg. *Ecocriticsm*. London and New York: Routledge, 2004.

Ghose, Vijaya,. "The Dilemma of Children's Books." *The Book Review*. 15.6 November-December 1991: 3.

Gist, N.P. and A.G. Dworkin, eds. *The Blending of Races: Marginality and Identity in World Perspective*. New York: Wiley Interscience, 1972.

Goethe, Johann Wolfgang Von, 1749-1832. *Torquato Tasso,* 1790.

Gokhale, Namita, ed. *Days of Innocence Stories for Ruskin Bond.* New Delhi: Roli Books, 2002.

—. "Eternally Innocent." *India Today.* 10 June 2002.

Gray, Martin. *A Dictionary of Literary Terms.* Essex: Longman York Press, 1988.

Harris, Judith Rich and Robert M. Liebert. *The Child: Development from Birth to Adolescence.* Englewood Cliffs, NJ: Prentice, 1984.

Hathi, Daksha. "No times for the Blue." *Sunday Deccan Herald.* 22 July 2001: 1.

Heyman, Michael. *The Life and Works of Ruskin Bond* (review). *Children's Literature Association Quarterly.* 28.4, 2003: 253-254.

Hogan, Patrick Colm. *Colonialism and Cultural Identity: Crises and Tradition in the Anglophone Literature of India, Africa and the Caribbean.* New York: State University of New York, 2000.

Hogarth, Basil. *The Technique of Novel Writing.* London: The Bodley Head Ltd., 1937.

Hoijer, H. "Linguistic and Cultural Change." *Language in Culture and Society.* ed. Dell Hymes. New York: Harper and Row, 1964.

Holbrook, David. *English for the Rejected: Training Literacy in the Lower Streams of the Secondary School.* University Press, 1964.

Hunt, Peter and Shelia Ray, eds. *International Encyclopedia of Children's Literature.* London and New York: Routledge, 1996.

Hunt, Peter, ed. *Children's Literature: The Development of Literary Criticism.*London: Routledge, 1990.

Hunt, Peter, ed. *International Companion Encyclopedia of Children's Literature*. 2 vols. London and New York: Routledge, 2004.

Hunter, Adrian. *The Cambridge Introduction to the English Short Story in English*. Cambridge University press: New Delhi, 2007.

Iynger, K.R. Srinivasa. *Indian Writing in English*. New Delhi: Sterling Publishers, 2006.

—. *Two Cheers for the Commonwealth: Talks on Literature and Education*. New Delhi: Asia Publishing House, 1970.

Jafa, Manorma. "The Indian Sub-Continent." *International CompanionEncyclopaedia for Children's Literature*. Ed. Peter Hunt. vol. 2. London: Routledge, 2004.

Jain, Jasbir. "The Plural Tradition: Indian English Fiction." *Spectrum History of Indian Literature in English*. New Delhi: Atlantic Publisher, 1997.

James, Sheila Pais. "The Anglo-Indians: Transcolonial Migrants and the Dilemma of Identity." Department of Sociology, Flinders University. The International Journal of Anglo-Indian Studies vol. 7 No. 2, 2004. <www.alphalink.com.au/~agilbert/ indexold.html - 15k>.

Jhon, Binook K. "Moving Memoir." *India Today*. 29 December 1997.

Kachru, B. Braj. *The Indianization of English: The English Language in India*. Delhi: Oxford University Press, 1983.

Kakar, Sudhir. *Indian Childhood: Cultural Ideals and Social Reality*. New Delhi: Oxford, 1979.

Kalinnikova, E.J. *Indian English Literature*. Gaziabad: Vimal Prakashan, 1982.

Kazmi, Nikhat. "Cinema of the Week: The Blue Umbrella." *Sunday Times of India*. 12 August 2007.

Keerti, Ramachandra. "An Evaluation of Themes and Style

in Children's Fiction (9-12 age group)." Diss. Centre of Linguistic and English. Jawaharlal Nehru University, 1985.

Kenan, Shlomith Rimmon. *Narrative Fiction*. New York: Routeledge, 2003.

Khorana, Meena G. *The Life and Works of Ruskin Bond*. London: Praeger, 2003.

—. "Ruskin Bond." *Twentieth Century Children's Writers*. Ed. Laura Standley Berger. Detroit: St. James Press, 1994.

—."The River is Eternal: Nature Mysticism and Vedanta Philosophy in Ruskin Bond's Angry River." *The Lion and Unicorn*. 19.2 December 1995: 254-268.

Kipling, Rudyard. *Kim Mohwah*. New Jersey: Watermelt Press, 1981.

Kirkpatrick, D.L., ed. *Twentieth-Century Children's Writers*. New York: St Martin's, 1983.

Krishnamurthy, Sarla. "Growing up with Nature." *Deccan Hearld* . 10 November 2002.

—. "In Nature's Abode." *Deccan Hearld* . 30 June 2002.

Kumar, Anju. "Beyond Word Length." *The Hindu*. 10 May 2007.

Kumar, Meenakshi. "Movers and Losers." *Hindustan Times Sunday Magazine*. 11 August 2002: 2.

—. "Ruskin Releases Book for Children." *Asian Age*. 16 November 1999.

Kurian, Nimi. "Life in the Hills." *The Hindu*. 22 November 2002.

Lakhani, Brenda. British and Indian Influences in the Identities and Literature of Mark Tully and Ruskin Bond. B.A. Thesis Prepared for the Degree of Master of Arts. University of North Texas. Aug. 2003 <http://digital.library.unt.edu/permalink/ meta-dc-4313:1.>

Lanser, Susan Sniader. *The Narrative Act: Point of View in Prose Fiction.* Princeton, New Jersey: Princeton University Press, 1881.

Lodge, David. *Language of Fiction: Essays in Criticism and Verbal Analysis of the English Novel. London:* Routledge, 2002.

Lucas, F.L. *Style.* London: Cossell and Company, 1955.

Marquand, Robert. "India's Pioneer of Modern Children's Tales." *Christian Science Monitor.* 92. 191, 24 Aug. 2000.

Matthew. *The Bible.* 2:37.

Mehrotra, Arvind Krishna, ed. *An Illustrated History of Indian Literature in English.* New Delhi: Permanent Black, 2003.

Mehta, Kamal, ed. *The Twentieth Century: Indian Short Story in English.* New Delhi: Creative Books, 2004.

Menon, Navin and Bhavana Nair, eds. *Children's Literature in India.* New Delhi: Children's Book Trust, 1999.

Merson, A.J. *Modern Short Stories: First Series.* Bombay: Macmillan India, 1981.

Morris, Pam. *Realism.* London: Routledge, 2003.

Mukherjee, Meenakshi. *The Twice Born Fiction.* New Delhi: Pencraft, 2005.

—. *Realism and Reality: The Novel and Society in India.* Delhi: Oxford University Press, 1985.

Murray, J. ed. *The Autobiographies of E. Gibbon.* London: Albemarle Street, 1897.

Nabar, Vrinda. *Caste as Women.* New Delhi: Penguin, 1995.

Naik, M.K. *A History of Indian English Literature.* New Delhi: Sahitya Akademi, 2005.

—. *Perspectives on Indian English Fiction.* New Delhi: Abhinav Publication, 1985.

Naik, M.K. and Shyamala A. Narayan. *Indian English Literature: 1980-2000, a Critical Survey*. New Delhi: Pencraft International, 2004.

Nehru, Jawaharlal. *The Discovery of India*. Delhi: Penguin, 2004.

Oken, Donald. "Alienation: Concept, Term and Meanings." *Alienation and Identity: Some Comments on Adolescence, the Counterculture and Contemporary Adaptations*. Ed. Frank Johnson. New York: Seminar Press, 1973.

Paranjape, Makarand. *Towards a Poetics of the Indian English Novel*. Shimla: Indian Institute of Advanced Study, 2000.

Pathak, Nilima. "Bonded to nature." <http://www.lifepositive.com/common/sharing/ruskin-bond.asp>.

Philip, Mariet. *Introduction to Jean Paul Sartre's Existentialism and Humanism*. New York: Philosophical Library, 1957.

Ranganathananda, Swami. *Universal Message of the Bhagavad Gita*. Kolkata: Swami Mumukshananda, 2005.

Rao, A. Ramakrishna, ed. *Comparative Perspectives on Indian Literature*. New Delhi: Prestige Book, 1992.

Rao, M. Subba. *Reading in Indo-Anglian Literature*. New Delhi: Kanishka Publishers, 1995.

Ray, M. Supryia. *The Bedford Glossary of Critical and Literary Terms*. New York: Ross Murfin, 2003.

Reddy, K. Venkata and P. Bayapa Reddy, eds. *The Indian Novel with Social Purpose*. New Delhi: Atlantic, 1999.

Reynolds, Kimberley, ed. *Modern Children's Literature an Introduction*. London: Palgrave Macmillan, 2005.

Rodrigues, Santan. "Book Review: Vintage Bond." *Free Press Journal*. Mumbai. 2 September 2001.

Rushdie, Salman. *Imaginary Homelands: Essays and Criticism 1981-1991*. London: Grant Books London, 1992.

Sadhu, Nirmal. *The Tribune*. 29 February 2004.

Saili, Ganesh. *Ruskin Our Enduring Bond*. New Delhi: Roli Books, 2003.

—. *The Hindu Metro Plus*. 8 January 2005

—. *The Hindu Metro Plus Delhi*. Online edition of India's National Newspaper. Saturday, 08 Jan. 2005.

—. "Well-Deserved Honour for Child of the Doon." *Garhwal Post Dehradun*. 3.27, 26 March-April 1999.

Scholes, Robert and Robert Kellogy. *The Nature of Narrative*. London: Oxford University Press, 1968.

Sehgal, Rashme. "A Bond with Words." *Times of India*. 3 January 1999: 2.

Sharma, R.S. and S.B. Shukla, ed. *Studies in Contemporary Literature*. New Delhi: Sarup and Sons, 2000.

Sharma, Sanchita. "Bonding for Ruskin, Between Covers." *The Hindustan Times*. 16 Febuary 2002.

Sheoran, Kamal. "Contemporary children's Literature in India." *Children'sLiterature*. 4, 1975: 127-137.

Short Oxford English Dictionary. Oxford University Press: 2002.

Sidhwa, Bapsi. *Ice-Candy-Man*. New Delhi: Penguin Books India, 1989.

Sigh, Sangeeta. "Bond with the Best: Scripting the Write stuff." *Times of India*. 22 February 2001.

Simpson, Claude M. ed. *Twentieth Century Interpretations of Adventures of Huckleberry Finn*. Gladys Carmen Bellamy, "Roads to Freedom." N.J. Englewood Cliffs: Prentice Hall, 1968.

Singh, Nripendra. *Contemporary Indian English Short Story: Ruskin Bond, Anita Desai, Shashi Deshpande*. New Delhi: Creative Books, 2007.

Singh, Prabhat Kumar, ed. *The Creative Contours of Ruskin Bond*. New Delhi: Pencraft Publication, 1995.

Singh, Sushila. *Feminism: Theory, Criticism, Analysis*. New Delhi: Pencraft International, 1997.

—. "Multiculturalism and Its Limits." *Indian Journal of American Studies*. 27.2. 1997.

—. ed. *Feminism and Recent Fiction in English*. New Delhi: Prestige Books, 1991.

—. "Haroun and the Sea of Stories: Rushdie's Flight to Freedom." *The Novels of Rushdie*. Ed. G.R. Taneja and R.K. Dhawan. New Delhi: Indian Society for Commonwealth Studies, 1991. 209-216.

Sinha, Achal. "A Study of Nature, Location and Childhood." Diss. Patna University, 2006.

Sinha, Krishna Nandan, ed. *Indian Writing in English*. New Delhi: Heritage Publishers, 1979.

Slote, Bernice, ed. *The Dimensions of Short Story: A Critical Anthology*. Harper Collins Publishers, 1964.

Son, Kenneth Kempton Pay. *The Short Story*. Cambridge: Harvard UP, 1954.

Spacks, Patricia Ann Meyer. *The Adolescent Idea: Myths of Youth and the Adult Imagination*. London: Faber, 1981.

Srinivasan, Prema. "Treasure Trove." *The Hindu*. 4 February 2001.

—. *Children's Fiction in English in India: Trends and* Motifs. Chennai: T.R. Publication, 1998.

Swift, Jonathan, 1667-1745. Letter to a Young Gentleman lately entered into Holy Orders. 9 January 1720.

Tanu, K. Thomas. "A Bond with Children's Minds." *The Times of India*. 25 May 2003.

Tharoor, Shashi. Writers on Writing: "Expanding Boundaries with a Colonial Legacy." <www.nytimes.com/books/specials/writersjuly 30, 2001>.

Tiwari, Shubha. *Children and Literature*. New Delhi: Atlantic Publication, 2006.

Tucker, Nicholas. *The Child and the Book: A Psychological and literary Exploration*. London: Cambridge U P, 1982.

—. *Suitable for Children? Controversies in Children's Literature*. Great Britain: Sussex University, 1978.

Twain, Mark. *The Adventures of Huckleberry Finn*. Britain: Penguin, 1884.

Walsh, William. *Indian Literature in English*. New York: Longman, 1990.

Wasi, Muriel. "Bond: Boy, Man and Writer." *The Hindustan Times*. 29 January 1994.

Wattas, Rajnish. "Bond with Ruskin". *The Tribune*., Saturday Extra. 13 May 2006: 1.

—. "Languorous Days in Landour." *The Tribune on Sunday*. 16 June 2002.

—. "Keep Writing, Never Despair." *The Tribune*. 6 December 1998.

Wilde, Oscar. Letter to the *Daily Telegraph*. 2 February 1891.

Index